From Hell to Paradise

From Hell to Paradise

DANTE AND HIS COMEDY

Olof Lagercrantz

Translated from the Swedish by ALAN BLAIR

WASHINGTON SQUARE PRESS, INC. • NEW YORK • 1966

851.15
L

Frontispiece by Harry Bennett

Preface

FOR MORE than six hundred years Dante has been acknowledged as one of the greatest writers of our Western culture.
Taine called Dante, Shakespeare, Michelangelo, and Bee-
thoven humanity's caryatids, thus distinguishing them before
all others. Stefan George saw Dante, Shakespeare, and Goethe
as the mightiest figures in the literature of the new age, and
his judgment has predominated in modern Germany. Eliot's
words have become famous: "Dante and Shakespeare divide
the modern world between them; there is no third."

It is easy to pile up expressions like these. In the minds
of innumerable people Dante has occupied, and still occupies,
a place in literature like that given to the lion in the world
of fable. He has been put in a class by himself, and when
he has been compared with others there have been very few
to choose from. "The greatest poetic work of all," says Umberto Cosmo of *The Divine Comedy,* and his tone is as
matter-of-fact as if he were talking of the sun's supremacy in
our sky.

Those who study Dante cannot help at first being over-
awed by his fame. There is only one person who can free
them from this burden—Dante himself. When we read the
Comedy we forget that it is famous, that the best minds all
down the ages have annotated the work, that a literature
exists on its problems so extensive that it can be equalled
only by the number of learned works about the Bible. We
forget this simply because the Comedy, as it exists on the
printed page, takes possession of us. Having waited, so to
speak, in a marble hall among gold-laced court dignitaries

for an audience with a dreaded ruler, we find after being admitted to the presence that he rules by spiritual authority and not outward pomp. Fear vanishes. Even the beginner feels confident.

I know enough about the Comedy as a living fabric of words, about its multitude of figures and its many dimensions, to be fully aware of the inadequacy of my own presentation. While working on it, I have felt like a country telephone exchange that has been commandeered by the army of a great power. The calls are far too many, and it is beyond my capacity to put them through. I have sought and found help from Dante scholars old and new. My gratitude to them is great and perhaps not always satisfactorily recorded. I have borrowed methods and viewpoints without always acknowledging the origin of the loan. That Erich Auerbach is a pioneer within the so-called *figura* school, that Singleton has shed new light on *Vita Nuova,* that Mazzeo has made it easier for us to find our way in the Elysian light, to take only three examples, is generally known within Dante research. Such things must be counted as public property. I have looked for keys and clues in many quarters, but the journey through the Comedy is my own.

The main source of my knowledge about the Comedy is the work itself, a work I have read over and over again. Each time I think I have come a little farther along the way of understanding, new paths and new perspectives have opened up. It is like climbing a mountain. The higher up, the bigger the world and the smaller one's relative comprehension. A consolation is that one is continually spurred on as the horizon widens.

I hope, of course, that my book will stimulate others to read the Comedy. Dante's other works also repay reading, especially the book about the universal monarchy and *Vita Nuova.* But comparing these works with the Comedy is like comparing the sums that Einstein did at school with his relativity theory, or like comparing Columbus' Sunday outings in a sailing boat in the Gulf of Genoa with his voyage across the uncharted Atlantic. At the same time, I am almost afraid of urging people to read the Comedy. It is not a book to be read, but rather a life to be lived. Reading the Comedy only once is hardly worth while. If we liken Dante to Shakespeare, we must bear in mind that Shakespeare had to win over his audience with *every* play. He also possessed, to an unusual degree, the ability to realize the whole of his talent at one bound. Dante, on the other hand, devoted all his life to the Comedy, worked all his experience into it, filled it with countless human destinies, grappled in it with the moral, political, and religious problems of every age. All this in a monolith whose outer dimensions are vast and inner ones immeasurable. Those who do not stay long with the work will get proportionately little out of it.

I am very happy that my book is now appearing in the United States of America. American scholars first acquainted me with the methods and results of modern Dante research. When I quote from the Comedy I have used the blank verse translation by Louis Biancolli in the Washington Square Press edition and the prose version in *The Temple Classics*. I have found that the Comedy in a good translation reveals itself, if not in all its grandeur, in something closely resembling it. Only when one seeks to penetrate the different episodes and compares them with the Italian original, does one see that the Comedy cannot be translated, that the natural rhythm of Dante's verse, his incredible precision and neatness, must defy any translator. When I quote in Italian I have made use of *The Temple Classics* text. The Italian edition I have used most is that of Scartazzini and Vandelli, *La Divina Commedia, Testo Critico della Società Dantesca Italiana,* 17th edition, 1958. This is an excellent edition, not over-expensive, with detailed and indispensable notes. There is also a rhyming index and an index of proper names.

Olof Lagercrantz

Contents

List of Illustrations

Inferno
Hell

1

MAN AMONG SHADES

THE POSTULATE is this: A man, Dante Alighieri from Florence, has made his way on foot through Hell, Purgatory, and Paradise, the three regions that await man after death. Some years later he tells of his journey, and the result is the great poem that has been known ever since the sixteenth century as *The Divine Comedy*. As in other autobiographical accounts, the storyteller is older and more experienced than the person he is talking about. It may be practical to distinguish them by calling the hero of the poem Dante the pilgrim and the writer of it Dante the storyteller. To some extent this terminology is supported by Dante himself, and it has been used by several modern Dante scholars.

Dante the pilgrim is in his thirty-fifth year. He was born in Florence under Gemini, the third sign of the zodiac—21 May to 20 June—in 1265. He is a cultured man of good family. He has studied the art, philosophy, and theology of antiquity and of his own age. He has written poetry, and he has been active in politics in his native city. The most important part of his life lies ahead of him. The dead he meets can see into the future, and the pilgrim will often ask them what is in store for him. He sets out on his journey on Good Friday of the year 1300, a year celebrated by papal decree as one of great rejoicing with special concessions for believers. A vast band of pilgrims are making their way to Rome. The pilgrim Dante's journey in the realms of the dead lasts for about a week. It is fifty years before the Black Death and seventy-four years after the death of St. Francis. The crusades are over but the thought of them lives on in many hearts.

Only nine years have passed since the loss of the last Christian possession in the Holy Land. The Pope is Boniface VIII and the Roman emperor is Albert of Hapsburg, the former the object of the pilgrim's and the storyteller's joint hatred, the latter of their contempt. This kind of data may be used to fix Dante's journey in history, but the reader who is preparing to go deeply into the Comedy should also bear in mind that the poem has the character of a vision and that it takes place simultaneously in timelessness and in time. The Comedy *exists,* and its story is outlined and completed at this moment; it belongs to the present just as much as the rain that is falling and the cold war that is going on.

Dante the pilgrim goes astray in a wood. The first lines of the poem are (*Inferno,* I: 1–3):

Nel mezzo del cammin di nostra vita
mi ritrovai per una selva oscura,
che la diritta via era smarrita.

Halfway along the journey of our life,
Having strayed from the right path and lost it,
I awoke to find myself in a dark wood.

We realize that the wood is an image of our life and that it is the pilgrim who is halfway along his span. He sees a sunlit hill, but as he makes to ascend it his path is blocked by three menacing wild beasts: first a leopard with spotted hide, then a lion with head erect, and last a she-wolf. This beast, far more terrible and frightening than the first two, drives the pilgrim down into a deep ravine. In this hour of need he meets a man whose voice is hoarse from long silence. The pilgrim begs the stranger to help him (*Inferno,* I:65–66): "Have pity on me, / Whatever you are, living man or ghost!"* The stranger replies that he *was* once a man, but is one no longer; his parents were from Mantua, he was born in the time of Julius Cæsar, he lived in Rome when the good

---

* The blank verse quotations are from the English text of *The Divine Comedy,* copyright, ©, 1966, by Louis Biancolli, published by Washington Square Press. The prose quotations, unless otherwise noted, are from *The Temple Classics.*

Emperor Augustus ruled there and people still worshipped false and lying gods. In keeping with the medieval convention that one should not mention, still less flaunt, one's own name, a convention which Dante adheres to for his own part, the hoarse stranger does not give his name but introduces himself to the lost pilgrim in an equally effective way (*Inferno*, I:73–75): He says, "I was a poet, and sang of that just son / Of Anchises who had come from Troy / When all proud Ilium went up in flames."

Blushing from shyness, the pilgrim exclaims joyfully (*Inferno*, I:79–90):

> "So you are that Virgil, and that fountain,
> Which spreads so broad a river of discourse,"
> I answered him with shamed and humble brow.
> "O light and honor of all other poets,
> May I now profit from the study and great love
> I long applied to fathoming your book.
> You are my author, and my teacher, too;
> You are the only one from whom I took
> That style of beauty which has won me praise.
> Look there, at that beast who forced me to turn back;
> Help me to escape her, O noted sage!
> She makes my pulses throb, and all my veins."

Virgil replies that the pilgrim, who in his anguish has burst out weeping, must take another road, for the wild beast is so savage and her greed so insatiable that she lets no one pass. Virgil offers to show the pilgrim another way which, though very long and devious, will lead him up into the light. Their journey will take them through Hell and Purgatory. If the pilgrim wishes to go further, he must seek another guide, for he, Virgil, was not a Christian and therefore cannot gain Paradise. Dante's grateful acceptance of the offer brings the Comedy's first canto, which is in the nature of a prologue, to an end. In the thirty-three cantos that follow, the two poets descend into the underworld, where they meet those who have been condemned to everlasting punishment.

Dante the storyteller is a middle-aged man; he began the Comedy when he was forty-five and worked on it for ten years. In the years since 1301 he has been banished from his native city, and a sentence of death hangs over his head. Boniface VIII is dead. Albert of Hapsburg was succeeded in 1308 by Henry VII of Luxemburg. In 1314 Louis IV became emperor, but the imperial power is only a shadow of its former self. With Clement V (1305-1314) began the popes' "Babylonian captivity" at Avignon. The Comedy was written in a period of decline for the two great powers—the papacy and the empire—to which Dante was to devote so much of his thought, energy, and writing.

In the epic the storyteller writes he lets his youthful self, the pilgrim, love a woman by the name of Beatrice. She is dead and lives in Paradise, and from there she guards and guides the traveler. It is at her request that Virgil breaks his long silence and comes to help Dante. Beatrice is the wanderer's good genius, but she is also the storyteller's. Here, as so often, it is hard to see the dividing line between the pilgrim and the storyteller. They live on separate planes and belong to different generations, but kindling sparks fly constantly between them. The older man's features, scorched by political and religious passions, emerge from the younger man's unmarked face. The younger one is led—often like a child guided by its father or mother—towards Paradise by Virgil and Beatrice. With power and insight the older man impels his poem towards the same goal under the protection of the same two persons. While Dante the storyteller is a highly cultivated man of his age, Dante the pilgrim has but little learning. He is the hero of a novel of development. He develops morally, politically, and religiously during the lessons that the journey of life gives him. It is a long time before he arrives at any definite knowledge. His struggle for enlightenment is one of the Comedy's main themes.

The reader can make no clear distinction between the thirty-five-year-old pilgrim and his older creator, and this uncertainty has a stimulating effect. We never quite know when wisdom and insight are speaking and when it is only a naïve questioner we have before us. This means that we are never trampled by dictatorial demands of the spirit. Dante the storyteller has Dante the pilgrim beside him at every moment. He never forgets that the pilgrim is full of vacillation, anxiety, and doubt. At the same time he knows that this doubt and this anxiety have been, and perhaps still are, his own. In the course of his story he often makes no distinction between the man he once was and the man he is now. In that he resembles all other men.

All whom the pilgrim meets on his journey have passed the gate of death and possess only phantom bodies. Dante alone is clothed in his flesh. Because it is dark in Hell the unfortunates who dwell there often do not notice that the visitor is different from themselves. Inattention is part of Hell's nature. Here live people who are beside themselves. How can they take any interest in their fellow beings! They have enough agony of their own. Each one is shut up within himself and herein often lies the punishment.

But on the Mount of Purgatory, which is situated on the other side of the earth in the midst of an endless sea, the sun is shining and the shadow cast by Dante's body betrays him. No wonder, therefore, that every meeting in Purgatory is filled with fright or amazement. When the shades of the dead see that Dante's breast rises and falls with his breath and that the rays of the sun do not shine right through him, they cry aloud in astonishment, point him out to each other, and rush up to him to satisfy their curiosity. This curiosity is a sign that they are in a more fortunate state than the doomed in Hell. They wish to increase their knowledge and enlarge their range of consciousness. But this amazement is also quite natural. No living human being has been in these regions; and the pilgrim has to keep on explaining how it is possible that he, who exists in the first life, is wandering among the dead.

Sometimes the pilgrim himself forgets the difference between his status and that of the others. Once, standing beside Virgil, his heart is in his mouth when he sees his shadow in front of him but not his friend's. He whips round to make sure that Virgil is there. He has forgotten that Virgil, unlike himself, has no body. On another occasion, upon meeting a dear friend who is dead, he embraces his friend three times and each time feels his own arms beat the air and encircle his own chest.

The storyteller has taken great care in his descriptions of confrontations between the living pilgrim and the shades of the dead. Some commentators complain that the scenes of surprise are too many. The answer to this complaint is that the story makes it necessary for us to keep the difference between the living and the dead in sight. No doubt it is as striking to have a heaving breast among spirits who no longer need air as it is to be the giant Gulliver among the Lilliputians. Who criticizes these small creatures for first reflecting on Gulliver's size and only later examining his other qualities?

But perhaps the scenes of amazement—for my part I feel the same delighted anticipation every time one of these scenes approaches—also derive light from a source other than the need of credibility. It is an extraordinary distinction to be the only one among millions to own a shadow, a distinction comparable with that of original personality and inimitable genius. Among the passions that rend the heart of the banished poet Dante is ambition. Perhaps his ambition and his self-confidence have tempted him to present so many meetings between the living pilgrim and the shades of the dead. The dead shrink in dismay and cry out: "Is he really alive? Why are the sunbeams broken when they strike him?" Behind the words the reader seems to hear echos of other utterances: "Is it really, is it really—Homer, Shakespeare, Einstein, Chaplin, Dante?" Can a mortal, by creating a work that is read throughout the centuries, overcome death and live when all others have become shadows? This longing for immortality sweeps like a fire through Dante's life and poetry. Virgil, walking beside the pilgrim, is a stimulating reminder of the chances Dante has of achieving immortality. *The Divine Comedy* comes into being in emulation of the guide and master, Virgil. One of the aims of the work is that Dante's name shall live. His wish has been granted in that those who read the Comedy experience his personality in the flesh and blood of the action. Dante still casts a shadow among myriads of dead.

All those appearing in the Comedy, except Dante, are spirits. Did Dante believe that spirits exist, that life goes on after death? Without any doubt. But even if we cannot share his conviction on this point, that is no reason for us to withdraw. Adam in the Bible, Cervantes' Don Quixote, Harry Martinson's tramp Bolle do not exist in the material world. They live by virtue of their creators', and our own, imagination. They too are shadows; we can neither embrace them nor speak to them. Nevertheless, you say, they are supposed to be human beings like ourselves: They breathe, they eat forbidden apples, they tilt at windmills, they bleed when they cut themselves, they feel the cold and seek warmth in brick kilns. Dante's humans, on the other hand, possess only illusory bodies. Does this not lend a touch of unreality to his work?

In accord with the belief of his age, Dante imagines that the soul, which is created directly by God and therefore cannot die, frees itself at the death of the body but takes with it, in its new form of life, all that is human and divine in a man. In the twenty-fifth canto of *Purgatorio* he lets the Roman poet Statius discourse on this theme to Virgil and the pilgrim as they pursue their way along a narrow mountainous road. When man's thread of life is cut, Statius says, the body, which belongs to the animal and vegetable kingdom, is left behind. The liberated soul has memory, intelligence, and will. In the realm of the dead, whether the soul goes to Hell or is taken to the purification of Purgatory, it assumes a new form, a shade which possesses equivalents of the senses that man had in his first life. This soul-shadow is to the soul as the flame is to the fire. The dead speak with the shade's help. The shade laughs, cries, sighs, and has all kinds of feelings and desires. Although the dead do not eat, they can feel hunger. Although they do not drink, they can feel thirst. Although they have no bodies, they are burnt by a flame and weighed down by a burden. Thus, in all things, the dead are like the living. They are distinguished from the living only by their having moved on into another form of existence. Yet is it not hard to accept them?

The answer is no. The feeling of proximity and immediate truth is heightened by the fact that in the Comedy only one person is in the flesh and all others are shades. When reading the poem we need not consider the question of the soul's immortality any more than when reading about Gulliver we need ask ourselves whether or not there are Lilliputians and giants. It is quite immaterial—Eliot has vigorously maintained this viewpoint in his little book on Dante— whether or not we are believers. All that is expected of us is that we are neither believers nor non-believers, that we read the Comedy as every book deserves to be read and every human being deserves to be treated—without prejudice.

No man thinks of another as being so real as himself. Moreover, during his life he associates just as much with shadows as he does with people who breathe. Dead relations, dead love partners, dead friends are with us in our daily life. They increase in number the longer we live. The writer of the Comedy is getting older. In the fourteenth century life was harder and swifter than now, and, if we disregard the unbeatable record of shades to which survivors from modern slave camps and extermination centers can testify, the shades of the dead in everyone's life then were more numerous than in our time.

Dead heroes and rogues from history, dead thinkers, artists, and poets play a decisive part in the life of a cultivated person. One of the purposes of Dante's poem is to revive a bygone culture. "But here, O holy Muses," he cries in the prologue (*Purgatorio,* I:7–8), "let dead poetry / Be resurrected." If one were to draw a realistic picture of man's life here on earth and to seek the most typical situation of all, would not one choose to depict a man of flesh and blood surrounded by shades who, out of their shadowy existence, groped for contact with someone who was still alive? Dante's poem is a conjuring up of the dead. The shades are called forth to take part in this present life, or they themselves push forward because they have messages which still concern us.

At the very moment that Dante enters his poem and begins his journey through the realms of the dead, he gains an enormous artistic and human advantage, and he knows how to make full use of it. Although everything is so strange, although the noise in Hell is so deafening and the light in Heaven so dazzling, we know where we are at every moment. The dead are ever present, and their presence is an essential part of our life. Their lives have ended, and they appear before us in a number of pictures and situations which during the course of our lives and the story take on an increasingly firm shape. Dante's meetings in the realms of the dead correspond to meetings we all have daily. The Comedy can therefore be conceived as the only truly realistic work in Western literature. It is a work in which the dead can join, in which dead writing is invited to come alive, in which all that belongs to the world of learning is granted a contemporary presence.

This does not mean that the Comedy is ordinary and familiar. This can perhaps be said of some of the *Purgatorio* cantos, but the *Inferno* reflects not only the agony inherent in the nature of the place but also the horror that anyone seeking contact with the dead cannot help feeling. Virgil is not merely a noble representative of the poesy of antiquity; he is also a seer, and he can conjure up the dead. Once before, when he wrote the *Aeneid,* he penetrated the underworld at Aeneas' side, and the same kind of incantations he used then come to his aid now. He personifies ancient knowledge about underground spirits and the art of catching them in snares of words and blood. It is he who rescues the pilgrim when the monsters who guard the various circles of Hell are about to hurl themselves at him. It is he who flings earth into Cerberus' gullet and silences him. It is he who rebukes the Minotaur by reminding him of Theseus who slew him. When nothing else avails he calls forth angels to help the wanderers or uses the magic formula that breaks down all resistance: "Thus it is willed there where what is willed can be done." A shudder of horror, which the old and new incantations can never quite overcome, goes through all the cantos of the *Inferno.*

In Paradise the blest yearn for the last judgment, the moment when they are to be united with their bodies and know an intensified bliss. In the world of the poetic word every figure depicted by the poet is a shade who longs to be filled with blood, to be changed from a phantom into pulsating life. Dante admits that his figures *are* shades, but to us they often seem to put on a living body. The dead live; but we know at the same time—and we are nauseated by the knowledge—that they are dead. One of the many wonders of this poem is that it has found a form and a growth resembling what we experience as truth. Dante conceives existence as multi-dimensional, and he breaks down the narrow confines we build around us.

2

THE ART OF BEING IN HELL

ALONG WITH VIRGIL, his friend and guide, Dante the pilgrim makes his way beneath the earth's surface into Hell. He crosses dark rivers of death. He wanders over burning deserts and desolate wastes of ice. He is not in a dream world and still less in an allegorical region; he is in a real landscape. He is in Hell in the same way as Sam Weller of *The Pickwick Papers* is in London on the day he stands in the yard of the White Hart Inn cleaning boots and exchanging banter with the chambermaids. Had anyone informed Mr. Weller that London was nothing but a city of the damned— not an unreasonable thought in view of the misery in the big cities of that age—it would not have prevented him from looking about him with a twinkle in his eye, always alert for the next tip. Dante the storyteller is fond of using images that suggest cosiness and idyllic surroundings in order to illustrate horrible and tragic events. I fancy, therefore, that he would not snub someone who compares the pilgrim's situation in Hell with Sam Weller's in London. The point of the comparison is that Dante the pilgrim is in Hell just as each one of us is present wherever his body happens to be.

The pilgrim might be an explorer who has arrived in a country where the inhabitants have peculiar customs. Some wallow in filth, others pass along the street clad in gilded copes of lead. Some bathe in boiling pitch, others engage in wrestling. He might also be a visitor to a hospital, who goes from ward to ward and from bed to bed looking at the swollen, crippled victims of hideous diseases. He might be a civilian who finds himself on a battlefield between two warring armies and sees thousands of deaths all around him.

The pilgrim knows that Hell is a penal institution and that it is the condemned who are in it. He is reminded of this the instant he enters, for over the gate is written (*Inferno*, III: 1–9):

> *Per me si va nella città dolente;*
>   *per me si va nell' eterno dolore;*
>   *per me si va tra la perduta gente.*
> *Giustizia mosse il mio alto Fattore;*
>   *fecemi la divina Potestate,*
>   *la somma Sapienza e il primo Amore.*
> *Dinanzi a me non fur cose create,*
>   *se non eterne, ed io eterno duro:*
>   *lasciate ogni speranza, voi ch' entrate.*

THROUGH ME YOU PASS INTO THE WOEFUL CITY:
THROUGH ME YOU PASS INTO ETERNAL PAIN:
THROUGH ME YOU PASS AMONG A PEOPLE LOST.
JUSTICE IT WAS THAT MOVED MY LOFTY MAKER;
DIVINE POWER BROUGHT ME INTO BEING,
THE FIRST LOVE AND THE HIGHEST WISDOM.
BEFORE ME ONLY SUCH THINGS WERE CREATED
THAT WERE ETERNAL, AND I ENDURE FOREVER.
LEAVE ALL HOPE BEHIND, YOU WHO ENTER HERE.

It is thus expressly stated at the beginning of both pilgrimage and poem that the divine righteousness has created Hell, and reader and pilgrim alike will find continual talk of punitive justice, as indeed there must be in a work that deals with life after death. It is plain to all that in this earthly life the evil often triumph and the good are made to suffer; therefore God, for the very reason that He is love and justice, must restore the balance after death.

The people whom the pilgrim is about to meet are justly punished. But he is a human being and not a robot. He reads the words which are inscribed "in dark colours" above the gate and says to Virgil: "Master, their meaning to me is hard." Virgil replies (*Inferno*, III: 14–18):

> "Here all suspicion must be left behind.
> Here every kind of cowardice must die.

A 16th-century illustration by Federigo Zuccaro (1539-1609).
Dante and Virgil are standing in the very portal of hell.
Uffizi, Florence.

R a loloco oue afcender la riua

venimmo alpestro: &perquel cheuera ancho

tal chogni ustane farebbe schiua

Quale quella ruina chenel fiancho

One of the most famous medieval Dante manuscripts is *Codex
No. 365 Urbinato in the Vatican Library*. This picture from
the end of the 15th century by an artist of Andrea Mantegna's
school shows Dante on the back of the centaur Nessus beside
the tyrants' river of boiling blood. Virgil follows on foot.

We have come to the place of which I spoke,
Where you shall see the people doomed to pain,
Who forfeited the good of intellect."

Virgil means that the damned in Hell have lost the knowledge of God's goodness and of the highest truth. We are not told how this could come about; but there is reason to think that it is the inexorable nature of the punishment, expressed in the words about the hope that one must abandon, which Dante considers hard and disturbing. There are Christian scholars who hold that the damned have chosen evil, have chosen Hell, but it is hard to understand how anyone could choose everlasting suffering. So we are forced to put it like this: In the infernal concentration camp, God's enemies have been disabled. Surely the believer, be he Nazi or Christian, should be content with this. He can stroll smugly about the great institution, delighting in its orderliness and the chastisement meted out to those rebelling against God the dictator. Is this what Virgil means when he banishes all doubt and cowardice?

A few seconds after their conversation about the inscription, Virgil takes Dante's hand in his. With a cheerful countenance (*con lieto volto,* line 20) which comforts Dante but bewilders the reader, Virgil leads Dante into Hell, and the starless vault echoes with sighs, wails, and screams. Virgil may look cheerful, but Dante begins to weep. He is incapable of remembering that every being he meets from this point on has been judged by the court that is part and parcel of the Christian religion.

Of course it is possible that the pilgrim bursts into tears despite the justness of the punishments, that he is seized with horror and compassion when he sees the awful ends to which sin leads. Each punishment is also a possibility and a threat for him, for his life is not yet over. But Virgil is obviously displeased with this weakness.

The pilgrim as we see him during his journey through Hell is a man who often forgets the punishments and looks on Hell as a place where, for some extraordinary reason, people suffer. On all sides he sees beings who are tormented by filth and rent by their passions. They have been banished from life on earth. Their bodies are covered with boils, swollen, gaunt, torn to pieces by savage dogs. He meets creatures entangled in their lies, besmirched with their vices, tortured forever by the thought that they have betrayed a great cause, that they have wasted their chances, that what is done cannot be undone, that one particular action irrevocably decided the course of their life.

The pilgrim remembers the inscription over the gate and cannot shake off the anguish he feels at its import. But he is not a step in a sum to be worked out by true Christian believers; he is a human being. So he reacts differently throughout his journey. Now he is frightened, now he is enraged. At the next moment he is merely curious, noting down almost gaily the habits of the inmates and the appearance of the guardian demons. But how can he help feeling sorry for the sick and being alarmed by the violent in the madhouse? Nor is it possible for him not to feel repulsed by wicked and odious people. What would we ourselves do if we met Himmler, the murderer of millions of innocent people, in Hell? Even if he, in common with other tyrants who have drenched the world in blood, were now being boiled in this same liquid as a punishment—see the twelfth canto of *Inferno*—might we not jeer at him or kick at his head if it came too near us? In theory, tolerance and sympathy are easy to practice, but transferred to Hell it is unlikely that many of us would stand the test. It would be hard for us not to feel smug when we came upon our personal enemies in degrading situations. Surely *Schadenfreude* would rear its ugly head. And what would be our attitude to those who in life threatened others with hell-fire and whom we now found caught in their own toils? We might not be able to help thinking comfortably that the punishment was just and that we ourselves were only guests in this unpleasant place because we always preached tolerance. Therefore we should not be surprised that Dante sometimes acts harshly in Hell, that he who cries over the unfortunates one moment should add to their torments the next. Those who judge the pilgrim for his cruelty show an embarrassing lack of imagination.

Dante writes of the highest things, of the struggle in man between good and evil, of the chances of gaining lasting happiness, of man's final destination. True, the Comedy is a journey undertaken at a definite time, plotted with the aid of the stars', the moon's, and the sun's positions. However, the real journey takes place outside time and consists of a kind of survey of man's life, not only as it is outlined in one particular case from the cradle to the grave, but as it can be conceived when every opportunity is improved and every talent developed for better or worse.

The storyteller has placed the pilgrim in a Hell where people are barbarically tortured. Did he believe that such a Hell really existed? Did he believe that in a region beyond all hope one could lose the knowledge of the highest good? Let us begin by putting the question aside. We shall return to it in a later chapter, strengthened by experiences gained during the long journey. It is certain in this world that disease exists, that war exists, that hatred exists, that measureless suffering exists. In the *Inferno* cantos of *The Divine Comedy* a human being comes to a region where his fellow humans are suffering without hope or meaning. His senses are highly strung; his mind is on the alert. At those times when we are faced with apparently meaningless agony, it is little comfort to be told that life on the whole is beautiful, grand, and full of meaning. The pilgrim receives just as little comfort from the inscription which assures him that those who abide in Hell are justly condemned. Perhaps he thinks there is some consolation in the hopelessness of Hell, for in hope that is ever renewed and ever created there can be greater torment than there is in the knowledge that a sentence is final.

The pilgrim lives under God's protection. He is guided by Virgil, whom he regards almost as a god. The pilgrim's beloved in Paradise keeps her eyes fixed upon him at every moment and awaits him within a few days. Neither Beatrice nor Virgil, neither the Catholic Church nor the Christian faith can save him from being drawn into and undergoing the suffering he encounters. The storyteller has great knowledge of suffering, its movements, its manners and customs, its language and philosophy. Carlyle has said that Dante gives voice to ten silent Christian centuries. In the matter of suffering, these words can be used for *all* centuries.

We cannot make sweeping statements about the Middle Ages; it is a far too extensive and varied period. But those centuries, far more than ours, were marked by war, famine, and plague; whole tracts were laid waste; devastation climbed over the city walls and into homes with knife in hand. Perhaps people were more familiar with pain in Dante's time. They saw murderers buried alive, head downwards and feet above ground. When the pilgrim reaches the circle of Purgatory where the lustful are purged in fire, he clasps his hands and gazes into the fire, vividly recalling human bodies he has seen burnt at the stake (*Purgatorio,* XXVII:16–18). How could Dante help thinking of this, the same punishment which he himself was condemned to suffer if he were seized within the walls of Florence? People saw blind beggars groping their way along with their hands on each other's shoulders and heretics being tortured by hangmen with faces of iron. The suffering of our time is just as great, perhaps greater; but most of us experience it at a distance, de-sexed and dematerialized. No starving creature falls dead at our gate; we see such events only in our newspaper or on our television screen. Perhaps that is why suffering in our world is dumb. No one has yet given voice to the inconceivable things that happened in the trenches of the First World War, in the Russian slave camps, in the bombed cities of the Second World War, and in the Nazi-dominated world when the Jews were persecuted, herded into death camps, and exterminated like vermin.

In the *Inferno* cantos Dante gives utterance to an unbounded suffering, and thereby offers the only remedy there is for meaningless pain—words, consciousness, memory. He does so with such intense power that we can be grateful for his occasional reminder that those who have their abode in his land of suffering are only shades and not creatures of flesh and blood. Otherwise it might be more than we could bear.

Therefore, to accompany Dante is not merely to receive answers to questions. Rather it is to be registered at a vast university of the emotions; a place where we enlarge our perception at every moment, and at the same time a place where we are constantly aware of our own inadequacy and long for the day when we will understand more, when our feelings will be quickened and strengthened.

3

FRANCESCA

IN THE SECOND CIRCLE of Hell the pilgrim recognizes
Francesca and her lover Paolo. The gate with the dire inscription lies behind him. In a kind of vestibule, which is neither
Hell nor not-Hell, he has come upon the contemptible people
who are too cowardly to take sides, a rabble Heaven disowns
and Hell will have nothing to do with. Now they are envious
of every other fate, whether it be good or evil. He has met
the ferryman Charon, a fierce old man with "wheels of flame"
round his eyes, who refused to ferry him across the first of
the rivers of Hades. In the first circle, Limbo, he has met just
and virtuous pagans who lived before Christ and are therefore denied bliss. Whereas the air in Hell trembles with
screams and curses, in Limbo it is silent. Only sighs float up
to the dark vaults, for those who abide here live in endless
longing without hope. In Limbo, Dante has met Homer,
Horace, Ovid, and Lucan and has been received into their
midst. He has seen, at a distance, the armored Cæsar with the
falcon eye, Hector, Aeneas, Aristotle, Socrates, Plato. Now
he is in Hell, where real punishments are meted out. At the
entrance to the second circle stands Minos, an infernal spirit
with grinding teeth and lashing tail, who sentences each
newly-arrived soul to the circle appointed by divine justice.
Having passed this monster, Virgil and the pilgrim find themselves suddenly in a storm. The damned are whirled about
in the darkness by fierce winds, which—as few Dante commentators fail to point out—are symbolic of the turbulence
and ecstasy of passion.

Here live those who have trespassed for the sake of love (*Inferno,* V:37–48):

> I learned that to this torment were condemned
> The malefactors of the flesh
> Who subjugate their reason to desire.
> Just as the starlings are carried by their wings
> In full and spacious flock when it is cold,
> So are those evil souls by that great breath.
> Now here, now there, now down, now up it leads them,
> Not once consoled by any hope at all,
> Not of relief, but only of less pain.
> And, like the cranes that, singing their refrains,
> Make of themselves a long stripe in the sky,
> I saw coming, dragging their laments

Oddly enough, two groups which our ethics separate seem to be brought together here without discrimination: the lewd and lustful and those who have felt love to be a passion for only one person. Instructed by Virgil, a specialist by reason of his depiction of Queen Dido's love story, Dante recognizes a number of historical and poetical figures famous for their love: Semiramis, who made lust lawful in her kingdom, and the wanton Cleopatra beside Helen, Menelaus' wife, who was seduced by Paris and was the cause of the Trojan war, and Tristan, who was joined forever to King Mark's wife Isolde by the love potion administered at sea. When the pilgrim heard his teacher (*il mio dottore*) enumerating all these ladies and cavaliers of old, pity assailed him and he felt lost and bewildered. In his rhyme scheme Dante uses the word *smarrito,* and the reader recalls that this word, in the form *smarrita,* occurs at the very beginning of the Comedy. The pilgrim, it says, found himself in the Dark Wood because the straight way was "lost," *smarrita.* Does the word here refer to the kind of offense that led the pilgrim astray?

Among those who have lived their life in love or amorous pleasures are Paolo and Francesca. As nearly always in the poem, these two are suddenly there, without any whys and wherefores. Dante does not bother to tell us anything about the figures in his Comedy; he assumes that they are familiar to us, in the same way that the modern journalist does when he is sent to the airport or station to meet Greta Garbo or De Gaulle. We are not told that the general is the dictator of France or that the actress has played immortal heroines and for some inexplicable reason has gone into retirement. The journalist takes for granted that the reader knows these rudimentary facts and does no more than hint at them. His method is to present the celebrity, and the statements made, as spontaneously as possible. He gives us a wax impression of the event, and we see the celebrity caught for a moment in flight. Dante works in the same way. The characters in the Comedy come towards us as people we meet on a journey or in the newspaper. This is the method used even with Dante, the pilgrim who is the hero of the poem. Suddenly, in the first lines of the great work, he is there, astray in the Dark Wood. We do not know who he is or where he comes from. Nor have we time to doubt his existence, for at that instant we are carried away by the story. We never have a chance to resist. It is like a film; we are swept along by the action, and we get to know the hero and understand his problems only by degrees.

The trouble with this manner of portrayal, of course, is that our circle of acquaintances must be more or less the same as Dante's. We must know who the people are that converse, weep, and smile in the Comedy. The poem is not hard to understand. On the contrary, Dante is always clear and, like a good teacher, ready at every moment to put the reader on the right track. He wrote in the vernacular, Italian, because he wanted to be understood by simple people. Our difficulty is that Dante, like the modern journalist, expects us to know the elementary facts about the people who appear on the printed page. We must be familiar with the cultural tradition in which Dante lived—the Bible, classical poetry, the fathers of the church, the great theological speculations of the twelfth and thirteenth centuries, and the countless historical figures in the international and Florentine scene during Dante's time. We are therefore dependent on commentators and learned interpreters of the text. Their task is primarily to serve as guides and reference books. We need their signposts, their *dramatis personæ,* on our way into the Comedy. However, the instant we get our bearings the commentators have vanished, and we are alone within the living organism of the poem.

We are therefore to know that Francesca was the daughter of a prince, Guido Vecchio da Polenta, and related to the Prince of Ravenna, Guido Novello, with whom Dante found a refuge during his last years. For political reasons Francesca was married to a member of the princely house of Rimini, a man deformed and ugly. She fell in love with his younger brother Paolo. The lovers were surprised by the husband, and he killed them. This happened when Dante was twenty-one and himself passionately in love with a woman. The whole affair caused a sensation; it was the big society scandal of the day.

When the whirlwind blows the lovers within earshot he calls out, addressing them compassionately as wearied souls (*anime affannate*). When they hear Dante's cry they hurry towards him, in their eagerness (*Inferno,* V:82–83) "As fly the doves, when beckoned by desire, / To their sweet nest on firm and upraised wings." The whole of this canto, the fifth, is full of bird imagery, which is anciently related to erotic passion. Francesca speaks. She thanks Dante for the sympathy he has shown in hailing her. She says that if God were to allow her she would pray for Dante's heavenly peace because he pities her despite her having stained the earth with the blood of an adulteress. The first thing we find out about Francesca, therefore, is that she feels despised; part of her torment is that she imagines that people think of her with hatred and severity. She has been beautiful, rich, and highborn. Now she is grateful for a single kind word.

Francesca goes on to tell where she was born and of her love for Paolo, how he was inflamed by the lovely person (*bella persona*) she once was. She also says that it afflicts her to think of the manner of her death. It is reasonable to suppose that by this she means that she and Paolo were caught in the very act of love, which, seen with hatred's

eyes, is ugly, absurd, and degrading, worlds apart from the
feeling of tenderness and affection that fills two lovers in
their love. Francesca speaks harshly, heatedly, of her husband
who murdered her; and she predicts that his punishment will
be more severe than hers, that Caina, one of the very lowest
circles of Hell, awaits him. For he is not yet dead; it is still
only Easter 1300, the date when the action of the poem is
thought to take place.

Dante listens. He has been in great distress ever since entering this circle. He bows his head and keeps it low until
Virgil draws his attention with the words (*Inferno*, V:111):
"What are you thinking of?" Dante replies (*Inferno*, V:113–
114): "To think that such desire and sweet thoughts /
Should bring these two to such a grievous end." Then
turning again to the lovers he says (*Inferno*, V:116–120):
"Francesca, all these sufferings of yours / Have roused my
pity to the point of tears. / But, tell me, how did love con-
trive that at / The moment of sweet sighs / You should know
what your vague desires were?"

Francesca answers (*Inferno*, V:121–123): "There is no
greater pain— / Your master knows this—than, in our misery,
/ To be reminded of a happy time." The words are an
echo from the writings of the late-Roman philosopher Boe-
thius about the consolation to be drawn from philosophy,
but as always with Dante the quotation blends naturally
into his poem. To us, therefore, it seems as if the words,
despite their age, had sprung to the unhappy Francesca's lips
at this moment. It may be added that Dante was one of the
first to use the stylistic device that many of our modern poets
are so fond of—the hidden quotation which brings with it
into the new poem a breath of some great past event. Francesca continues: "But if you are so anxious to learn the root
of our love, I will do as they who speak and weep at the same
time." When the reader of the Comedy enters Paradise he
will do well to remember Francesca's readiness to speak. It
shows that she is related to those beings who are redeemed,
for nothing is more characteristic of them than their willing-
ness to increase the knowledge and insight of those they

The great French painter Ingres (1780-1867) did several paintings of the immortal lovers Francesca and Paolo. Here is one of his versions. The seductive love story falls from Francesca's hand and she is joined to Paolo forever. *Hyde Collection, Glens Falls, New York.*

The Farinata episode in the tenth canto of *Inferno*—see the chapter *Exile*—has fascinated many artists. Here the Englishman John Flaxman (1755-1826) has illustrated the moment when Farinata in the burning tomb and Dante exchange words about their exiles. The old Cavalcanti interrupts them, lifting his head over the edge of the tomb.

Sandro Botticelli (1444-1510) illustrated the Comedy toward the end of his life, having this, if nothing else, in common with Blake. Some of his drawings belonged to Queen Kristina. Here is a picture of the same scene as the previous illustration: Farinata in the tomb and Dante beside him.

meet. In the Comedy every scene, every word, and every gesture is correlated to all the rest, just as the lines and facets of a crystal correspond to each other. And that is why no one can ever get a proper idea of the Comedy merely from a quotation or an account of a particular episode. The part gains its deepest significance when seen in relation to the whole.

"One day for pleasure," Francesca says, going on with her story, "we read of Lancelot and of how love constrained him." Lancelot was one of the knights of the Round Table in the old French version of the saga, the one popular in Dante's time. He loves King Arthur's beautiful wife, Guinevere; it is of their love story that Francesca speaks (*Inferno,* V:129–138):

"We were alone and wholly unsuspecting.
Many times that reading drew our eyes together
And drained the color from our faces.
But it was just one place where we succumbed.
When we read how those wanted lips
Were kissed by such a lover,
He, who never will be separate from me,
Kissed me on the mouth, trembling all over.
Galahad was the book and he who wrote it.
We read no more of it that day."

Galahad, it should perhaps be mentioned, is the go-between who, by means of guile, kindles the love between Lancelot and the queen. While Francesca is relating this, Paolo stands beside her, weeping. Dante is so moved by what he hears that he thinks death is near. He falls to the ground in a swoon, "as a dead body falls" (*come corpo morto cade*) and this brings the canto to an end.

With sparing means—Dante has a streak of austerity and almost crabbed taciturnity which none of his bird imagery, however charming, can take away—Francesca's passionate nature is shown in her own words. Why is she punished? Why do we find a person of this quality in Hell?

Marriage was a sacrament. Bride and groom pledged themselves at the wedding ceremony not only to love each other till "death us do part" but also to strive in their union to emulate the union between Christ and the Church. Those who act against this holy sacrament destroy their marriage and also assail the unity between the Saviour and his Church. Forgiveness would have been possible for Francesca, but she died unrepentant. One tradition has it that she flung herself forward and received in her own breast the dagger intended for Paolo, thus showing that at the last moment of her life she was thinking more of her lover than of God. Therefore, Francesca is in Hell for good reason, and she continues to be the same proud woman she was in life.

But no one, surely, who reads about Francesca in the Comedy is willing to judge her. Even the upholders of objective morality who consider that adultery in any circumstances is wrong, must admit that the maximum extenuating circumstances are present here—compulsion, the deformed husband. According to one version of the story, Paolo was his brother's proxy during the marriage negotiations, and Francesca thought that he was to be her bridegroom.

The pious theologian and Dante translator Dorothy Sayers, who during a less pious phase of her life wrote detective stories and who—I devoutly hope—is now in the heaven she so firmly believed in, maintains that Francesca gave in too easily, that she was incapable of saying no, and that she nurtured an exaggerated self-pity. But I cannot find one iota of support in Dante's text for these accusations; they seem to be contrived in order to make the crime fit the punishment and Francesca's placing in Hell seem acceptable to us. In older Dantean research, particularly, efforts of this kind were very common. But has not Francesca reason to weep, and is it unseemly for her to thank anyone who feels sorry for her? If Dorothy Sayers' charges against her for not being able to say no are at all valid, only those who have never loved can go free. If, assessed subjectively, it were right to send Francesca to Hell for adultery, then we can understand the medieval poet who imagined Hell as the only place after death where you could count on meeting respectable people, among them the noble knights and high-born ladies who have lived and died for the sake of love. It also seems plain that Dante the pilgrim did not condemn Francesca. He swoons for pity and—it says so explicitly—is near death.

What is it that distinguishes Francesca from other women who have loved and been unhappy? Ophelia in Shakespeare's drama sings her mad song and takes her life because of love. Isolde loves Tristan even though she is King Mark's wife; and the writer of the story—at any rate in Josephe Bédier's version—is passionately on Isolde's side and puts love before convention and the external moral commandments. Tolstoy's Anna Karenina is also seized by a guilty love which she cannot resist. At the end she is driven to throw herself in front of the train which crushes her.

Looking at these women—Ophelia, Isolde, Anna—and bearing in mind the pain that clouded the end of their lives, we see that they, just like Francesca, are in a kind of hell. There is no life for them outside the books that tell about them. They love; they go to clandestine meetings with terror in their blood and nerves. They are tormented by the prejudices of society and the censure of their fellow humans. They are rent asunder by their feelings and mauled to death by society's envy and abuse. Each lives in her own circle of Hell and each one's agony is everlasting. The writer has sentenced them to this existence forever.

Francesca is a woman who loves. When we meet her she is fused together—she says so herself—eternally with the man she loves. She says also that love, "that in gentle heart is soon aglow," took Paolo captive and fired him with the same feeling for her. The agony of this love was that the two lovers could only snatch at stolen bliss, dreading discovery at every moment. We might therefore say that Francesca is not in Hell any more than Isolde and Anna are. It is her nature and her situation which are the punishment. Punishment—I use Eliot's term—is a state and not a consequence. Francesca is simply presented to us as a human destiny. She suffers because she is capable of a great passion. Ezra Pound says that Dante shows us people's inner self, their mental state, such as it was in life, immortalized after death. If this is correct, then we see Francesca in the Comedy as she was in life.

But neither Dante nor we who read can be unaffected by the fact that the place is Hell and not St. Petersburg or medieval Denmark. Francesca in Hell does not offer us *merely* a picture of illicit love. If we are to acquit her, we must make up our minds about another question as well.

Every human being wants to be availed of, used—to death, if need be—by life. But if we are to pay with our own blood, we must know that what we sacrifice ourselves for is worth the price. Was it really a sacred duty for me, who was born Orestes, to slay my mother in order to avenge my father? That question pierces deeper after the judgment than any of the Furies' claws. Was I right to betray my country for my political convictions? Was it a just death to die when my country called me? Was I right in giving up everything else in life for the love of this mortal body which will soon grow old?

Dante knew the ancient Greek tragedies and the inexorable stars that guided the characters' destinies. As politician, thinker, and lover he had himself been tempted to give up everything for the sake of a single thought or passion. His Comedy takes place on many planes simultaneously. On one of these planes Dante wanders into his own soul. When he meets Francesca he is at a crossroads in his life. He is writing his great poem which—of this he has no doubt, as he wrote in the famous letter to his friend and patron, the Prince of Verona—is to guide people to a richer and happier life for hundreds of years. He could raise the span of his poem only if he gave up everything else for its sake.

Paolo and Francesca in the Comedy are not only reflections of the two lovers, Lancelot and Guinevere, in the Arthurian legend, they also act as foils to the leading pair of lovers in the Comedy: Dante and Beatrice. Like Francesca, Dante had also been seized with love for a *bella persona,* and this love determined the course of his whole life. When Francesca tells of her love and of how she was joined to Paolo, the pilgrim bows his head. When Virgil asks what he is thinking of, we hear him answer: "Alas, so many thoughts, so many desires that led them—Paolo and Francesca—to the woeful pass!" It is easy to understand Dante's thoughtfulness and the personal background to his reflections. He had seen Beatrice in the full bloom of her youthful beauty, and his heart had stirred to life within him. He must have longed for the kind of happiness and the union that Francesca sought and found. Beatrice had died, and in the poem her beauty leads him, not to sensual pleasures and earthly bliss, but to a broadened insight and the soul's redemption. He is so upset at Francesca's words because he recognizes himself, his own life. He could have abandoned himself to his passion and let it rule his life. He might have been here in Hell now, in eternal damnation, fused together with a being who could offer only a temporal happiness. He chose to love a woman who was dead and who, from her heaven, guided him as he wrote the great work. But the choice was hard, for it meant denying himself some of the sweetest and loveliest things that life has to offer. That is why such a violent tremor passes through the story of Francesca, the unhappy shade blown about by the fierce wind.

4

THE MORAL MUSEUM AND BRUNETTO LATINI

DANTE'S HELL is arranged according to a strictly moral system. Each sin has its appointed place. The primary rule is that the farther down we come in the conical abyss, the more heinous are the sins we find. The pattern is easy to remember, for what is more natural than that those who are farthest away from God bear the heaviest burden of guilt. Lucifer, chained at the center of the earth, is as far away from God as it is possible to be.

Francesca dwells in the second circle because of unbridled love. The gluttonous wallow in filth like swine in the third. The avaricious and the prodigal roll great weights against each other in the fourth circle. In the fifth, submerged in the mire of the Styx, the river of death, are the wrathful and the sullen. Out of their abasement they cry (*Inferno,* VII:121–124):

> "In the sweet air
> That is made happy by the sun, we were
> Corrupt, and harbored slothful fumes;
> And now we sorrow in this black morass."

The Swedish poet Vilhelm Ekelund, who loved Dante and has spoken so many apt words about him, writes that those who were sullen in the warm sunlight seemed to him to represent the most grievous sin of all.

Then follows the lower Hell, the Inferno proper, surrounded by a high wall guarded by demons, where the blasphemous, the violent, the suicides, the thieves, the wizards,

the flatterers, and the seducers are punished. In the ninth
and last circle the traitors lie frozen in eternal ice.

Whereas in the upper Hell the sinners do not offer
enough resistance to temptation and their sins are mainly
the result of incontinence, drunkenness, gluttony, lust; in the
lower Hell the damned are downright evil. They have had
a wicked will and acted as the tools of evil. Therefore they
are punished more severely.

There exists an enormous literature on Dante's hierarchy
of sins and on this hierarchy's dependence on antique and
medieval speculation. Dante comes into a great inheritance.
He has had an opportunity to listen to hair-splitting discus-
sions on rank and status in sin, on the nature and origin of
evil, and on the chances of atonement and purification. Many
older interpreters regarded the Comedy as minutes of court
proceedings in which Dante has noted down God's judgments. When the pilgrim shows compassion for several of
the damned, a man like Edward Moore, who has done so
much for the study of Dante, is eager to emphasize that it is
not the particular person's sin that Dante is overlooking, but
that even a man guilty of a serious crime can have likeable
qualities.

To the moralist, Dante's Hell is a museum in which the
zealous official, Dante, has classified the sins in accordance
with certain set rules. The visitor goes from showcase to
showcase, reading each label to see what kind of animal is
exhibited. It is not punishment he sees, but different species
of sin arranged by a Linnæus of morality. The basis of the
grouping is not a subjective evaluation, but a moral scale
which Our Lord has presented to humanity through the Bible
and the Church. Every human weakness is pictured vividly
and clearly, so that even those with little education can follow the wholesome instruction by object lessons. Many of the
sins are clad in allegorical dress that can be understood at
once. The hypocrites wear gilded copes of lead. The violent
boil in blood. The flatterers are smeared with human excre-
ment because they have defiled the world with their lies.
Dorothy Sayers is convinced that Dante has made room in

this flatterers' abode for our present-day gossip writers and yellow-press journalists who distort the truth and paint triviality in colors of importance.

Hell, seen from this angle, is a macabre exhibition hall where queer human specimens are displayed. The visitor moves around and is given salutary reminders. He sees his own sins epitomized, to the extent that he is capable of perceiving any faults in himself and does not smugly declare that useful, if rather hard, lessons are given here to people who indulge in vices in which, fortunately, he does not. Naturally, he sometimes questions the scale of values. By that, of course, I do not mean the valuation that has condemned the sinners to eternal punishment, but that which lies behind *the order of precedence*. But while the visitor, passing from one exhibit to the next, gives himself up to ethical reflections as far as lies in his power, he is seized by doubt and distress.

Francesca was a noble and lofty woman and even the most rigid moralist is shaken at the sight of her. True, the pilgrim encounters many unpleasant, not to say repulsive, beings: for instance, the glutton Ciacco in the sixth canto, and the arrogant and wrathful Filippo Argenti in the eighth. But a greater impression is made on him by shades like Francesca whose appearance in Hell comes as a shock. Among these shades are the Ghibelline chief Farinata, who is punished for heresy in a burning tomb (I shall return to him in the chapter on Dante's political mission), the Emperor Frederick II's chancellor Pier della Vigne, who has become a stunted tree in the wood of suicides and whose only crime is that in an attack of bitterness he has taken his life, and the writer and politician Brunetto Latini, who lives naked in a sandy waste where flakes of fire rain down incessantly.

Brunetto is in the seventh circle of Hell, and he and his like have been put together with the usurers, because, according to an old annotator, the usurers make fruitful what nature intended to be sterile (gold), while the homosexuals make barren what nature has created fertile (the sexual urge). Dante and Virgil have just emerged from the suicidal wood and pass along a dike that skirts the river Phlegethon. On the other side extends the fiery desert which they dare not step down on for fear of being burnt. A modern reader is reminded of the sunbaked earth that sets the scene for the two wretches in Samuel Beckett's *Happy Days*—a natural association, for Beckett is one of the writers in this century who is closest to Dante and who has been strongly influenced by him. The pilgrim and Virgil walk along the dike in the same way as a guard walks along a wall surrounding a prison yard. Down below they see a troop of people coming towards them, who, because of the glare and the distance, peer at the pilgrim's face, thus—as Dante says with one of those vivid everyday similes (*Inferno,* XV:21): "Like an old tailor at a needle's eye."

One of the figures recognizes Dante (*Inferno,* XV:23), stretches up his arm, seizes the hem of the pilgrim's garment, and cries: "What a miracle!" (*Qual maraviglia!*) His face is scorched by the flakes of fire, and Dante does not at once see who it is. Bending down—he is standing so high that his feet are on a level with the other's head—he gazes into the shrivelled face and exclaims: "Are you here, Master Brunetto?" (*Siete voi qui, ser Brunetto?*) The other says in reply: "O my son!" (*O figliuol mio*) "do not be offended if / Brunetto Latini lets the others go ahead / And in your company turns back a little."

Brunetto Latini was born in Florence in 1210 and was therefore fifty-five years older than Dante. He was one of the most illustrious men in Florence. He died there in 1294 after having held a number of the highest public offices. In common with Dante, he spent much of his life in exile, mostly in France. When he meets his young compatriot in Hell, he has been dead for six years. Brunetto was famous chiefly as a scholar and writer. According to the Florentine chronicler Villani, Brunetto was the first in Florence to introduce a more serious study of oratory and political science. His principal works were a prose encyclopædia in French, *Livre dou Trésor,* and the didactic poem *Tesoretto,* which he wrote in Italian and which had some influence on Dante's great poem. Several facts in Dante have, as research has shown, been taken from Brunetto's works.

In other words, Brunetto Latini was an elder colleague of Dante's. Tradition says that they were neighbors in Florence. In any case, during his childhood and youth, Dante's imagination was stirred by this eminent man. A number of the great figures in the Comedy are, in fact, people whom Dante sees for the first time on the stage of his childhood. It is natural that this should be so. None are so huge as those we see when we are children, and often we retain an after-glow of this original splendor all through life. Dante can say the words he uses about the three great citizens of Florence about many of his childhood's memorable figures (*Inferno,* XVI:58–60):

> "I come from the same land as you do
> And always with affection heard proclaimed
> Your accomplishments and estimable names."

Brunetto is one of these. In Hell the two Florentines walk together for a distance. Dante is ashamed of being above Brunetto on the causeway and reverently inclines his head as much as he can. We can presume that he is bent almost double, while Brunetto walks along with his head on a level with Dante's coat-tails.

Brunetto asks what chance or destiny has brought Dante down here before his last day and who is the man showing him the way. Dante answers in detail, and it is the first time he tells any of the lost souls how it is that he began his journey through Hell. He seems to feel duty bound to give his revered compatriot an explanation (*Inferno,* XV:49–52):

> "Up there above in the clear, calm life" I said,
> "Before I had attained the age of fullness,
> I found myself wandering in a valley,
> Which only yesterday I put behind me."

Now, Dante goes on explaining, with Virgil's help he is on his way home along this road. It is in order to reach the

sunlit heights—Paradise, man's real home—that he has undertaken this pilgrimage through Hell. Brunetto takes his words
to mean that Dante is speaking of the work he was engaged
on and the renown he hopes to gain thereby. And not without reason, for as the pilgrim presses on, so does Dante the
storyteller (*Inferno,* XV:55–60):

> "By following your star,
> You cannot fail to reach the port of glory—
> If I judged rightly in that beautiful life.
> If I had not died so early, I would have
> Given you encouragement in your work"

Brunetto behaves as befits an old and famous man in the
presence of a young follower. He does not lament his own
fate but is full of friendly encouragement. There are doubts
as to whether he really was Dante's teacher. He is in any
case a teacher in spirit, a model who inspires by his example.
He too has known the curse of exile. He utters harsh and
bitter words about the ungrateful and malevolent Florentines.
He predicts that Dante will be banished from the town where
they were both born and that the two parties—the blacks
and the whites—will snap and snarl at him.

Dante replies with a passionate outburst of gratitude and
affection (*Inferno,* XV:79–87):

> "If my own wishes had been gratified,"
> I replied to him, "you would not yet
> Have been exiled from humanity.
> For that dear and good paternal image
> Of you when, from hour to hour, in the world,
> You taught me how man gains eternity,
> Is fixed in my mind and now desolates me;
> And while I am alive it shall be on
> My tongue what gratitude I owe to it."

And we can imagine how he bends down even lower towards
the old man in the prison yard.

After some further speech, and after Brunetto has commended his *Tesoro,* the encyclopædic work in which he still

lives on earth (*nel quale io vivo ancora*) to Dante's care, the
two friends part. Brunetto must hurry in order to catch up to
his companions. He has run the risk of more severe punishment by talking to the traveler. Dante gazes after him and
recalls the famous annual foot-race at Verona: the prize was
a green cloth. At this moment, despite Hell and the unlovely
haste, Brunetto seems to him more like the winner than the
loser.

This meeting between teacher and disciple gives a picture of the spiritual sonship that every human must seek.
Dante the son up on the dike is not yet menaced by the rain
of fire, by age, and by death. Brunetto the father is scarred,
old, and seared, but has works behind him that will make him
immortal. Their meeting in the fiery desert sets in blazing
focus the cultural torch-race that is one of the Comedy's great
themes. No wonder T. S. Eliot was so fascinated by this
scene that he let it rise anew in the greatest of his quartets,
Little Gidding. With London burning in the air raids of
1940, the English poet confronts a man who seems to him
like a dead master. The stranger's face, like Brunetto's—or is
it Dante's? they had both been in the desert of fire, one dead,
the other in the vision of his poem—is unrecognizable owing
to burns, and the words of the Comedy are blown back on
the wind: "Are you here?"

At his meeting with Brunetto, Dante acts not only reverently but bravely. Since Brunetto is punished for homosexuality, Dante must be aware that a shadow could fall upon
himself. It is true that *O figliuol mio*—"O my son," "O my
dear boy," or however one cares to translate it—Brunetto's
form of address, can be construed quite innocently. But a
suspicious person might jump to conclusions. Nevertheless,
Dante admits his debt of gratitude to Brunetto and promises
to defend him in the world above. There is no allusion in
the Comedy to Brunetto's homosexuality. Were he not rele-
gated to the place where the homosexual is punished, we
should not even know of his "sin." Are we then to think that
Dante the poet considered the sentence on Brunetto Latini
so unquestionably just that he did not even think it worth-

while to discuss it? It was not Dante who had sentenced Brunetto to the desert of fire, but God. It is God who has meted out the punishments in Hell, and these decrees of God's are recorded in the Bible and in the other sacred writings of the Church. When Dante marks out Hell and its different circles, therefore, he is—as I have already implied—not an independent creator but a copyist. Actually, Dante is in exactly the same situation here as each one of us is in today. We too have organized *our* hell just as strictly as the Middle Ages ever did. It is just that we have no name for it. Shall we call it Public Opinion, subdivision Condemnation! In the various condemnation circles of this hell we place our fellow humans in accordance with our moral rules, our prejudices, and our conventions.

There is a stock exchange of sins, where prices rise and fall. When war threatens, treason is the worst sin of all and the traitor is thrust into the ninth circle. The more lasting the peace, the greater the understanding for the man who sacrificed all for another idea. The difference between us and Dante is possibly that we live in a somewhat less mono-political world. In the democratic world at least, many kinds of hell exist, so that the representatives of these institutions cannot make demands that are *too* tyrannical.

Therefore, Dante places Brunetto in the burning waste because the prevailing moral system enjoins him to do so. Dante was under compulsion in the same way as the Soviet writer is forced to repudiate Trotsky if he should come across the great revolutionary during his travels in the history of the Soviet Union. We can also picture Dante in the presence of Brunetto as a Victorian visiting Oscar Wilde in prison. He admits that the punishment is justified but remembers that the man *also* had a good side and was a genius. He is not so petty as to disclaim his debt of gratitude. It stands fast, even if it is owed to a sinner. This thought has been put forward by several learned Dante scholars.

But the meeting between the two great Florentines can be interpreted in another way. There is no connection—and this is often the case in Dante's world—between the punish-

ment and the inner status of the condemned. This is partly
due, no doubt, to a naïve narrative tradition that has left its
mark in the Comedy. But Dante knows how to make this
naïveté serve his ends. We are not above suspecting that he
is ashamed of God's judgments and that he makes use of
Hell as an alibi behind which he can preserve his inner
freedom. It was dangerous to be a heretic, and for Dante
the risk of such an accusation was especially great, as all his
life he was a critic and enemy of the papacy. In his political
writings he defends thoughts that come near to blasphemy.
Taking the part of suicides and homosexuals could also lead
to extremely unpleasant consequences. When Dante confesses
he is a friend of Brunetto's he is taking a risk similar to that
taken by a Soviet citizen under Stalin who spoke of his friend
Trotsky. Before the court of God, Brunetto was a loser, yet
Dante is bold enough to liken him to a victor.

In the culture of the ancient world that Dante revered,
love for boys was counted as something higher and more
beneficial to the soul than love for women. Dante, with Virgil
at his side, belonged to this culture, sat at the feet of Socrates,
Plato, and Aristotle and had recently been received into the
circle of the foremost antique poets. Was not Florence an
ancient city with an unbroken tradition from the illustrious
days of Greece and Rome? Was not the affection that arose
between teacher and disciple a fertile soil for fellowship and
growth? Did not the vulgar gossip of the common people
often give a distorted picture of this *eros,* which shunned
perchance all coarser forms of expression? The gentle, sympa-
thetic touching of a dear and ravaged face may have been
all that this feeling desired.

Brunetto Latini is a victor in Hell, and the meeting between him and the pilgrim is full of tenderness. Should
some medieval reader with very little feeling for naïve effects
be indignant because this prisoner, this teacher and seducer
of youth, punished for homosexuality, was described in these
rapturous terms, nothing would be easier for Dante the storyteller than to give a courtly bow and say: "But do you not
see, dear sir or dear lady, that Brunetto is in *Hell* and that

it is *I* who have placed him there? You surely don't believe that there are victors in Hell?" The words would be followed by a smile of both pride and contempt.

The Comedy has an objective moral pattern. But Dante is ill-suited to be an official in a moral exhibition hall. Having passed through the building at his side, we see that all the showcases have been broken. Or let me be a trifle more cautious—most of the showcases; for it would be wrong to imply that Dante is exclusively an evangelist and altogether lacks a stern moral strain. But in this fifteenth canto of *Inferno,* as in many other places, the rigid pattern is loosened, and the living water of compassion and understanding wells up. In it we see reflected Brunetto's noble face.

5

THE DEVILS

i

IN DANTE'S Hell, demons, devils, and monsters do service as guards. There are three-headed dogs, ferrymen with flames round their eyes, dragons with human faces, giants, and creatures that are half-man, half-bull. These beings from sloughs and subterranean caverns in nature and in the soul are very old. Every culture has had its fantasies about them, has feared them, and sought to ensnare them. During the centuries called the Middle Ages, they can be glimpsed everywhere. They are walled up in churches, they crawl about in old paintings, and the folklore and the drama of the common people are full of them.

Dante uses some of these creatures not only as guards but also as clowns and practical jokers. In the twenty-first and twenty-second cantos a gang of waggish devils with wings on their backs and long forks in their hands prowl along the edge of the broad ditch where venal officials are plunged into boiling pitch. If any sinner tries to rise above the surface to ease his scorching pain, the devils rush to poke him down again. They are like the scullions set by the cook to watch the meat boiling in the cauldron (*Inferno,* XXI:55 *et seq.*). Coarse jests and shameless remarks are bandied about. One devil trumpets with his rump. Another wants to prod the pilgrim with his fork. Two devils who have flown out over the lake of pitch start quarreling in the air. They clutch at each other with sharp talons like sparrow-hawks, get tangled up, lose height, and fall into the pitch, where their wings get so stuck together that they cannot rise again. The others try to rescue them with their forks.

In a scene like this the action is driven along with a circus whip. The demon jesters pop up with racy jokes between their teeth. Not even Bellman in his most boisterous poems has more movement and spontaneity. The sinners are there, of course, lying in the pitch like toads in the mud on a summer's day, but the black humor that is given free rein here chases compassion away. It is the fool who has his say and steals the show. The reader accepts the thought that Hell is also a place for farce, that next door to the greatest suffering is the emergency exit of gallows humor.

The devils represent a moral zero. They are members of a club of gangsters and hangmen who amuse themselves with absurd pranks while they work. They stand for absolute evil, and we find it hard to believe that they exist other than in our imagination. They are terminuses on the road of suffering. They have left all that is human behind and belong solely to the realm of demons. In the moral scheme, therefore, they cannot be used for anything but farce or decoration.

One would expect them to take to Hell like a duck to water. And there is no doubt that the scullions with their forks do feel at home, but other demons are tormented. Many of them have a great past; at one time they were gods, demigods, kings, or heroes in ancient mythology or history. The judge in Dante's Hell, as in Virgil's *Aeneid,* is King Minos of Crete. Together with his family—Pasiphaë, who crept into a wooden heifer and offered herself to a bull, was his wife, and Ariadne, who rescued Theseus with the clue of thread, was his daughter—this resplendent ruler over a mighty sea kingdom played a big part in Greek fantasy. In the underworld he has been transformed into a monster with a lashing tail. He indicates the sinners' place in Hell by the number of times he coils his tail round his body. His tail is thus so outrageously long that it can be entwined about him at least nine times. Plutus, god of riches, guards the fourth circle of Hell where the avaricious and the prodigal roll stones with their breasts, and he is depicted as a wolf with a swollen snout. The noble centaur Chiron, who taught Achilles, stands guard by the tyrants' river of blood. Hell is a place of assembly for those who have sunk to the level of demons. Dead gods, misshapen creatures, the nightmare serpent-women and bull-men, the deformed, and those who are utterly lost in the dark caverns of nature and the soul, all gather here. Hell is a demon kingdom that existed long before Christianity but which has also admitted into itself the Jewish and biblical infernal spirits with Lucifer, the fallen morning star, at the head.

But before the demons got as far as the terminus of suffering, before the light was snuffed out in their souls, where were they? When does the hangman become so perfect that he can joke as he works? There are paintings from these centuries in which one sees hangmen whose faces seem to reflect an utter callousness to the plight of the condemned. Were these hangmen so hardened that they no longer reacted, or is their callousness due to their conviction that they were serving a just cause? The real hangmen whom Dante and his contemporaries saw were servants of state and church. The victims of torture and execution were very often people accused of heresy. The first half of the thirteenth century saw the hideous massacres of the Albigenses. The hangmen dispensed a divine justice, and those who protest are weak and thoughtless.

In the twentieth canto, which precedes the scene with the devils at the chasm of boiling pitch, the pilgrim sees a crowd of weeping people coming slowly towards him. At first he thinks it is a liturgical procession, but when they come nearer —it is dark in Hell so mistakes are natural—he sees that their heads have been twisted around. As they cannot see in front of them, they are forced to walk backwards, and this accounts for the slow pace. Their tears stream down their backs and into the crack between their naked buttocks. The punishment has been meted out according to the simple symbolic rule of which the age was so fond. Those who are thus tormented have tried to pry into the future. Therefore God has twisted their heads around. Among them is Tiresias, who with the aid of sorcery prophesied the fate in store for Ulysses. Dante the storyteller urges the reader to profit by this sight and tells us that he himself burst into tears.

Leaning against one of the hard rocks in the sorcerers' valley, he weeps. Virgil, otherwise so moderate, flares up. "Are you another of those fools? / Whatever pity lives here is better dead" (*Inferno*, XX:27–30). And he goes on: "Who is more blasphemous than he who feels / Compassion where God's justice has prevailed?" Several scholars have asserted that Virgil's vehemence on this occasion is due to the reputation for sorcery that he had during the Middle Ages. Dante wants to show how unwarranted this slander is by making Virgil particularly zealous when it comes to putting down witchcraft.

But the hangmen in medieval paintings may also have been people who listened devoutly to words such as those spoken here by Virgil. Anyone feeling pity is guilty of dereliction of duty, guilty of a weakness which cannot be tolerated in working hours. The commandant of the extermination camp at Auschwitz, Rudolf Höss, who jotted down his memoirs before he was executed, shows qualms of this kind. He did feel queasy when supervising the gas-chamber murders, but regarded his pity as treachery to his Führer. If the Jews were not exterminated, it would be impossible to make the fair dreams of an Aryan millennium come true. The hangman in the concentration camp whose hand shook was a cowardly soldier in a righteous war. It was not pleasant to murder, but your conscience was clear so long as you did your job.

But the demons and hangmen in Dante's work are not happy. Though living in Hell as soldiers and officials under the institution's ruler, Lucifer, they know that there is a power greater than his. Did Rudolf Höss also know that his ruler's power was limited and did this cause him torment? I am not thinking now of the risk that Hitler might lose the war and the millennium might never come about. I am thinking instead of the possibilities Höss would have had in a victorious *Reich* of living happily as a retired hangman, tending his garden, and listening to the bleating from the sheepfold he dreamt about. We all live, it must be admitted, as retired hangmen in that we are sons and daughters of victors. History is about the downfall of peoples and civilizations, and might and not right has triumphed everywhere. But history also shows how a certain pattern, which is not that of might and violence, constantly recurs. It is difficult, and goes against the grain, to give it a name or even to sketch in its outlines. The abuses in this field are many and appalling. Yet in *The Divine Comedy* one cannot bypass this pattern.

ii

In the twenty-fourth canto of *Inferno* Dante and Virgil reach a chasm. The climb is so steep that the pilgrim sinks down panting and exhausted. He can be made to go on only after Virgil has admonished him, pointing out that men never come to fame without effort. The incident serves to show not only that ambition is an essential spur to the pilgrim and the poet during the journey, but also that the more terrible his experiences, the greater his inner resistance. It is a road of self-knowledge he is traveling, and now he is deep down in the abyss, hence the heavy breathing.

He pulls himself together, and the two wayfarers continue their climb. Down below them they hear a voice, but the speaker is so enraged that he cannot articulate the words. The pilgrim sees that the chasm below him is full of hideous serpents. People, naked and terrified, are running about among the reptiles with no hope of escape. Their arms are tied behind them with snakes. Snakes are coiled round their hips and chests. Dante sees a snake bite a man in the neck. At the same instant the man takes fire and within a few seconds is burnt to ashes. Out of the ashes, like Phoenix rising from the funeral pyre, the man resumes his former shape. He resembles, we read, a man who has fallen down in a faint and does not know whether it is evil powers or a stoppage

The monster Geryon, symbol of duplicity, who serves the pilgrim and Virgil as an airship. Illustrator: Gustave Doré (1832-1883). See *Inferno* XVII. The seemingly honest face is offset by a dragon's body.

The German Josef Anton Koch (1768-1839) is one of the painters who have devoted a great part of their lives to Dante. Here is a picture of the lake of boiling pitch into which barrators are plunged. *Inferno* XXI. The devils are equipped with long forks, with which they poke the sinners down under the surface. See the chapter *The Devils*.

William Blake (1757-1827) started working on the Comedy in 1824, having specially learned Italian despite his age. When he died three years later he had illustrated all the cantos in the Comedy, though most of the pictures were only sketches. This drawing shows a man and a six-footed serpent merging together in the snake-infested valley of the thieves. See *Inferno* XXV and the chapter *The Devils*.

William Blake: The theme of this picture also is taken from the valley where the thieves are punished. Man and serpent exchange shapes. *Inferno* XXV.

of the blood that has caused him to swoon. He rises, looks round in fear and bewilderment, and sighs heavily (*Inferno,* XXIV:97 *et seq.*):

Not far from where we stood, a serpent sprang
Upon one wretch, transfixed him at the place
Where the neck is knotted to the shoulders.
Never was "O" or "I" so quickly written
As he burst into flame, and, thus consumed,
Fell in a heap of ashes on the ground;
And after he was thoroughly demolished,
The ashes reassembled by themselves,
And in a flash he was himself again.
So—according to the great savants—
The Phoenix dies and then returns to life

Dante tells us that this is Vanni Fucci, a man of violence and a thief, who has stolen church plate and allowed another to be blamed. Fucci is as savage, brutal, and debased in Hell as in life, and Dante declares that this thief has been justly punished. The pilgrim and Fucci converse, and the latter says that "life of the brute, not man, delighted me" (line 124). It grieves him that Dante sees him in his misery, and in order to forestall any malicious enjoyment of his plight he predicts Dante's coming misfortunes. Fucci gives vent to his spite and fury by making an indecent gesture with his fingers, explaining that he is thus insulting God. Without delay a snake coils itself tightly around his neck so that he cannot get another word out. The pilgrim's words are the cruelest he utters in the whole Comedy: "From that moment on the serpents were my friends,"—*Da indi in qua mi fur le serpi amiche"* (*Inferno,* XXV:4). Dante's words, it should be added, are given extra force and venom by the fact that Fucci belonged to the black party which had driven Dante out of Florence.

The valley of serpents is reserved for thieves. That is why we find Vanni Fucci there. The pilgrim and the reader have not been in this place long before their senses are befogged as though by drugs and snake venom. The pilgrim sees a centaur with serpents entwined about him and on his neck a dragon with outstretched wings. It vanishes. At the same

moment, in a stealthy and dreamlike way, three spirits approach (*Inferno,* XXV:35 *et seq.*) and address the pilgrim
and his guide. Dante lays a finger across his mouth to draw
Virgil's attention to the newcomers. A six-footed snake fas-
tens itself on one of the spirits, clinging to him as tightly as
ivy to the bark of a tree. The forefeet seize the man's arms,
the middle feet his belly, the hind feet twist round the thighs,
and the tail is thrust between them, entwining itself round
the loins. The fangs gash his cheeks. Reptile and man begin
to melt and stick together as if they were of wax. It looks
the same as when paper is set alight and a brown color runs
before the flame. The white dies but the black has not yet
appeared. The man's and the snake's heads become one. Two
new extremities are formed from the man's arms and the
snake's forefeet. Thighs, legs, belly become members "such
as never man beheld." Of the original being nothing is left,
and the horrible new creature moves slowly away.

Dante the poet has not yet had enough. A snake rushes
at the second of the three men as swiftly as a lizard darting
from hedge to hedge in the heat of the dog-days. The snake
bites the man in the navel and falls to the ground. The man
gazes silently at the snake. He begins to yawn, as if overcome with sleep or fever. Man and snake eye each other.
Smoke issues from the fang-wound in the belly and from the
snake's mouth. The two plumes of smoke mingle. Reptile
and man begin to exchange shapes in the smoke that unites
them. The snake's tail is cleft in two, and the man's legs
grow together: the snake thus acquiring legs, and the man a
tail. Where scales grew, there is now human skin, and the
reverse. The human arms withdraw into the armpits, and the
reptile's short legs lengthen. The snake's hind feet take on
the form of a penis, and the man's genitals are divided. While
this transformation is taking place the two beings stare hyp-
notized into each other's eyes. The man falls to the ground
and the serpent gets up. The man's brow sinks in, the ears are
drawn into the head like the horns of a snail, the tongue is
cleft. When the exchange of form is complete, the smoke

ceases. The snake glides away, hissing, and the man spits after it.

The reader knows that the people undergoing these hid eous transformations are thieves. Dante, however, is tactful enough not to say a word about it in the text. We felt un certain about Vanni Fucci. Despite his savage brutality, the punishment seemed far too inhuman. We could perhaps con sole ourselves with the thought that the fire which consumed him and out of which he rose again was a symbol of a bestial nature's mad rage. At the same time, we saw that the wretch was a prey to something that resembled an epileptic fit depicted by an artist who, even at the sight of this pain, was capable of making realistic and detailed notes. The text itself hints at a disease, for Dante uses the simile of a man who falls prostrate because of a stoppage of blood—*oppila zion* (*Inferno,* XXIV:114).

As for the other two, the thought of their punishment grows more and more repugnant. If this is the fourteenth century's idea of how thieves should be treated, we must turn away in disgust. We are told very little about the kind of people who suffer such horrible transformations. We know that one of them belonged to the black party in Florence, but we shrink from the thought that Dante is here indulging in an act of revenge. Nor does the scene make sense to us if we try to interpret it allegorically. A person who gives himself up to vice is changed into a reptile. It may be effective as imagery, but it is trivial as an interpretation of a soul. What does exist in the poem and cannot be explained away is that people are broken down. They are not punished here for some extrinsic crime, and the punishment they suffer comes not from outside but from inside. What happens to them is inexplicable to Dante. He refrains from any comment other than that with which the transformation canto ends. His eyes are perplexed and his mind dismayed by the weird spectacle.

Those with changed shapes are threatened to their very core. They are about to slide out of every human fellowship. They resemble the insane rather than the punished. The in articulate cry that Dante first hears might just as well come

from a madhouse. The desperate creatures running about
naked might as well be bound with ropes and strait jackets
instead of with snakes. Those who dwell here are human
spawn who have been kicked out of their homes and disowned even by their mothers. They are brothers and sisters
of Kafka's Gregor Samsa, who was changed into a beetle, of
the mad women in Agnes von Krusenstjerna, who felt claws
growing out of their eyes, and of Dostoievsky's shattered
creatures, who regard their misfortune as a diabolic con-
tagion.

Whether those we find here are robbers, murderers, and
traitors or not, is of no account. Their punishment is the
result of an inexplicable threat under which they live. We
recognize them from plague-stricken zones that our thought
seldom enters. As we regard them, we also look down into
our own soul as we look down into the depths of the sea
when someone turns a searchlight on it. Creatures are moving there which we have only dimly imagined.

Dante's Hell is also a madhouse where evil changes take
place, and all that is human dies. Here, as elsewhere, the
pilgrim is a tourist but at the same time a fellow actor. It
happens that he is drawn into what is going on and must
defend himself against those who attack him. He is infected
by Vanni Fucci's insane hatred and wickedness. Is that why
he declares his liking for the serpents which stifle evil? Or
is it that, when he sees brutishness emerge in humans who
have their origin in God, he is seized by the conviction that
Hell really is an institution of justice? Those who have
chosen bestiality have thereby chosen eternal torment. The
pilgrim's avowals of love would then be a sign that he had
recovered his mental health. He begins to understand that
Virgil was right to put on a cheerful countenance when
entering the chasm. It is worth noting that the twenty-fifth
canto's description of how snake and man exchange shapes
is interrupted by an aside to the reader (*Inferno*, XXV:94–
102):

> Let Lucan be still where he treats of Sabellus
> And Nassidius, and listen carefully

To what comes next; and let Ovid be silent
About Cadmus, and Arethusa, too:
I do not envy him if, as a poet,
He turned them into snake and fountain;
For he never changed two beings, front to front,
In such a way that both forms readily
Exchanged one substance for the other.

In other words: Dante admits he is writing in conscious emulation of the very poets into whose circle he has been received in Limbo—Ovid was renowned for his transformation scenes, his metamorphoses—and is thereby following an antique tradition. One deliberately competed with one's predecessors, often challenging them in the text itself. This kind of contest also plays a large part in modern writing, but the challenges, the mention of prototypes and the exulting in having excelled them, have fallen out of fashion.

But whether we interpret the transformation scenes in these *Inferno* cantos as descriptions of diseased states, as depictions of the power of evil in man, as artistic showpieces in an astonishing *genre,* or as these three alternatives together, we still do not exhaust the significance of the scenes or account for their powerful effect. We turn the light on the men who are being transformed and seek an explanation. When the analysis is complete, the big scenes go back into the mysterious gloom in which they are enacted. They exist. They show the breaking down of the human forms. People have had such experiences in all ages. Dante's boast that he excels his predecessors is not unwarranted. Is it true of his successors?

iii

The devils and monsters who serve as hangmen in Hell are also the beings that have been transformed, that have been excluded from the circle of brothers and sisters and disowned by their mothers. They are at once executioners and victims, murderers who fuse together with the condemned on the scaffold. Some of the most moving scenes in the

Comedy show us dying demons. When Virgil utters the
name of the archangel Michael, the wild beast Plutus, who
guards the fourth circle of Hell, falls to the ground as instantly and definitely as the sails of a ship that collapse in a
tangle when a storm breaks the mast (*Inferno,* VII:13–15).
At the encounter with the two pilgrims, the Minotaur acts like
a bull which, at the moment it feels the death blow, plunges
helplessly to and fro (*Inferno,* XII:22–25). Anyone who has
seen a bullfight knows how brilliant this image of loneliness,
rage, and utter hopelessness is.

The demons' fury is understandable in the light of their
duties. Dante, in traversing their realm, is trespassing on
their rights. Normally they have power over those who come
to the infernal regions. With Dante and Virgil, who are
under the protection of a higher power, they are forced to
give way. They are jailers in the service of the commandant,
Lucifer. In Dante's presence they are reminded that there is
a power greater than the commandant's. Is their rage partly
due to their knowing that love is more powerful than hate?
When they meet the pilgrim, who is sent by God, does some
memory stir within them that they themselves once belonged
to a world which in a double sense was a world of light? Is
the Minotaur a hangman who is pierced by a ray from this
world just as the bull's heart is pierced by the point of the
sword? For those in the world of *The Divine Comedy* it is
natural to answer yes to such a question.

When Dante the pilgrim has journeyed all the way
through Hell and in its last circle crosses the eternal ice, he
fancies he sees a turning windmill ahead of him in the mist
(*Inferno,* XXXIV:6). He makes the same mistake, only in reverse, that is made three hundred years later by Don Quixote,
who mistook real windmills for giants. For this *is* a giant the
pilgrim has in front of him—Lucifer, the Evil One himself,
king and ruler of the infernal regions. Lucifer resembles not
only a windmill but also (Professor Charles Singleton has
shrewdly analysed this scene) a cross. The four huge sails of
a windmill can, in fact, easily be confused with a large cross.
Lucifer wanted to be like God, and he has gained his end.

He is a copy of God but in reverse. He has three heads and is therefore triune like God. The wind of hate that blows out of him makes everything in his realm freeze over and die, just as God in His kingdom makes everything grow and live with the aid of sunlight and love. Lucifer was the fairest of the angels, and he was a servant of God. He is still a servant in Hell. Everyone who sees him knows what God is like. Lucifer is a sign which stands and points to God. He illustrates the words of St. Augustine: "As an artist God makes use even of the devil. If God could not make use of him, He would not let him exist at all." In other words, Dante has the highest possible sanction when he makes use of the devil in the Comedy. In its allegorical pattern it is therefore right that the pilgrim, by climbing Lucifer's body, gains the abyss which leads him up out of Hell.

Lucifer is like God because he is crucified, he suffers. Tears stream from his six eyes and bloody froth dribbles from his mouths. He—and all the servants in his realm share his fate—has the sign of the cross branded forever in his soul. Dante, in common with the age in which he lived, believed that man's soul was created by God and that every human being retained a memory of the bliss he felt at the moment he left God's hand. In the universe built by Dante, this conception of a sign of the cross remembered seems realistic.

Even the most wretched of creatures is an angel that has fallen. Here, too, some words of St. Augustine apply: that a nature in which there is no good cannot exist. We all keep—though it be only as a far-off dream—the memory of goodness, security, rippling water, vicarious suffering, a love that does not seek its own. Those who feel definitely shut out suffer the most. They are demons who die when the light strikes them, when the memory of the security they have lost passes by in their hell. The greatest torment in Hell is the dream of liberation, but because that dream exists, there is no Hell. It is merely an image of pain and a sign that points away from it.

6

ULYSSES

DANTE ENDS the twenty-fifth canto of *Inferno*—his account of the hideous transformations—by saying that he feels faint and is bewildered by what he has seen. The transformations take place in a dream state. In the twenty-sixth canto the pilgrim is still very upset. He and his guide are now passing through a rocky tract between the seventh and eighth pit of Hell located in the sloping series of ten concentric pouches known as the *Malebolge*. Below him he sees a chasm filled with flames. As so often, Dante illustrates his narrative with a simile drawn from everyday life, and there is a frightening contrast between the idyll of the simile and the horrors it is used to elucidate. As the peasant, resting on the hill in the evening, sees the dale beneath him full of fireflies, so the eighth pouch of Hell is alight with flames (*Inferno,* XXVI:25 *et seq.*).

When Dante understands what he sees, he is greatly troubled. He says—and suddenly Dante the pilgrim and Dante the storyteller are demonstratively on the scene together—that he sorrowed then and that *now,* i.e., when he is writing, he sorrows again: *"Allor mi dolsi, ed ora mi ridoglio"* (*Inferno,* XXVI:19). He goes on to say that he must curb his genius more than he is wont lest he go astray from his kindly star.

Each flame contains a human being. The punished are entirely wrapped in fire. As they burn they move forward, and the poet is reminded of the prophet Elijah, who, with chariot and horses, vanished in a cloud—a fitting image here, as the whole canto is about a great journey. The pilgrim sees a flame cleft at the top and asks his guide who lives inside it.

He is told that it is Ulysses who is being tortured there together with his companion Diomedes. They are being punished, Virgil goes on, because they counseled guile: It was Ulysses who thought out the ruse of the wooden horse which helped take Troy, and Virgil makes special mention of this "crime." He adds an allusion to the hero of his own great work, Aeneas, who was a son of Troy and became the founder of Rome and thereby the progenitor of all Italy. Virgil wants to underline the justice of the sentence passed on Ulysses, a man who outraged one of the instruments God himself had chosen.

Still very much disquieted, Dante asks Virgil if it is possible to communicate with those inside the flames. Three times he repeats the word *prego* when begging Virgil to let him await the horned flame. Virgil answers that Dante's request "deserves all praise" but urges him to hold his tongue during the encounter. Ulysses and Diomedes are Greeks and might not want to listen to what Dante has to say. It is hard to understand why Ulysses would better tolerate Virgil, who had so rapturously sung of his enemy, but the problem, discussed by many Dante scholars, will not be gone into here. It is at any rate Virgil who addresses the ancient double flame as it approaches. He calls upon the two heroes to stop and asks Ulysses to tell them how he died. It may seem surprising that he enquires about this and not about the sin for which Ulysses is punished, but the author of the Comedy is unusually fascinated by the moment of death—understandably in an age when everlasting bliss or everlasting damnation might depend on the circumstances at the last moment of earthly life.

For other reasons too, it is essential to the Comedy that the moment of death should often come to the fore. The dead are occupied in reflecting on their lives. Time has stopped for them; only the past and the eternal torments they are now suffering exist. But these eternal torments often consist of this past petrified—a fossil inside the stone of eternity. Their lives come to a focus at the moment of death when the final decision was made. They *must* look back through the very aperture provided by their death scene. In this they resemble each one of us who is still alive. We look back on our life through the window of the present moment. Every *now* is really a moment of death, for we do not know if we shall live any longer. We therefore have reason constantly to look back on our life as though for the last time and to think over what we have done. It could thus be said that tact and psychological insight make Virgil ask Ulysses about the manner of his death. This must be what Ulysses wants to speak of most, even if it causes him pain.

At Virgil's exhortation the larger horn of the divided flame begins to quiver and crackle as though torn by the wind. The tip of the flame moves as if it were a tongue. Painfully—he has been silent for so many centuries and should be even more hoarse than Virgil was in the first canto of the Comedy—the hero within speaks. Ulysses tells them that soon after he returned to Ithaca from his wanderings after the fall of Troy, he set out on his travels again. Neither reverence for his aged father, affection for his son, nor love of his wife Penelope could conquer his ardor to gain experience of the world and of human vices and virtues. With a small company of those who had not deserted him, he put forth to sea with only one vessel. He sailed through the Mediterranean, saw the coasts of Sardinia, Spain, and Morocco, and reached the sound known today as the Straits of Gibraltar. When they came to this "narrow pass" where Hercules set up his pillars to stop men from venturing farther, Ulysses and his shipmates were old and slow. He says a few words to his friends (*Inferno,* XXVI:112–120):

> "O brothers," I said, "who through a hundred thousand
> Perils have reached the Occident at last,
> Do not forbid your senses, in this
> So brief vigil that remains to you,
> The adventure of the world without
> Human beings that lies beyond the sun.
> Consider the nature of your origin.
> You were not made to live like beasts, but for
> The pursuit of virtue and of knowledge."

Ulysses, inside the flame, goes on to tell Virgil and the pilgrim the rest of his story (*Inferno,* XXVI: 121–142):

"With this short address I made my companions
So enthusiastic for the journey, that
I would scarcely have been able to restrain them.
And, having turned our stern around at morning,
We made wings of our oars for that wild flight,
And continued making headway towards the left.
Already the night beheld all the stars
Of the other pole, while ours was so low
That it did not rise above the ocean floor.
Under the moon the light had burned again
Five times, and just as many times gone out,
Since we had penetrated that deep strait,
When a mountain, dark and blurred by distance,
Came into sight that seemed to me
The highest mountain I had ever seen.
We were overjoyed, but that soon turned to tears,
For a great whirlwind sprang up from the new land
And started battering the vessel's prow.
Three times, with all the waves, it made the ship
Spin round; the fourth time it lifted up the stern,
And sent the prow down—as Another willed—
Until the ocean had closed over us."

No similar account of Ulysses' death is known; it may be entirely a fabrication of Dante's. In his youth, several daring Genoese set off on a voyage in search of land on the other side of the ocean but were never heard of again, and Dante may have been influenced by this leap in the dark that predated Columbus. For us, Ulysses is an obvious symbol of the love of adventure and thirst for knowledge. The eminent Italian Dante scholar Bruno Nardi has suggested that Dante got the idea for the episode with the sirens from Homer. Dante was not directly familiar with Homer, but of course saw frequent references to him. Cicero in one of his books says it is unreasonable to think that the enchantment that took Ulysses captive consisted merely of empty singing tricks. "It is knowledge which the sirens offer," Cicero goes on, "and it is not surprising that he who loves wisdom holds such song dearer than his home." These are words which seem to echo those of Ulysses in the Comedy. Knowledge entices more irresistibly than anything else does. The siren, as a giver of knowledge, is the most dangerous of all women.

Ulysses is aware that he is defying the will of the gods. He is prepared to sacrifice everything for the sake of knowledge. Not to seek knowledge of countries and people, of good and evil, is to exist like brutes. He goes in search of experience independent of divine decrees and human taboos. He is well aware that a higher power does not want man to penetrate to the other side of the globe. In his story he hints several times that his voyage was a sin. He calls it "the mad flight" and his comment on the final foundering is that "Another"—that is, God—desired it. Nevertheless, he made the voyage and does not regret it. In no respect has he changed his attitude in Hell. He is like an athlete who has been beaten and alludes without the least sentimentality to his defeat and to the victor's greater ability, but who does not let that keep him from thinking proudly of his own efforts and from taking credit for his ambitions.

Several Dante scholars have regarded Ulysses as the personification of striving after knowledge for its own sake. He is a genuine representative of the spirit of outward and inward conquest which is the prerequisite for all human progress. Even when age and death approach, "the evening of the senses," as it is called in the poem, he continues to gather facts and to push on. He is an example to all who sink into despair at the end of life. For Ulysses the way is full of meaning, even if the goal is annihilation.

Ulysses is opposed to the conception of the universe commonly associated with the Middle Ages. God has created the world and set a limit to man's knowledge. The world is an ingenious clock which one day will strike the awful hour of doomsday. Man can learn how the cogs interlock, how the hands move, and how the pendulum swings; but in his quest for knowledge he must, of course, remember that it *is* clockwork he is studying, that there is a controlling hand behind it, a meaning in the times and images shown on the dial,

and a final goal. The watchmaker's name is God. It is for His
sake we seek knowledge of the clock—the world. St. Augustine prayed to God to save him from the temptation of seeking knowledge for its own sake, and that prayer often rose
to Heaven during the centuries that followed.

But Ulysses has forgotten this. Despite the divine inter-
dict he decides on his voyage and sets sail. He behaves like
a man with nothing to lose, who begins from the beginning
and questions not only the fruit but also the root and the
origin. He is the most dangerous man in the whole Comedy,
and it is really he who should be lord of Hell, not Lucifer.
What is Lucifer beside Ulysses but a wretched juggler and
mimic! Lucifer wanted to be like God. That was his pride,
and in this he was actually the most pious and humble of all
God's servants. For can one pay greater homage than wishing
to be exactly like the person one loves? Lucifer is an ingrati-
ating flatterer who has suffered under a delusion, who has
never understood that when God made man in His own image
and likeness, he kept the power for Himself. On that point
God wanted neither images nor relations. And Lucifer's punishment was the most shameful and ridiculous of all—he has
attained nothing and at the same time is forced to play the
part of a God in reverse, testifying in everything to the one
he defied.

God's real enemy, on the other hand, is Ulysses, a man
who considers knowledge and freedom of search more important than God. When he grows old, and more than ever
should be thinking about saving his soul, he continues his
seeking and is overtaken by death in the middle of his foolish
exertions. Ulysses despises God and wants to be as unlike Him
as possible. Many fancy they recognize in him the hero of
the Western world *par excellence.*

With the exception of Francesca, the pilgrim is more
upset at the sight of Ulysses than of anyone else in Hell. It
is easy to understand his disquiet. The Comedy itself, and
not only Ulysses who appears in it, tells of a journey to a
forbidden realm. No one is allowed to descend into the abode
of the dead. There are not many cantos left before the pil-

grim is to climb the Mountain—Purgatory—which Ulysses saw after voyaging for five months and which was the origin of the destroying whirlwind. Although Ulysses is a heathen and lived many centuries before Dante, we have to accept the fact that in the Comedy he embraces the same view of the universe as the people of the Middle Ages. It is one of the fictions that offer the imagination little difficulty. Dante, like Ulysses in the poem, is a man who penetrates to unknown tracts and now, in the autumn of his life, seeks knowledge of human vices and virtues. Was his journey also in defiance of God's will?

The pilgrim has worried about this. In the second canto he asks Virgil where he is to get his authority to go down into Hell while still alive. He recalls that Aeneas, while clad in the flesh, descended into the lower world. But Aeneas had been chosen by God to found the Roman empire and in "the immortal world" was to learn things necessary to his appointed task. He also remembers that Paul, according to a medieval legend, had gone down into the infernal regions, but this descent, too, was for the purpose of founding a mighty kingdom—the Church. Paul and Aeneas had been empowered by God to penetrate to the realm of the dead. What reason was he, Dante the pilgrim, to give for his journey? Even if Dante had not read Homer, he probably knew that Ulysses, who is standing before the pilgrim, had also forced his way down into Hades and that the recklessness he showed then was akin to the feelings that drove him across the ocean.

Virgil has reassured the pilgrim—in the second canto of *Inferno*—by telling him that he has been sent to guide Dante by three holy women in Paradise. The Virgin Mary, Lucia, the saint of light, and Dante's beloved Beatrice, overcome with compassion for the pilgrim when they saw him menaced in the Dark Wood, have resolved to save him. The journey takes place at their request. Just as Christ once descended into Hell in order to break its power, Beatrice descends to see Virgil, tell him of her anxiety for Dante, and ask Virgil to help him. She says it is love which prompts her to speak.

Dante's journey therefore takes place with the sanction of both love and God.

When the pilgrim, who has doubted and despaired, hears Virgil's account of the meeting with Beatrice, his heart, the poem tells us, responds like flowers which have closed and drooped in the chill night but raise their stems and open their petals to the morning sun. "So much good daring" (*tanto buono ardire*) runs to his heart that he feels like a man set free (*Inferno*, II:133–139):

> "O she who out of pity has aided me,
> And you who with such gallantry and speed
> Obeyed the true words she addressed to you,
> You have roused in my heart, with what you say,
> Such a great eagerness to go ahead
> That I have come back to my first intention.
> Let us go; we two have but a single will"

The journey to the lower world begins in this mood. In other words: There is a striking resemblance between the feelings that animate the pilgrim at the start of his journey and the feelings of Ulysses' companions. A further similarity is that the adventurers are roused to their daring by an adviser, guide, and friend—the pilgrim by Virgil, the seafarers by Ulysses. They are all seeking knowledge and virtue.

Dante and Ulysses' shipmates are thus in the same situation, but Dante is also closely related to Ulysses himself. It is no exaggeration to say that they are like two brothers, one of whom has been blessed and the other cursed. In Ulysses—particularly in the opinion of Benedetto Croce—Dante recognizes himself. When Ulysses comes towards us in the mantle of flame he personifies ambitions and temptations familiar to Dante. The pilgrimage is not only a journey to the bowels of the earth and to lands on the far side of the globe, but also a journey inwards into the land of the soul, and there the traveler runs a greater risk of trespassing than he does in the world of outer reality. Had not Dante just looked into the forbidden world of madmen and sorcerers and been seized with dizziness? One wonders whether Dante himself was sure which of the two brothers, the blessed or the cursed, was the nearer to him.

Virgil tells the pilgrim that Ulysses is being punished for his guile with the wooden horse. Most readers will surely find the sentence barbarous, for it is based on the assumption that Troy was on God's side and that Troy's enemies were therefore to be punished. Aeneas is in the right camp and Ulysses in the wrong one. There are persons in the Comedy who have both counseled guile and been treacherous themselves, but who are rewarded with celestial bliss because their treachery benefited God's chosen people. One example is the harlot Rahab, who betrayed her countrymen and let Joshua's men into Jericho. For this piece of infamy she is commended in Paradise. Like other tyrants, God looks with pleasure on every fraud that profits Himself. The same law applies here as in the totalitarian state. The traitor is a louse to be crushed, and he is to be denied any human greatness. On the other hand, he who betrays for the sake of his country and the party is a true hero and is placed in the nation's pantheon. Such acts go unquestioned in every tyranny.

When Dante equips Ulysses with human greatness—for his story bears witness to the intractability and fire of his spirit—he is acting as he did with Brunetto Latini. Ulysses is the same in Hell as he is in life. If we wish, we can see the flame in which he is wrapped as a symbol of his ambition, of his constant desire for more and more knowledge. It drives him forward, giving him no peace, burning his soul night and day. The flame is the very nature of striving, seeking man, a curse which dogs him all his life, yet at the same time it is a blessing. Ulysses, we could also say, is the Renaissance man, a representative of unconditioned search immured in a medieval prison of faith. The fierce strength he possesses is proof that his liberation is near.

In his monograph, *The Ulysses Theme* (second edition 1963), W. B. Stanford draws a parallel between Dante's Ulysses and Faust. Dante, Stanford says, has realized that it was immoral to condemn Ulysses because of the wooden horse. It was the victorious Romans who spread the myth of

Ulysses as a sly magician who should be cast out of the company of decent people. Ulysses had not in fact offended against any internationally recognized moral code when he hit on the ruse of the wooden horse. Rather it was his duty as one of the Greek leaders to make use of every possible means of victory. Dante has accepted Ulysses as an example of an evil counselor but has deepened the guilt that rests upon him. Ulysses was a false and bad adviser, for he persuaded his companions to seek forbidden knowledge and was thus the cause of their death. For Stanford, Dante is a man who wants to warn his contemporaries against seeking knowledge unconditionally. Stanford sees him transferred to our time as a man who is trying to check the atomic physicists before their experiments have blown the earth to bits. Dante has been tempted by Faust's craving for knowledge but has resisted, and in the person of Ulysses Dante condemns his craving. Joseph Mazzeo has much the same idea. According to him, it is Dante the pilgrim who is impressed by Ulysses and glorifies him in the Comedy, for the pilgrim, as he makes his way through Hell, is still a sinner who knows no better. Dante the storyteller, on the other hand, has reached a higher moral level. He therefore places Ulysses where he belongs—in Hell.

Both Stanford and Mazzeo seem to forget that the traveler is not only Dante the pilgrim but also Dante the storyteller. In the fancied framework of the Comedy, in which we study Ulysses and Dante the pilgrim, things go badly for the former and well for the latter. The pilgrim, if one is to believe Stanford and Mazzeo, learns that his admiration for Ulysses was wrong. But what about Dante the storyteller? Is he too, when he writes of the three realms of the dead, under divine protection?

He believed—of this there can be no doubt—in a punitive God, an order of rank for sins, and a plan of salvation which humanity had to follow. He believed in the clockwork. But perhaps, in his artistic inspiration, he also experienced some of the same things that distinguished Ulysses when he defiantly set out on his own course and navigated unknown waters. Was Virgil right when he assured the pilgrim that the journey was prompted by a divine love? Yes, in the Comedy Virgil is certainly the prototype of a good counselor and thus the opposite of Ulysses. Virgil was even considered in his works to have foretokened the coming of Christianity. The fact that the matter of Dante the pilgrim's and Dante the poet's authorization is taken up in the Comedy must in the last resort mean that authorization was necessary, that Dante the poet had moments of doubt when he overstepped forbidden limits and forced his way into spheres reserved for God and the angels. Perhaps he noticed that in *his* poem, in *his* Hell, all did not conform to the great pattern. When the word is made flesh, when living beings spring up on the basis of the great design, then theories no longer hold good and the dogmas of faith are burst asunder. The writer who lets Ulysses tell his companions that they are created not to live as brutes, but to seek virtue and knowledge, cannot allow these words to echo in his poem without also, if only for a moment, investing them with truth and sovereign power.

Arnold Norlind, one of the few Swedes who has devoted productive years of his life to studying Dante, says that the difference between Ulysses and Dante the pilgrim is that the former's motive in seeking the Mount of Purgatory is "selfish at heart, even if it gives itself such fine names as 'to seek virtue and knowledge.'" Dante on the other hand, Norlind says, sets out for Purgatory in order to free himself from his own lower self. But if Norlind is right in saying that Ulysses' motive is selfish, so is the poet's motive in writing the Comedy, for it is his own salvation and his own glory he is seeking. If Mazzeo is right in his view that it is the pilgrim who glorifies Ulysses, it is the storyteller who lets him do so. And if Stanford is right in maintaining that Ulysses' fate is meant to be a warning to the Fausts of humanity, then the poet must be accused of having equipped the condemned man with the most brilliant and demoniacally attractive qualities. If Ulysses is to be punished, Dante the storyteller should also be punished. If Ulysses is a captive in a medieval prison, Dante the storyteller is a captive too, a captive who is filing at his chains.

The picture of Ulysses in the Comedy is so vivid because it shakes with terror of damnation. Does Dante see his poetic self in Ulysses? One thing is certain: He has portrayed Ulysses' companions as men who perished because they took the advice of setting out on a great voyage of discovery, and in this they have been deliberately contrasted with the pilgrim, who was exhorted by Virgil to undertake a no less hazardous journey. There is an affinity between the journeys. Dante lets Ulysses and his men go under, but the actual account of Ulysses' greatness in life and in death is not without elements of risk. Dante the artist places Ulysses under two curses at the same time: that of deceitful advice and of a godless quest for knowledge. But at the instant Ulysses' ship is dragged down into the deep, some reader may fancy he hears a cry. Throughout the Comedy let the reader remember that its hero and author bears the name not only of Dante, but also of Ulysses, and in this guise, wrapped in an everlasting flame, wanders the world.

7

FINALE IN HELL

THE PILGRIM is near the bottom of Hell, and it is getting darker and more difficult to see. To a corresponding degree his mind is dimmed and his feelings are confused. In the valley of the thieves he has seen men changed into reptiles. Despite swirls of horror and pain he was able to keep his human and artistic balance, but he stressed the fact that his mental powers were enfeebled by what he had gone through. In the following cantos we witness a gradual infection of the feelings.

The thirtieth canto begins by evoking images of two figures who are utterly broken and stricken insane. King Athamas of Thebes was seized by the delusion that his wife was a lioness and his two sons cubs. He shouted to his huntsmen to spread a net to capture them, grasped one of the boys, and dashed him against a rock. The mother drowned herself with the other child. Priam's wife, Hecuba, whose tragic fate also plays a part in Hamlet's life, was carried off as a slave after the fall of Troy. Her daughter was slain on Achilles' grave. Her son was washed up dead by the waves. Hecuba's mind is unhinged by grief, and she rushes around barking like a dog. These two scenes, described as usual with words which seem torn from the breast and are therefore very few, illustrate the mental state in the last chasm of the *Malebolge*. Here dwells Myrrha, who seduced her father after taking leave of her senses. Here the pilgrim also meets two notorious falsifiers: Adam of Brescia (*Inferno*, XXX:49), who counterfeited florins, the gold coins of Florence, and Sinon, who by lies and deceit persuaded the Trojans to drag the wooden horse into Troy and thus caused the city's capture. These two, the forger of coins and the falsifier of words, begin quarreling and wishing each other increased torment. Dante listens intently to this vile scene between the two men, one of whom suffers from maddening thirst and the other is bloated with dropsy. Virgil interrupts, telling the pilgrim that it is "a vulgar wish" (*bassa voglia,* line 148) to want to listen to such base wrangling. Dante is so filled with shame at this rebuke that at the moment of writing he feels it again. The episode shows that the pilgrim's own mind is now seriously threatened. He has entered a world where he is drawn into evil and frenzy and very nearly goes under.

The thirty-first canto describes the descent into the last circle of Hell, the ninth. The pilgrim and Virgil move silently through the thick gloom. In the distance they hear a mighty blast on a horn, and Dante recalls the most famous horn blast of the Middle Ages, the one blown by Roland in the pass at Roncesvalles as a signal to Charlemagne to come to his aid. The image is aptly chosen, for the help came too late and Roland and all his host were cut down by the Saracens. In the same way, the two travelers are now approaching a zone where help is far away and perdition near.

In the distance the pilgrim thinks he sees a number of lofty towers and he asks his guide if they are coming to a city. The medieval towns of Italy were dominated—as our big cities are by skyscrapers—by towers up to two hundred feet high, which were the combined dwellings and fortresses of the great ruling families. When he gets nearer he sees that what he took to be towers are giants sunk to the waist in stone wells. They are standing around the ninth circle, or central pit, of Hell, bound with strong chains and thus serving more or less as watch-dogs. It is one of them who has blown the horn.

Dante remarks that we can be thankful that the race of giants has died out on earth, for no mortal can stand against those who combine "the instrument of the mind" with force and evil will. It strikes the reader that the giants' guilt consists mainly in their large size. They are as extinct as the mammoth and the dinosaur. Chained in their wells, they are representatives of people who have perished because they could not adapt themselves to the demands of a new age. They are symbols of innocent losers whom history has rolled across and crushed. One recalls the dire inscription over the gate of Hell—that it was supreme wisdom and primal love which built this city of pain and woe. It is quite plain here that this supreme wisdom is speaking the language of sheer might. He who is born a giant shall not be left among the living, for he is a menace to those who are not giants and who happen to be identical with the people of average size who build cities, till the soil, organize churches, rule kingdoms, and write mundane or divine comedies.

When the giants loom up in the half-light they are therefore a kind of liberation. True, it is said of one of them, Nimrod, that he showed defiance when he built the tower of Babel and of another, Ephialtes, that he wanted to try his power against the gods. A modern reader is more familiar with another of the giants—Prometheus, who stole fire from the gods and gave it to men, and who is punished for his "crime" by being chained forever to a rock on Mount Caucasus. But the whole of the thirty-first canto, in which the giants are placed before us, is chiefly the account of a guilt which is no more than a destiny inflicted by the gods and has nothing whatever to do with punishment. In this sense Oedipus was also guiltless, for he did not know that it was his father he killed and his mother he married. Orestes, fated by the laws of a blood feud to murder his mother, was not guilty either in our sense. He and Oedipus were giants inasmuch as the feeling of duty towards the role that fate had assigned them grew to gigantic proportions and overshadowed all else. The giants in Dante are outside every moral pattern, outside the verbatim record of the trial proceedings. Something mysterious adheres to them, something that points far back to times before all civilization. Apart from their tremendous decorative effect in the infernal landscape, they serve in the Comedy as heralds of the last great human drama in Hell. The blast on the horn announces the entrance of Count Ugolini della

Gherardesca and the savage natures that are tortured with him.

One of the giants on the brink of the pit is Antæus, who drew new strength each time he touched his mother, Earth, and whom Hercules overcame by lifting him high into the air and strangling him. At Virgil's request—to gain his ends Virgil makes use of flattery—Antæus picks the two pilgrims up in his huge fist and lowers them down to Cocytus, the ice plain comprising the last circle of Hell. There, frozen into the ice, lie the traitors. Just as the frog in the summer heat has only its nose above the water, so these wretches have only their heads above the ice. When they weep, their tears turn to icicles. Two of these beings are frozen together and keep butting each other like he-goats with interlocked horns.

Something extremely unpleasant now happens to Dante. He is making his way, shivering, across the ice, while below him are thousands of faces grinning with the cold. By mistake he strikes his foot against a head. With a shriek it yells at him (*Inferno*, XXXII:79–81): "Why do you kick me? / Unless you come to wreak more vengeance for / Montaperti, why must you molest me?" The pilgrim, seized by a suspicion, stops. At the battle of Montaperti on September 4, 1260 between the Guelfs and Ghibellines of Florence, one Bocca degli Abati played a vile trick. He belonged to the Guelf army, whose success the Alighieri family fervently desired, but had been bribed by the Ghibellines. The battle had hardly begun when he cut off the right arm of the Guelf standard-bearer. The standard fell to the ground, and this helped to confuse the Guelf forces, which suffered a crushing defeat. Dante has an idea he has stumbled on Bocca and asks Virgil if he may stop to confirm his suspicions. He asks who the man is and receives an angry answer. The man in the ice will not give his name. The pilgrim then bends down, seizes the man by the hair and says (*Inferno*, XXXII:98–102):

"Either you tell me what your name is,
Or not a hair will be left standing here!"

And he said: "Even if you leave me hairless,
I shall not tell or indicate who I am,
Though you pounce on my head a thousand times."

The pilgrim has already coiled Bocca's hair round his hand
and pulled several tufts out of the scalp, the wretch howling
up at him and keeping his eyes downcast, when one of the
others in the ice spitefully shouts Bocca's name. Dante lets
go of Bocca's hair, calls him an accursed traitor, and threatens
to increase his punishment by telling of his shame in the
world above.

Several times during the journey there have been indica-
tions that the pilgrim cannot pass through Hell mentally un-
scathed. We have seen him struggle against agitation of mind,
and here he is overpowered. At this moment he loses all dignity and appears mean and cruel. For even if Bocca's treachery was base and brought disaster to the party that Dante
and his family traditionally belonged to, the punishment was
horrible enough and should have prompted the pilgrim to be
moderate.

It is possible, of course, that this argument is a romantic
psychologizing of the encounter between Dante and Bocca.
When we find the pilgrim acting with such cruelty towards
Bocca we are tempted to imagine ourselves in his shoes and
refuse to accept what is offered us simply and directly. Perhaps the meeting with Bocca reflects an implacability and a
savagery that was a natural component of Dante's nature,
but we find it hard to reconcile with the magnanimity he
shows on other occasions. What are we to do if it is true that
Dante gloated over the recollection of this encounter, of the
kicks he gave the traitor's head, and of the hair that he tore
from his scalp? What if Dante thought his own conduct was
fair and that when writing the canto he was justly exposing
Bocca to the loathing of the reader? What if he did have a
temperament of this kind and if, even before God, he believed he could judge so harshly and behave so cruelly? Or
rather: What if, as so often before, he applauds God's sentences and acts as hangman's mate?

Even older interpreters, Edward Moore for instance, who

lay more stress on the objective, moral framework of the Comedy than we do, hesitate before the pilgrim's inhumanity on this occasion. But Moore solves the problem for himself by reminding the reader that Dante often appears in the guise of an Old Testament prophet. The pilgrim's experience and behavior, which are presented as belonging to his person, are actually the experience and behavior of mankind. The curse Dante utters is uttered in the name of mankind, and Moore ends by recalling Tennyson's words: When the poet says *I*, it does not always mean that he is speaking of himself. The whole human race is speaking through him. According to this view, therefore, when Dante meets Bocca he is supposed to be carrying out a divine sentence. Such an interpretation is all the easier since Moore makes no distinction between the Dante who is the poem's hero and the Dante who writes the pilgrim's adventures.

I am, of course, aware that my own interpretation is influenced partly by the modern acceptance of the difference between the narrator and the self he is telling about and partly by the desire of this age to see a faltering "human" in every writer. Many have written about Dante as though it were possible to penetrate to *the truth* about him. They imagine Dante in much the same way as Dante imagined the created world. To God everything was quite clear, but man had to search long and laboriously to find any clarity. So too with Dante. He sketched out his world: the three realms of the dead and all their teeming destinies. He worked with great precision and always knew what he was doing. The reader approaches Dante's work and makes an effort to understand. One day he arrives at Dante's own conception.

Interpreters like these—they are many—forget that the Comedy is a poetical work and that it would have no interest for us if it contained ready-made solutions. It has unrelieved tensions within it; hence it is alive. Here, as we pass across the ice, we are in one of these inexplicable zones of tension. We are compelled to keep many ways open. It is certain that Dante the storyteller, though not perhaps Dante the conscious human being (the writer who is quite clear as to every movement is no writer), has known that here in the last cantos the ground was undermined. That is why madness, a frenzy that is beside itself, forces its way nearer and nearer to the surface.

The biggest scene in the frozen regions remains. A man is biting into a head stuck in the ice immediately below him. He resembles a starving mongrel that seizes a bone in its teeth. Aghast at this cannibalistic savagery, Dante stops and asks the tormented spirit his identity. The sinner lifts his face from the horrid meal (*fiero pasto*), wipes his mouth on his victim's hair, and begins his story. He says that desperate grief wrings his heart, but he wants to tell of his fate in the hope that his words will bring infamy to the traitor he gnaws.

His name is Count Ugolino della Gherardesca and the man he is chewing is Archbishop Ruggieri. The Count had treacherously been taken captive by the Archbishop and shut up with his children in a cage meant for falcons. After being there for several months he had a dream which foretokened his fate. He saw the Archbishop hunting a wolf and its cubs. Savage dogs took part in the chase and soon the he-wolf and the cubs seemed to tire. In an instant their flanks were ripped open by the sharp fangs.

When the Count awoke with the dream pounding in his head, he heard his sons crying in their sleep and asking for bread. The same morning the dream began to come true, for as the hour approached when food was usually brought to the captives they heard the door being nailed up. They were sealed in, and their fate was to starve to death. The Count says that he turned to stone within, so great was his horror. He gazed at his children, unable to utter a word. His little son Anselm wept and asked why his father was staring so wildly, but he could not answer him. The day passed and night came.

Next morning, when a feeble ray of light crept into the prison, the father saw four white faces, reflections of his own. He bit his hands in anguish, but the boys thought he did so from hunger. They rose from the floor where they

Robert Rauschenberg, born in Texas in 1925, one of the innovators of "pop" art, has illustrated all of the *Inferno* cantos. He exemplifies a newly-awakened interest in Dante among the *avant-garde* artists. Of the writers, Samuel Beckett is the foremost. The theme of this picture is taken from *Inferno* XXXI: the imprisoned giants in the wall around the lowest pit who are symbolized by the Olympic winners in hammer-throwing. Dante and Virgil can be seen in Antæus's hand. The horn is the one the travelers hear in the darkness and which sounds as terrible as the blast on Roland's horn at Roncevaux. *Collection, The Museum of Modern Art, New York.*

William Blake: Dante compels the traitor Bocca to reveal his name by pulling his hair. *Inferno* XXXII. On the left, Count Ugolino, who is frozen into the ice and is digging his teeth into the neck of his mortal enemy, the archbishop.

Auguste Rodin (1840-1917) worked on Dante themes for many years. Here is Count Ugolino, with his dying children in the sealed-up hunger-tower at Pisa. *Musée Rodin, Paris. Inferno XXXII and XXXIII.* © SPADEM 1966 by French Reproduction Rights, Inc.

Virgil and Dante ascending from the underworld through the narrow passage. Lucifer's clawed feet sticking up. *Codex 365 Urbinato, Vatican Library.*

lay and offered themselves to their father as food (*Inferno,*
XXXIII:61–63):

> "Father, we would suffer much less
> If you would eat us instead; you clothed us
> In this wretched flesh; take it from us now."

The Count then calmed himself in order not to make them
still more unhappy. That day and the next they were all silent.
On the fourth day without food and water Gaddo fell at his
father's feet and said: "O father! why don't you help me?"
Then he died. Between the fifth and the sixth day the Count
saw his other three sons die one after the other. For the
next three days the Count, now blind from hunger, groped
about over the dead children's bodies, calling their names.
"Then," he says, "hunger did what sorrow could not do"
(line 75). The Count was dead at last.

This story is perhaps the most terrible in the whole
Comedy. It becomes still more so if, as some annotators do,
we infer that the Count was so overcome by hunger that he
was tempted to try and eat his dead children's bodies. It is
thought that the words "hunger did what sorrow could not
do" hint at this. In any case the Count really does turn
cannibal in Hell when he digs his teeth into his mortal
enemy's neck.

Like the Archbishop, the Count had been treacherous on
several occasions in his political career. In Dante's moral
system, therefore, he belongs in the ice. But here is a case, if
ever there was one, of punishment being a state and not a
penalty. For the Count, gnawing like a starving dog at his
enemy's neck, is so beside himself with anguish at the
suffering inflicted on his children that no other pain can
touch him. Remove him from the ice in Hell and place him
in a flower garden with birds singing and bees humming
and his agony would be just as great, his lust for revenge
just as fierce. Is it not a balm for him that he is tormented
physically, for this bodily torment may be palliative in the
same way that physical pain gives a moment's relief to a
person numb with melancholy.

What are the feelings of Dante, the pilgrim and poet, as he stands before Ugolino? Only a few steps earlier, face to face with the traitor Bocca, he was seized with a fury and vindictiveness almost as savage as the Count's. Like the Count, he was thrown into a state of brutish cruelty by this fury. The canto goes on to say that Pisa, the town where Ugolino starved to death, should feel shame and disgrace for having put not only the Count but his children to such torture. The reader cannot help agreeing. But Dante too behaves harshly. He places Ugolino, despite all his suffering, in the last circle of Hell and suggests that Pisa should be punished by damming up the river Arno so that everyone in the city is drowned.

After parting from Ugolino, the pilgrim shows yet another mark of brutality. A shade addresses him. It is Fra Alberigo, a contemporary of Dante, with several heinous crimes on his conscience, one of them being the murder of his brother and nephew. He invited them to a banquet and towards the end of it he called out, "Bring in the fruit!" This was the agreed signal to the servants to rush in and kill the guests. His crime is therefore of the same nature as that of Ugolino's enemy. Fra Alberigo is now a captive in the ice, and as a sign that his crime is even worse than those of the others on the icy plain, his face is turned upwards. His tears freeze to a crust which, his hands being locked in the ice, he cannot remove.

In the dark Fra Alberigo mistakes Dante for a criminal who has been sentenced to the same punishment as himself. He begs him to lift the ice crust off his face so that he can vent some of his sorrow in tears. The pilgrim replies that he is willing to do so if, in return, he may know the sinner's name, adding: "If thee therefore I do not extricate, may I go to the bottom of the ice" (lines 116–117). We already know that those sentenced to the worst punishment do not—unlike those living higher up in Hell—wish to have their names disclosed. Fra Alberigo is convinced by Dante's solemn assurance. He reveals his name, which is well known to Dante, and alludes to the "fruits" he once served. Now, he says, dates are given him in return for the figs he offered his brother. The pilgrim is astonished, for he has not heard that Fra Alberigo is dead. In fact, this fratricide is still alive on earth. It is only his soul which has been cast down into Hell. Fra Alberigo tells Dante that the circle of Hell he is now in contains souls of this kind. The criminal's soul has already begun to serve its sentence in Hell while his body still lives on earth and is there governed by a devil. It is thus possible for a man to eat, drink, sleep, and wear clothes while his soul exists in Hell.

When Fra Alberigo has revealed this horrible secret to Dante he claims his reward. "Reach here thy hand and open my eyes," he says. But the pilgrim does not keep his promise, for, so the poem says, it was only right to act meanly to a man such as Fra Alberigo. Like the sly crofter's son of the fairytale, the pilgrim knew how to trick Fra Alberigo. He promised to free him from the crust of tears or else go to the bottom of the ice. Fra Alberigo, who thought Dante was a sinner, naturally took this to mean that Dante pledged himself to incur an even worse punishment if he broke his promise. The pilgrim knew that he was on his way to the bottom in any case.

Is the pilgrim's renewed baseness yet another proof of his mental contamination? Psychologically it is natural that he, who has just shrunk back in horror at the agony endured by Ugolino, should grow callous at the sight of a man who acted as vilely as Ugolino's murderers and let even innocent children suffer. Alberigo is from Genoa, and Dante the storyteller calls down a horrible curse on the city, as he did a moment before with Pisa, wondering why it has not been wiped off the face of the earth because of its viciousness. But to me it seems as if the meeting with Ugolino completed the pilgrim's development. That is, the infernal part of his development is at an end. When he meets Fra Alberigo and himself makes use of lies and treachery, he has for a moment been transformed into one of the devils who torment the sinners and find their pleasure in doing so. The story of Fra Alberigo, who has been given hellish dates instead of blood figs, has a farcical streak. It is a satyric drama which is a sequel to the Ugolino tragedy. As a sign of this, the poem alludes to the prankish demons who prowled along the edge of the chasm where the venal politicians were plunged into boiling pitch. Alberigo mentions a man whose soul is in Hell though his body is still on earth. This man, Branca d'Oria, had murdered his father-in-law, Michael Zanchë, who was one of the barrators in the twenty-second canto. Sudden associations like this are one of the secrets of Dante's art. A bow of electric sparks is stretched between the place where we are and a scene in a previous canto. The whole Comedy—*Inferno, Purgatorio,* and *Paradiso*—is simultaneously present in the poet's imagination. At any moment he can call up any figure or any scene he likes in order to illustrate any other situation. On top of the most grievous pain comes the grim humor of the hangmen, and all at once we find ourselves beyond good and evil.

Thinking back to Ugolino, we see that he, like the giants, is guiltless. He is a human being furnished with superhuman passions, a giant of pain, paternal love, and hate, a man who cannot be fitted into any moral system. We bow to his awful greatness. For such a nature, Christian filiation and Christian humility are unattainable. Devoured and blinded by his political passions, by his lust for vengeance on his opponents, Dante the pilgrim tore out Bocca's hair in the same way as the Count tore hair and scalp from *his* victim. There is a connection between these two savage scenes. It was necessary for the Count to be imprisoned in the ice, for a sentence to be pronounced on him, and a punishment meted out. Until that had happened, the pilgrim, Bocca's furious tormentor, could not go on towards Purgatory and Paradise. In the Christian doctrine that is Dante's, this can happen only by a miracle, only by the intervention of grace. Even we realize that the pilgrim, who tricks Fra Alberigo into revealing his secrets, is not going to find it easy to make his way up into the world of light and human fellowship by himself.

In the thirty-third canto of *Inferno* Count Ugolino tells of his and his children's death in the hunger tower. Only one canto remains, the thirty-fourth. Here, we meet Lucifer. He looms out of the mist on the icy plain, and tears are pouring down his three faces. He is a creature petrified in despair. It is perhaps a touch of exaggerated allegory when the pilgrim and Virgil, as a sign that even Lucifer testifies to God, must climb down the monster's body in order to reach the narrow passage leading from the center of the earth up to the Mount of Purgatory on the other side. The two travelers lower themselves down Satan's hairy flanks. When they reach the thigh, Virgil turns himself head downwards, a procedure that causes him severe effort. The exertion is all the greater because Dante, at this dangerous and critical point, is clinging to his neck. Virgil begins climbing up and the pilgrim's heart is in his mouth, for he thinks they are about to return into Hell. In fact, they have now passed the center of the earth and Dante sees Lucifer from below. In the allegorical pattern this indicates that Hell is an upside-down world, that everything there has only to be turned inside out for God's love and God's Heaven to emerge.

Dante has been a visitor and a tourist in Hell. But he has also been a fellow actor and has himself shared the experience of many of those doomed to live there. And, of course, he has been a prophet and a moralizer, who, fired by God's wrath, has demonstrated the different kinds of sin and brandished his scourge over his contemporaries. But it is as a fellow actor and a fellow human in Hell that he moves us most, because we think it more important to understand than to judge. When the pilgrim takes his leave of Hell, he does so thanks to the grace that Beatrice, who is keeping watch over him, mediates. As a sign that he is incapable of anything by himself, he is borne by Virgil during the last steep climb. The ability of Dante the storyteller to continue is due, as Brunetto Latini hinted, to his genius and his ruthless determination to penetrate into the depths of the soul and extract its secrets so that he and his readers shall not have to go on living in isolation, knowing nothing of themselves or of the hidden power of motivation that governs our words and deeds. *Inferno* concludes with this passage:

> Along that secret path, my guide and I
> Began our journey back to the bright world;
> And, without thought of pausing for a rest,
> We kept climbing up, he first, I second,
> Until, through a round opening, I glimpsed
> Some of the beautiful things the sky carries:
> And then we came out to see the stars again.

Purgatorio
Purgatory

8

THE DELECTABLE LIFE

DANTE AND VIRGIL have come out into the open air.
The pilgrim has breathed the underworld's "dead air which
had afflicted eyes and heart" (*Purgatorio*, I:16–18). Now he
is back in the "pure light," and it is a great relief to him.
The reader of the Comedy feels this relief in the very character of the verse, which now changes. The journey through
Hell began in a Dark Wood. The description of Purgatory
opens with a sea image:

> Per correr miglior acqua alza le vele
>   omai la navicella del mio ingegno,
>   che lascia retro a sè mar sì crudele.

> To cruise in better waters, the small vessel
> Of my imagination now hoists its sails
> And leaves behind it such a cruel sea.

It is just before dawn on the morning of Easter Day, the third
day of the pilgrimage. On the horizon shines the morning
star, Venus, brighter than the constellations of Pisces (*Purgatorio*, I:19–21):

> Lo bel pianeta che ad amar conforta
>   faceva tutto rider l'oriente,
>   velando i Pesci ch'erano in sua scorta.

> The fair planet that emboldens love
> Was making the entire East smile, and was
> Veiling the Fish that were her retinue.

The smile that is kindled in the east, the messenger of dawn,
lingers throughout all the cantos of *Purgatorio*.

On this spring morning the pilgrims have reached the foot of the Mount of Purgatory. It lies in the southern hemisphere in the middle of the sea. The placing is Dante's own idea. With his passion for geometrical precision he has made Purgatory an antipode to Jerusalem. The medieval mind conceived the center of the world as the city where Jesus was crucified, and thought that the inhabited world spread out around it. In Dante, Purgatory floats in the center of the southern ocean. At the top of the Mount lies the Earthly Paradise from which Adam and Eve were once driven forth. This the pilgrim will finally attain after his ascent of the Mount.

The sun has not yet risen. The travelers are standing on the shore of the ocean. I will leave them there in this and the next chapter; they are in any case in need of rest after their harrowing experiences in Hell. Instead, I should like to try first to indicate the nature of the place they have now come to, and then to discuss the fundamental features of *The Divine Comedy*.

According to Roman Catholic belief, Purgatory is the abode of souls departing this life in grace but requiring to be purged before they can enter Paradise. It is the second of the realms of the dead Dante passes through with the help of Virgil. He climbs the Mount and, just as in Hell, he finds that strict moral rules are in force. The Mountain rises in terraces and each ledge is devoted to the purging of a particular kind of sin. The same principle applies as in Hell: the farther down the more grievous the sin and the greater the resistance sensed by the traveler. Once again pilgrim and reader find themselves in a moral museum, the difference being that in Hell no development took place—the sinners, unchanging and unchangeable, were imprisoned like flies in the amber of perdition. In Purgatory, on the other hand, the souls are purified. Purgatory is a hatchery where membranes break and buds burst.

Dante the pilgrim arrived in Hell and made his way through its nine circles just as a stranger wanders through a large town by night. He knew it was a penitentiary he had come to, but he did not walk along with the code of laws in his hand. He was a human being with a heart in his breast. At one moment he reacted with compassion, at the next with loathing. Sometimes he wept, sometimes he smiled in scorn. He is the same person now that he has come to Purgatory. He is in a real place and not inside a theological speculation. The stars that shine down on him when he emerges from the underworld are real stars. The sea that stretches towards an endless horizon is a real sea. When the sun rises, the shadow cast by his body is real. He is in Purgatory in the same way as Huckleberry Finn is on the great brown Mississippi River, floating along on his raft at night under the stars.

To us, Hell is strange and hostile as a penitentiary, but familiar as a state. It was through a realm of suffering people that the pilgrim passed. It is the same with Purgatory. An institution for the correction of souls after death seems irrational and absurd to most of us. But as a state, what is more familiar to us than Purgatory, for it is identical with our life such as we live it here on earth.

It is, therefore, a stroke of genius on the part of Dante that he has located Purgatory not in the underworld next door to Hell, as was mostly done during the Middle Ages (Thomas Aquinas is one of those who embraced this view), but up on the earth's surface. For in some respects it is his own life the pilgrim is now starting. Purgatory, as Umberto Cosmo puts it, is Dante's notebook.

Or to put it another way: The story has been brought back to everyday life from nightmare and agony without hope. In Hell, pain has no meaning. In Purgatory, on the other hand, suffering does have a meaning, and thus despair never gains a foothold. It is like the pangs that rend a woman at childbirth. Even if she is to be pitied, even if she moans and begs for an anaesthetic, a smile is never far away. She, like those standing around her, knows that something great is happening to her, that a new life is being brought up from waters a thousand fathoms deep.

The members of a family gathered round a deathbed hang on the doctor's lips and speak whatever words of comfort enter their minds. But in their hearts they all know this comfort to be a sham—stage scenery and paper flowers which they grasp at in this hour of utter despair. What a relief it would be if someone were to speak the truth! In Dante's Hell this relief is felt. There is comfort in the very hopelessness. The truth, however terrible, tastes better than lies. Pain put into words gives even the most wretched of us courage to endure. Those who embody pain, sustain life, because pain, were it to stay mute, would overwhelm us.

When a child is born, on the other hand, comfort is a reality, a live bird which flies through the room. The woman in her torment merely has to be told that an anaesthetic might harm the child, and she gladly gives up all thought of it. Here it is a question only of a trial. Every instant a larger perspective presses into the smaller. It is life which is being created, and nothing momentary, however disrupting, can shake assurance and hope.

This is how things are in Purgatory, where we proceed from pain to happiness. A mightier and greater life is not far off. One day we shall awaken to it. If in Hell there is a dream of something better, of something else, it is a lie. When the lie vanishes, the soul sees with renewed intensity that all is stone, desert, and death. In Purgatory the dream is real, for even if death does at last dig its claws into the heart of one not yet born, none can doubt or deny that the newborn, if he lives, will first go to meet the sunlight and a loving glance.

The pilgrim, now arrived in Purgatory, will find that the spiritual conditions prevailing here are the same as those on earth. Whoever looks into the Medusa's eyes is turned to stone and is forever captive in his melancholy. But nobody can live without in some way yielding to the illusion that life has a meaning. This is particularly true of childhood and youth, and it is these two ages of man to which the *Purgatorio* cantos are mainly devoted. Purgatory is the very will to live, the urge to press on. Extending on one side of it is the wasteland of death—Hell, where people who have lost their souls live; on the other side is the dream of salvation and

eternity—Paradise. *Purgatorio* is the middle section of the
Comedy, and it is in the center that we now find ourselves.
Some people see death in everything, and the people of the
Middle Ages did not forget this perspective any more than
we do. But everyone at some time or other has lived in life
as a child and a trusting disciple.

Purgatory is our life. As soon as Dante takes us with
him, we recognize it all. The scenery we knew on earth
extends on all sides. The pilgrim strolls through vernal land-
scapes which are familiar to us from Italy. Dante the poet,
who recently showed his talent in describing parched deserts
or icebound wastes, now musters all his skill to depict nature
at its loveliest. He has a fondness for imagery which brings
to mind moments of joyous change and repose in nature. At
the beginning of the seventeenth canto he illustrates a new
spiritual insight with the metaphor of a man who is overtaken by a mountain mist and sees his surroundings as dimly
as a mole through the skin. Then the sun breaks through,
the mist is dispersed, and the valleys appear far below. In
the twenty-seventh canto the pilgrim, Virgil, and Statius
each lie down to sleep on a ledge. Above them bright stars
are burning. They rest like goats which, after their nimble
leaping among the rocks, ruminate quietly in the shade during the heat of the day guarded by the herdsman leaning
on his staff. In the twenty-eighth canto, when the pilgrim
reaches the earthly paradise where thousands of birds are
singing in the trees and the air is laden with the scent of
flowers, the breeze stirs in the branches as "through the pine
forest on Chiassi's shore" (line 20). Chiassi was a place and
a river near Ravenna, where we know that Dante spent a
long time. After the excursion to the underworld, after the
reminder of a life without a gleam of hope, we have come
home to our life at its best, to our life as we once knew it or
as it is when we still think it worthwhile to bring up children,
combat the stupidity in the world, or penetrate into a great
poetic work.

In Hell the people Dante met were convicted, but spiritu-
ally unaffected by their punishment; they were captive, but

not broken; they held out, because they went on being themselves; they made up a proud race. The reader of the *Inferno*
cantos stops with a shudder before one great figure after
the other and experiences the dramatic conflict between the
ghastliness of the punishment and the stubbornness of the
sinner. In Purgatory, on the other hand, the people that
Dante meets—although they too are punished, and many of
them have to endure great torment—all accept the pain with
joy because they know that it develops them and makes them
worthy of Paradise.

The principle of justice that applies in Dante's Hell is
that of retribution: An eye for an eye, a tooth for a tooth,
a life for a life. In the huge place of correction the prisoners
themselves are well aware of this. Bertran de Born carries his
own head in his hand like a lantern because he has incited
father and son against each other and thus parted what naturally belongs together. He tells Dante that his punishment
testifies to the law of retribution (*lo contrapasso, Inferno*,
XXVIII:142). In Purgatory a more humane and modern
administering of justice prevails. Thomas Aquinas thought
not only that Purgatory was situated next to Hell in the
underworld, but also that the punishments in both places
were of the same kind. Of recent years Bernard Stambler has
written of this in his work *Dante's Other World*. In Dante,
however, there is never any question in Purgatory of meting
out punishment which is to weigh against this or that sin.
Instead, Dante seeks ways of correcting those who have gone
astray, of restoring the sick to health. In his Purgatory there
is no retribution. It is all a matter of how the sins can be
blotted out.

It is natural that Dante's method of presentation now
changes. Hell is rough, old-fashioned, and dramatic. At every
moment it maintains contact with an ancient realm of death
and demons and is that part of the Comedy which depends
most on prototypes. In Purgatory the poet takes a bolder
grip, his outlook is more lyrical. He is navigating virgin
waters and he breathes with greater freedom. It is no longer
the great destinies of other people which predominate. The

light falls more strongly on the pilgrim himself, on his development and his wrestling with moral and religious problems.

The vernal Italian landscape is the frame for the superb pictures from the world of friendship, love, politics, culture, and poetry that follow.

9

TO WRITE LIKE GOD

MODERN DANTE SCHOLARS, in their study of the unique artistic quality of *The Divine Comedy,* have reached new conclusions, conclusions that are the result of a deeper penetration into the medieval conception of the universe. In this I am only an amateur, a follower who has listened to a number of masters. I am indeed grateful to such men as Erich Auerbach, Etienne Gilson, Charles S. Singleton, Joseph A. Mazzeo, Johan Chydenius, Umberto Cosmo, Ernst Curtius, and others. When they put forward different views, I find it hard to choose. The most important thing to me is finding fruitful starting points—paths into the great work, viewpoints and clues which make it easier for me to understand and explain. My presentation is very concentrated, and I have allowed myself a certain stylization. As I write, I am not always clear as to the source of the knowledge I use. Nor do I know where to draw the line between what I have borrowed and what is my own. What I say here is mine only in that I feel myself to be in possession of it.

Dante had the highest of exemplars when he wrote the Comedy—God Himself. Dante and his age took God's creation of the world in a spirit of perfect love for granted. The creation, with soil, trees, animals, and people; and history, with battles, assassinations, and the rise and fall of mighty nations, exist in a simple and unmistakable way and can be grasped by reason and the senses. But nothing in the world exists only for its own sake. Each thing and each event is also a sign and has a meaning outside itself. Creation and history are a book written by God's hand. A man of insight reads the huge pages and sees God's meaning in everything.

God has written another book—the Bible. It is written on the same principle as the book of creation. The Bible begins with Genesis, God creating Heaven and earth, and ends with the Revelation of John, the last judgment, when the time that God has allotted to man has run out. Between the creation and the judgment comes the greatest happening of all —God's incarnation in Jesus, His crucifixion, His sacrifice of atonement, His overcoming of sin and death, and His resurrection. The writing of God's first book, the created world, is not yet finished, and will not be finished until doomsday. But because we have the Bible, we know what the end will be.

The Bible is also to be read in two ways. What it says is literally true. Cain killed Abel. David in a linen ephod danced before the ark of the Lord. Jesus raised Lazarus from the dead. But there is a deeper, hidden meaning as well. This meaning, again, is threefold, so that actually the Bible is enacted simultaneously on four planes. The first plane, the literal one, is a straightforward account of what happened. Let us call it the historical plane. The second plane instructs us in what the account means. On this plane the historical facts we are given can be regarded as allegories concealing truths which any man of intelligence can find out for himself. The third plane is the moral one, instructing man as to how he should live. The fourth plane is the most remarkable. It is called the anagogic, and it teaches man about coming events and heavenly matters.

This method of reading seems strange to the man of today. Let me therefore try one or two exemplifications. I will get Dante himself to help me. Towards the end of his life Dante wrote a letter to his benefactor Can Grande della Scala. No one today doubts the authenticity of this letter. In it Dante discusses his Comedy—the letter was accompanied by a dedication of *Paradiso* to the Prince—and indicates how it should be interpreted.

For the elucidation, therefore, of what we have to say, it must be understood that the meaning of this work is not of one kind only; rather the work may be described as 'polysemous', that is, having several meanings; for the first meaning is that which is conveyed by the letter, and the next is that which is conveyed by what the letter signifies; the former of which is called literal, while the latter is called allegorical, or mystical. And for the better illustration of this method of exposition we may apply it to the following verses: 'When Israel went out of Egypt, the house of Jacob from a people of strange language; Judah was his sanctuary, and Israel his dominion.' For if we consider the letter alone, the thing signified to us is the going out of the children of Israel from Egypt in the time of Moses; if the allegory, our redemption through Christ is signified; if the moral sense, the conversion of the soul from the sorrow and misery of sin to a state of grace is signified; if the anagogical, the passing of the sanctified soul from the bondage of the corruption of this world to the liberty of everlasting glory is signified. And although these mystical meanings are called by various names, they may one and all in a general sense be termed allegorical, inasmuch as they are different [*di-versi*] from the literal or historical; for the word 'allegory' is so called from the Greek *alleon,* which in Latin is *alienum* [strange] or *diversum* [different].

This being understood, it is clear that the subject, with regard to which the alternative meanings are brought into play, must be twofold. And therefore the subject of this work must be considered in the first place from the point of view of the literal meaning, and next from that of the allegorical interpretation. The subject, then, of the whole work, taken in the literal sense only, is the state of souls after death, pure and simple. For on and about that the argument of the whole work turns. If, however, the work be regarded from the allegorical point of view, the subject is man according as by his merits or demerits in the exercise of his free will he is deserving of reward or punishment by justice.*

Dante, in this interpretation of his own work, follows a set pattern. Yet he seems to use the term "allegory" in a wider

* Oxford University Press, translation by Paget Toynbee.

sense than usual. In Thomas Aquinas, for instance, it is only the second plane of meaning which is called allegorical. This interpretation is more in agreement with our terminology. Two other examples of the fourfold method of interpretation, both taken from Johan Chydenius' thesis, *The Typological Problem in Dante,* may help to throw light on the matter. God created the Garden of Eden. The flowers that bloomed in it were real. The birds that sang in it were real, and the apple Eve held out was just as real as any that we pick from a tree. The allegorical meaning of Paradise before the fall was to show a picture of the Church. The harmony in Paradise was an allegory behind which the pious could see how God had imagined the life of the Church on earth. The moral meaning, on the other hand, was that Paradise portrayed the peace of mind that every human being should strive for. Finally, the fourth meaning—the anagogic—is that Paradise on earth shows us a picture of the greater bliss that awaits us in Heaven. There are thus two Paradises, an earthly and a heavenly, and both are real.

In the Song of Songs the bridegroom sings the praises of his bride. One tradition has it that the theme of the poem is Solomon's wedding. The young woman is a real woman. Her lips really are "like a thread of scarlet," and the smell of her garments is "like the smell of Lebanon." Of course, God cannot mean that the song should be only a love poem. In the fourfold scheme, therefore, we find that the Song of Songs, on the allegorical plane, depicts Christ's union with the Church. Christ is the bridegroom, every rightful Christian is the bride. On the moral plane the Song of Songs is about the soul which unites with God. On the anagogic plane, finally, we see how the soul in Paradise enters into an everlasting marriage with the bridegroom Christ.

Whether God creates with people of flesh and blood as material within the framework of history, or whether He creates with words through the Bible, He is serious about all four planes of meaning. The things He allows to develop, the words He writes, are real on the literal plane, but at the same time they are pictures for man to ponder on the three mystical planes. God is fond of the analogous method. He creates Paradise on earth but has His heavenly kingdom as model. He creates Moses, but Moses is in fact only a rough draft, a type, a design for Christ who is to come. Christ will not be content merely with leading the chosen race out of Egypt but will show all mankind the way out of earthly bondage to a heavenly Canaan. God creates Job and smites the righteous man with afflictions; he is a harbinger of Jesus' suffering on the cross. God creates a bride in her sweet spring. She is also a sketch of the bliss that awaits the redeemed after death. Everything God creates is a sign to be interpreted. God has laid clues in history and in the Bible. Man's task is to search for them. God is a keeper of the seals—Dante uses this metaphor in the Comedy—who stamps His holy device in the wax of humanity. The impress is not always a clear one, but those who search carefully can glimpse perfection even in the faulty imprint.

Faced with a historical personage we ask: What kind of upbringing did he have? What ideas were implanted in him in his youth? On the basis of the answers we draw conclusions as to character and actions. We seek the motives, the causes. A medieval man must also have asked these questions. But more important to him was this: What does this historical figure represent? Whom is he a model for? We think we can explain a man's actions when we are in possession of all the reasons. Tell us what the Egyptian princess who adopted Moses was like, and we shall tell you the secret about the great prophet. The medieval man, aware that Moses was a rough draft of Jesus, studied Jesus in order to explain Moses. The best way of understanding the sketch is to go to the finished masterpiece! It is the same with Paradise and with the bride in the Song of Songs—only in Heaven do we understand their real nature.

To return to Dante's letter to Can Grande. Dante did not choose just any example to illustrate how the Comedy was to be interpreted. He quoted the first verse of Psalm 114: "When Israel went out of Egypt. . . ." As we shall see and hear in the next chapter of this book, when the souls arrive at the Mount of Purgatory from over the sea they are singing this very psalm, the pilgrimage theme of which is an essential part of the Comedy. But does Dante really expect us to interpret his poem in the same way as we interpret the Bible? Two obstacles, both apparently insurmountable, present themselves. The poet has no difficulty in creating a poem which is allegorical. Indeed, the Middle Ages put an allegorical interpretation on all poetry. The method is older than Christianity, but during late antiquity it became predominant: It offered moral and religious readings of heathen works which would otherwise have had to be sacrificed to Christian fanaticism. Virgil's *Aeneid,* present throughout the whole Comedy and as much a part of it as the watermark in a sheet of notepaper, was subjected during these centuries to the most refined allegorical interpretations.

It goes without saying that the profane poet is inferior to God in power of expression and facility of invention. But he is inferior to God also in this: He cannot create a work which is fully concrete and true on all four planes at once. In his prose work *Convivio,* the philosophical-esthetical tract which Dante worked on but did not complete during the first years of exile, he speaks of the poet's dilemma and cites an example from Ovid. Ovid, Dante says, writes a poem about Orpheus, who charmed the wild beasts with his song and even caused the trees and rocks to move. This is not literally true, but is an allegory which shows that art can move the hardest heart. If God had written the poem, the literal plane would have been true and the rocks really would have moved. So, Dante continues, the poet offers "truths draped in beautiful lies." The allegorical plane is the *true* plane while the literal one is a lie. The poet, compelled to use disguises and masks, cannot avoid spiritual contamination.

In a period of a strongly developed tyranny of faith and thought, the writer must of course be circumspect in all that concerns moral, political, and religious matters. The interest therefore shifts from the literal to the allegorical plane. The writer is locked in an allegorical prison. If he has once admitted that every poetic work has an allegorical meaning and that its *truth* is to be sought on the allegorical plane, then at every moment he must be prepared to say what kind of truth this is. The story, the literal aspect, loses in importance. The characters are drained of blood and become merely allegories, transparent disguises for ideas and dogmas.

We cannot go to God and ask Him what He means by an event in history or an episode in the Bible. God is inscrutable, and when we read Him we must often be content with the literal, the historical meaning. Sensuous pleasure is obvious in the Song of Songs, but the pious reader has unshaken confidence that enjoyment is not all—there is a deeper meaning even if he cannot always find it. But the man who tried to write a poem of this unashamed nature might be suspected of being far too taken up with the things of this earthly life. God is good, and we cannot doubt His goodness even when we see the lost souls in Hell writhing in eternal torment. For even if this torment is real, it will be explained when the higher planes of meaning are revealed to us. The human author, on the other hand, must be prepared to tell us what he means. He can and should be held accountable. In his poem about Orpheus, Ovid meant that art ennobles, that Orpheus was a personification of poesy and the rocks an image of rough natures which become refined. If the poet is now forced by the laws inherent in his art to lie, then of course he is not only far beneath God, but also beneath the philosopher and the theologian, who can serve up truths direct and unadorned.

If it is difficult, not to say impossible, for the writer to be truthful on the literal plane, the fourth plane of meaning puts equally great obstacles in his path. His characters should be types, symbols, and figures who, in a purer form, recur farther on in his portrayal and whose real nature is apparent only on the other side of death. Even the poet must create in analogies.

Several modern scholars—Charles Singleton is vehement on this point—hold that Dante makes a unique, an epoch-making demand by declaring in the Can Grande letter that the Comedy is to be interpreted like the Bible. This would be tantamount to saying that his poem is unlike any other, that, as opposed to Ovid, he does not offer truths draped in beautiful lies but that he is to be taken seriously on all four planes of meaning.

When we read a poem, what is our attitude to its meaning? We realize that it is taking place on several planes. Baudelaire's albatross limps about on the deck with the debasing cutty in front of its beak. Goethe's Prometheus hurls his defiance at the gods and fashions human beings out of his own strength. In the Swedish writer Erik Lindegren's poem about Icarus we see the mythical hero fly up towards the sun with the aid of his borrowed wings. We see that each of these poems has its allegorical and its symbolic meaning. The albatross poem is about the genius who is incapable of adjusting himself, the chosen one who is made the object of mockery. Goethe's poem deals with the liberation from "the tyranny of the gods." *Icarus* is about the possibility of ecstasy, about the moment when the foetal membrane is burst and a new reality is born. But this is not what strikes us as the essential part of the poem. Instead of speaking of "allegory" we use the concept "symbol," meaning thereby a poetic image which is not created by reason alone and is not to be explained by reason, but which is born down in the depths of the soul, forming its pattern from forces which the poet himself is not always aware of, a pattern which analysis can never quite explain.

In order to understand the three poems I have mentioned, it is necessary for us constantly to move from one place of meaning to the other. And we do this. Now we see the myth's real Icarus in the Lindegren poem, now we are flung out in the imageless ecstasy which is part of the poet's vision. We could also easily understand if someone told us that these poems have an anagogic meaning as well. For even if we do not believe in a life after this one, we like to believe that when all the planes of meaning that our reason can grasp are exhausted, something remains which points towards a region that is as yet uncharted.

Can *The Divine Comedy* be regarded as true on the literal

plane? The poem is about a man—Dante himself at the age of thirty-five—who journeys to the realms of the dead. This journey is of course a fiction. Even if Dante believed that the realms of the dead existed as factual realities, he could hardly believe that a human being of flesh and blood could travel through them. The poem's fictional character is also apparent from the poetic licence Dante allows himself as regards the organization of these realms. I have already mentioned that he locates Purgatory on the other side of the globe, despite the contemporary belief of leading theologians that it lay deep in the earth next to Hell. On the other hand, it is possible, even probable, that the visions we shall see in *Paradiso* are based on real visions. Dante maintains this in the Can Grande letter:

> And after he has said that he was in that place of Paradise which he [Dante here speaks of himself in the third person] describes by circumlocution, he goes on to say that he saw certain things which he who descends therefrom is powerless to relate. And he gives the reason, saying that 'the intellect plunges itself to such depth' in its very longing, which is for God, 'that the memory cannot follow.' For the understanding of which it must be noted that the human intellect in this life, by reason of its connaturality and affinity to the separate intellectual substance, when in exaltation, reaches such a height of exaltation that after its return to itself memory fails, since it has transcended the range of human faculty. And this is conveyed to us by the Apostle where he says, addressing the Corinthians: 'I know a man (whether in the body, or out of the body, I cannot tell; God knoweth) how that he was caught up to the third heaven, and heard unspeakable words, which it is not lawful for a man to utter.' Behold, after the intellect had passed beyond the bounds of human faculty in its exaltation, it could not recall what took place outside of its range. This again is conveyed to us in Matthew, where we read that the three disciples fell on their faces, and record nothing thereafter, as though memory had failed them. And in Ezekiel it is written: 'And when I saw it, I fell upon my face.' And should these not satisfy the cavillers, let them

read Richard of St. Victor in his book *On Contemplation;*
let them read Bernard in his book *On Consideration;* let
them read Augustine in his book *On the Capacity of the
Soul;* and they will cease from their cavilling. But if on
account of the sinfulness of the speaker they should cry
out against his claim to have reached such a height of
exaltation, let them read Daniel, where they will find that
even Nebuchadnezzar by divine permission beheld certain
things as a warning to sinners, and straightway forgot
them. For He 'who maketh his sun to shine on the good
and on the evil, and sendeth rain on the just and on the
unjust,' sometimes in compassion for their conversion,
sometimes in wrath for their chastisement, in greater or
lesser measure, according as He wills, manifests his glory
to evil-doers, be they never so evil.

But even if Dante, in common with Paul, who is cited
here and whose paradisian rapture played such a big part in
the whole of the Middle Ages, really did behold God—that
is, had a vision which bore all the signs of hallucination—
the journey described in the poem must be regarded as fictitious. This does away with any chance of interpreting the
Comedy's literal plane in the same way as the theologians
interpreted the Bible. Or did Dante in the Can Grande letter
mean something else by the four planes? Does not the claim
he makes imply that he has stepped out of the allegorical
prison and once more found the deepest secret of all writing?
Throughout the entire Comedy we sense the dead poetry
of antiquity coming to life. Dante writes in conscious emulation of the great poets of old. What is the secret that he has
stumbled upon? It is this: *A poetic work exists.* It has a
right to exist even when a deeper meaning cannot be dis-
cerned or accounted for. Its literal plane is true in the same
way as the Bible's. As material, the poet uses people, nature,
and happenings, all of which, in the last resort, are created
by God. Since everything created is also a sign, he can be
sure that even his work points above itself. On the literal
plane the poem, such as it exists at this moment on paper,
is just as important as what it expresses. The poem *is,* and
this alone matters. What it has to say is not subordinate to

what it is, but the poet can no more be held responsible for
what it is than God can. He is a sovereign who makes his
own laws and not a servant who can be summoned to his
master to give an account of his stewardship. He should have
God as an exemplar and therefore allow his work to take
place on several planes at once. But when he is incapable of
this—for he is not God but a human being—the literal plane
is just as important, and has the same right to develop freely,
as the other three. The literal plane may not be historically
true judged by human standards, but there is a poetic truth,
a poetic flesh and blood.

And with it, a new feeling of self-esteem is present in
every line of the Comedy. Also, we must now pay more attention to the fourth plane of meaning. Dante chose the
autobiographical form partly because he himself is a sign,
because his own life is enacted in analogy to the only proper
life, that of Jesus.

God has created the world from a great pattern. In the
midst of creation is the earth, and around it revolve the ten
heavens. In the center of the inhabited hemisphere is Jerusalem, where God, at the focal point of history, was crucified.
God is the number three, for He is triune. He dies in order to
be reborn. He overcomes death by voluntarily taking suffering
upon Himself. The Comedy is fashioned analogous to God's
great pattern. In *Purgatorio* there is the green earth, in *Inferno* the black abyss, and in *Paradiso* the ten heavens. The
basis of the Comedy is the Holy Trinity, which can be seen
everywhere, even in the rhyme scheme. Above the Trinity
rises the still holier decade, for three multiplied by itself is
nine and God, a unit in Himself, makes ten. The holiest of
the holy numbers is ten times ten—a hundred. Therefore the
Comedy has a hundred cantos, its very structure thus reflecting the mathematical balance which is God's unique quality.

Just as God descended into the underworld, so does the
pilgrim in the story. Like Jesus, he starts his journey of death
on Good Friday and returns to the earth's surface on the
morning of Easter Day. Jesus is the Saviour of mankind. In
Dante's fictitious world, Beatrice is the saviour. Everything

that happens in the Comedy is analogous with God's creation. But the vital part of God's two books is that He caused the word to be made flesh. He created the world out of His love and let Himself be incarnated in Jesus. So, too, in the Comedy the most important part must be the incarnation, Dante's God-given vision, which puts on flesh and blood.

If we read the Comedy by following Dante's own directions but keep in mind that the four planes of meaning cannot always be valid at the same time, we find a way of moving freely about in the vast world of the poem. We need not hunt for the allegorical meaning at all costs, because in that particular passage the poet may have a moral, an anagogic, or an analogous thought in his head. The pilgrim is in the Dark Wood at the moment we first catch sight of him, and the allegorical meaning is clear. The animals—the leopard, the lion, and the wolf which turn him from the path— are "beautiful lies" behind which we see the rank sins which lead mankind astray. Virgil appears and tells of the greyhound which shall drive off the wolf, a symbol of the insatiable avarice and lust for money which Dante abhorred above all else. We see that the greyhound, "That nourishes itself on neither land nor wealth, / But feeds instead on wisdom, love, and virtue" (*Inferno*, I: 103–104), is a harbinger of the Saviour to come. But when the pilgrimage begins, when the traveler enters the gate of Hell, Dante the storyteller is a man who is an instrument of his inspiration. What he has conjured up in his imagination takes form and can no longer be controlled at every moment by his reason. The allegory is filled from below with blood and goes its own way. Thus the shrieks that reach the pilgrim's ears are not symbolic but real. Francesca is a real person and not an allegory on the theme of illicit love. The trees in the suicides' wood are, admittedly, souls which have been turned into trees because they have not respected the bodies God gave them; but when the pilgrim stretches out his hand and breaks off a twig, when the tree starts to bleed, when, "a green firelog / Blazing at one end, whines and whistles / At the other, as the wind blows through it, / So from that splintered limb there issued words / And blood" (*Inferno*, XIII:28–44), it is as overwhelming as an immediate experience, and the symbolic meaning is swallowed up and vanishes. There is a similar scene in the *Aeneid,* but a comparison could only result in the prize being awarded to Dante.

Virgil, who guides the pilgrim, has been cast in many different parts by Dante scholars—a representative of human reason, of ancient poetry, of the Roman Empire, and so on. It is possible, indeed likely, that Dante did intend to do something of the sort with Virgil. But when we regard him in the poem, we see that he is the very person he gives himself out to be—a Roman poet, now dead, who has become the pilgrim's paternal friend. When he turns pale, we see that his pallor is real. When he becomes angry, the rage that shakes him is unmistakable. He is very human, and his deeply felt compassion seems only natural to us as, in the fourth canto of *Inferno,* he approaches Limbo, where his own fellow poets are and where he himself must return. If we regard Virgil as a hanger for an allegorical costume, as a riddle which we are to solve, he loses all interest for us. And if he is meant to represent human reason, we suddenly see him forget his part and peep out behind his mask with wise and mournful eyes.

At the entrance down to one of the infernal circles—see the end of the sixteenth and the beginning of the seventeenth canto—the pilgrim and Virgil encounter a monster by the name of Geryon. It has the face of a just man and the body of a dragon. They have before them a personification of fraud. The next moment they climb onto Geryon's back and are carried deeper down into Hell. Although Virgil is sitting behind him, the pilgrim is so terrified that his nails whiten and his whole body shivers as if with ague. He tries to beg Virgil to clasp him tight, but his tongue is locked in his mouth. But Virgil, as so often before, comes to his aid and throws his arms about Dante. At this moment Geryon is no allegory, either to the pilgrim or to the reader, but an airship of flesh and blood, and Dante the poet marshals all his artistry to describe the perilous, wheeling descent into the abyss. The monster, twisting in the air like an eel and using its paws as fins and the poisonous scorpion tail as a rudder, sinks at last like a falcon weary from the chase. The two travelers dismount from the reluctant creature, which has been quelled by Virgil's superior will and magic arts, and see it bound off like an arrow from the string. An allegory as simple as the riddle in the ABC book turned into a mysterious living being.

In the fiery waste the pilgrim meets the homosexual writer Brunetto Latini, and it would not be hard for us to give the scene an allegorical interpretation. But it is a moving scene just as it is. It shows us a man who, even in misfortune, retains his human greatness and dignity, and we need ask no more.

The reader of *The Divine Comedy* must learn to move from one plane of expression to the other, to understand that no one key fits every lock, that there is no Ariadne thread to follow. Dorothy Sayers, who had a ready wit, said that you can get through the Comedy in the same way as you can get across the Atlantic with completely different means of transport. You can go in a submarine. You can take a steamer. Or you can fly. You get there, whichever way you go. But the simile is misleading, for in the middle of the Comedy's Atlantic it may often be necessary to change the means of transport, a procedure not to be recommended on the real Atlantic. At one moment in the Comedy we see the chrysalis of the literal meaning trying to spread its butterfly wings. At the next moment an idea, an abstraction, takes on the flesh and blood of the poem, thus losing its entity and becoming something else. Now we have an allegorical riddle to solve; next we have an analogy in which borderline discrepancies are of no account next to the one vital theme at the center. The interpreter must hold the reins loose the entire time and ride forward with the greatest caution.

When Dante the poet decides to write his poem as God wrote the Bible, he finds the most fruitful of postulates. He moves from one plane of meaning to the other but allows none of them to be subservient to the other. He places himself as he was at the age of thirty-five at the center of the poem. He is present in the poem as a real person, but since he too is created by God, God's pattern has been woven into his life. Therefore he goes through the agony of Hell towards the bliss of Paradise. Therefore he is saved by his beloved just as mankind is saved by Jesus. Therefore he is, at one and the same time, Dante the Florentine, Everyman, and God who was incarnated in a man's shape.

Dante's great poem was a success because he made use of myths which are an integral part of everyone's life. He goes down into Hell and ascends again, just as Christ did. But Christ's descent was also in keeping with an ancient myth of rebirth that had existed long before him. The biblical myths that Dante follows are true even when regarded from a non-Christian angle. There are modern psychoanalytical scholars whose starting-point is the trinity of father, mother, and child. They hold that every son loves his mother and hates his father—Oedipus—and every daughter loves her father and hates her mother. Similar tensions and conflicts are to be found in all great writing. The pattern of the Comedy, surely, has no less validity, and it owes some of its power to the fact that we recognize ourselves in it.

The two pilgrims are standing on the shore. They are in Purgatory, which is a picture of our own life and analogous with life on earth. The stars pale and the sun rises. The travelers, with the darkness and curses of Hell behind them, resemble people who have been saved from a shipwreck. Or perhaps it is more correct to say that they resemble people who have been raised from the dead. It is the morning of Easter Day, and spring has just come. Thus in a fourfold sense we are witnessing a resurrection. The pilgrim has escaped Hell. The grip of winter is broken. The dead god awakens and rolls away the stone. The poem, *The Divine Comedy,* having sojourned so long in the realm of the dead, moves on to the realm of life. Each one may choose the plane he desires while the journey continues.

10

THE WONDERFUL FRIENDSHIP

AS EASTER DAY DAWNS, Dante and Virgil are walking across a green meadow that slopes down towards the shore where the waves are rippling in the morning breeze. In a month the pilgrim will be thirty-five. If Giotto, his contemporary and friend, has correctly drawn his likeness in the only picture extant, he had clear-cut features, a thin, curved nose and deep-set eyes. "He was," says Boccaccio, who wrote not so many years after Dante's death, "of medium height. He had a rather long face, aquiline nose, large chin and his underlip protruded beyond the upper one. His shoulders were a trifle sloping. The eyes were large rather than small. His complexion was dark. Hair and beard wavy and black. He always seemed melancholy and thoughtful." Boccaccio also tells us that Dante walked with a stoop towards the end of his life. Perhaps this is what he has in mind when, in the nineteenth canto of *Purgatorio,* he describes himself bent like "the half arch of a bridge" (line 42). Presumably at this moment he is walking upright. It is Dante the storyteller who is bent and his once black hair has turned grey. He sees himself in the poem as he *was.* He paints a portrait of the artist as a young man.

Dante the pilgrim is the leading character in an epic work which deliberately vies with those of antiquity. But he has little in common with Achilles, Ulysses, and Aeneas. Nor does he resemble the heroes of medieval poesy, Roland or Lancelot. Like Ulysses and Aeneas, he ventures out on a great journey and makes his way down to the underworld. But he never relies on his sword or his good head. The journey is an inward one, and what help then are weapons and stratagems? Nor does he bother about his dignity and his manly honor. He lets himself be turned from the path by wild beasts. In Hell he hides behind rocks when danger threatens. He laments, wails, faints, and weeps. The storyteller takes pains to show how irresolute, tormented, and helpless he once was, how easily his courage forsook him. The pilgrim is rather like the hero of a modern autobiographical novel. He is the first leading figure in a large epic who does not follow the pattern of the exalted style. He breaks with the demand for heroic behavior. He is a Rousseau four hundred years before *Confessions* and a Proust's alter ego in the great autobiographical novel. There is no distance between him and us. The pilgrim is one of the first great human portraits.

Dante and Virgil, whose friendship after their long journey together through the infernal circles is tested and firm, meet the warden of Purgatory, the Roman, Cato the younger, an old man with grizzled beard, fatherly and venerable to behold. They converse under the four stars of the Southern Cross, symbols of the four cardinal virtues of prudence, justice, fortitude, and temperance; and Virgil, who has paid many a tribute to Cato in his works and who is therefore responsible for Dante's choice of this steadfast person as guardian of Purgatory, alludes to Cato's biography and to his longing for freedom. He begs for Cato's protection, and when Cato hears that a lady of Heaven is interested in Dante, he agrees at once. He tells Virgil to cleanse Dante's face with dew and bind a rush around his brow as a sign of humility. Just as the rush bends to the waves, so should man's heart be—a simile dear to the Middle Ages and used by St. Birgitta, among others.

Dante the poet is describing a spring morning on earth; and since we have not yet shaken off the paralysis that overcame us in Hell, wind, light, and color seem all the more delightful to our senses (*Purgatorio* I:115–136).

> Dawn was vanquishing the morning breezes,
> Which fled so fast before it that from afar
> I could make out the quivering of the sea.

We walked along the desolate expanse
The way a man walks, seeking a lost pathway,
And seems to walk in vain until he finds it.
When we came to where the dew still struggled
With the sun because the air there was so cool
That very little evaporated,
My master spread out both his hands
And placed them tenderly upon the grass.
Knowing what it was that he was doing,
I turned my cheeks up to him stained with tears:
And he restored to me completely
The color that had been concealed by Hell.
We then came to the deserted strand, which had
Never seen a man navigate its waters
Who was able to find his way back after.
And he twined me round as that other wished:
And what a miracle! Exactly as
It was the humble plant was born anew
In the same place, the instant that he plucked it.

Watching the scene on the shore reminds us of the nursery. Small children are washed like this when they have fallen down. Children hold their faces up as the pilgrim does here. Dante calls Virgil father, leader, master, doctor, fount of knowledge, and Virgil calls Dante his son. Virgil guides the pilgrim, protects and exhorts him, and urges him on. He has taken upon himself the obligations not only of a teacher but also of a mother, a nanny, and a mistress. He puts his hands over Dante's eyes as they approach the city of Lucifer so that the Medusa's eyes will not turn him to stone. He holds him tight when they ride on the monster Geryon's back. On several occasions he carries him in his arms. In one of the infernal circles he carries him on his hip as a mother does her child when it is too heavy for her arm.

On the realistic plane the relationship between the two would be understandable if Virgil were a youth of eighteen and Dante his little brother of seven or eight. It is absurd if we think of them as the same size. How does one carry a person as big as oneself on the hip? Perhaps it is a picture of himself as a child that Dante wants to suggest. Augustine said that the Christian should be *little* as a child, not *innocent* as a child, in order to enter Heaven. An older friend, a poet of immortal fame, bends with fatherly tenderness over the disciple and wipes away the stains of dirt and tears. It takes only a few seconds and we catch a glimpse of the nursery. The next moment Virgil and Dante are standing side by side again as two grown men. It is these swift changes of scene which are one of the secrets of Dante's narrative art. His thought flies out like a bird from the nest and finds a new element.

Virgil wrote an epic which has lived through the centuries. Dante had been familiar with the *Aeneid* since his childhood. Probably this was the schoolbook from which he learnt to read. When the pilgrim first met Virgil he said that it was "he from whom I took the good style that hath done me honour." For Dante, Latin was just as much his language as Italian. He was a Roman, a Latin, an Italian, a Florentine all at once. But more important was that, in his great poem, Virgil had shouldered complete responsibility. The *Aeneid* is a work which treats of the individual's relation to his destiny as well as all mankind's. It depicts man both as a member of society and as a timeless being faced with love, righteousness, and death. With Virgil present in the Comedy, Dante is reminded at every turn that these are the ambitions a proper writer should attain.

Virgil, the poet of the Roman empire, lived at the time of Augustus and died in 19 B.C. In the *Aeneid* when he prophesies the reign of peace that is to come, he, like Dante thirteen hundred years later, chose universal peace and a righteous world ruler. Without being aware of it, he predicted the Christian millennium.

In the twentieth canto of *Purgatorio* the two travelers, who are high up on the Mountain on the ledge of the avaricious, hear a mighty shout—*Gloria in excelsis Deo!* The ground shakes as with an earthquake. The travelers quicken their steps in alarm. In the next canto a shade appears beside them, and polite words of greeting are exchanged. Virgil asks why the Mount shook as it did. The stranger replies that each time a soul is ready to ascend to Heaven the ground trembles, and all the other souls join in a mighty song of praise. He tells them that he, for whose sake the Mount quaked just now, lived during the first century A.D., at the time of the Emperor Titus, that he was a poet and wrote works about Thebes and about Achilles, and that his exemplar in the art of poesy was Virgil. Had it been vouchsafed him, he says, to be contemporary with Virgil, he would gladly have paid the price of another year in Purgatory.

At these words Virgil and the pilgrim exchange a look, and Virgil's eyes admonish him not to reveal who he is. Dante cannot help an amused smile. The three poets continue on their way together; and the stranger, who is none other than Statius, asks Dante: "Wherefore did thy face but now display to me a flash of laughter?" (*Purgatorio*, XXI:113–114). Dante is abashed. His teacher bids him be silent, and Statius bids him speak. With Virgil's permission he says, after hesitating (*Purgatorio*, XXI:121–126):

> And so I said: "Perhaps, O ancient spirit,
> You marvel that I laughed the way I did.
> But I wish to make you marvel even more.
> This one who is directing my eyes upward
> Is that very Virgil from whom you once
> Derived the strength to sing of men and gods."

At these words Statius falls on his knees at the master's feet and stretches out his arms to embrace him. Virgil raises him and says: "Brother, do not so, for thou art a shade, and a shade thou seest." And the canto ends (*Purgatorio*, XXI:133–136):

> And, rising, the shade said: "Now you can see
> How great is the love for you that burns in me,
> When, forgetting our emptiness, I treat
> A shade as if it were a solid thing."

During the Middle Ages Statius was greatly renowned. Now he is forgotten. When he kneels at Virgil's feet he gives a picture of Dante himself, who is aware of his debt of gratitude at every moment. A medieval tradition has it that Statius was a Christian, although he kept his faith a secret on account of the persecutions that raged against the Christians during his lifetime. Virgil had been his guide not only in moral and esthetic things, but also in religious matters. Statius tells Virgil of this (*Purgatorio,* XXII:67–75):

> "You acted as one does who walks at night
> Bearing a light behind him, useless to himself
> But making wiser those who follow after,
> When you said: 'The whole world is new again;
> Justice is back, and humanity's first time,
> And a new progeny comes down from Heaven.'
> I was a poet and a Christian, thanks to you.
> To make you see what I have traced the better,
> I shall put out my hand and start to color."

Statius quotes a famous passage from Virgil's fourth Eclogue here, words which were interpreted as a prophecy of Christ all during the Middle Ages, though originally the verse was a congratulation to a friend on the birth of a son.

The meeting between the three poets is important to the understanding of the Comedy. Virgil had written of a golden age to come without knowing its nature. He had sketched a figure which, most wonderfully, came to life only after he was dead. He carried a light behind him which showed the way not only to himself, but to those who came after. In this he showed that the poet was an instrument of God, that poetry contained more than the poet himself knew. Even in this he was Dante's teacher and example, for the Comedy too held truths which only the future would understand.

After this digression up the Mountain let us return to its foot. As the pilgrim stands on the shore and the rush is placed upon his brow, his thoughts are of Ulysses and his fate. Ulysses saw the Mount of Purgatory but never reached it; he was drawn down into the deep. He perished "as pleased Another" (*com' altrui piacque*). Exactly the same words recur in the account of Virgil's girding of the pilgrim. Was it pride that brought about Ulysses' fall, while the pilgrim was saved by humility?

A drawing of the portrait by Giotto (1267?-1337) of his contemporary, Dante, in the *Bargello Church, Florence.* Drawn by the Englishman Seymour Kirkup.

Josef Anton Koch: Virgil and Dante at the foot of the Mount of Purgatory see the angel-guided boat of souls arriving. Dante kneels. His ascent of the Mount in a state of humility is about to begin.

Dante and Virgil at the foot of the Mount of Purgatory. Illustration from a 15th-century manuscript, *Codice Vaticano Giraldi*. The terrace formation of the mount is clearly indicated.

Dante, Virgil, and the newly arrived souls listening to Casella's song. Cato approaches in order to exhort them to waste no time in climbing the Mount. On the sea in the distance is the boat propelled by the angel's wings. *Purgatorio* II. *Codex 365 Urbinato, Vatican Library.*

The two friends see a light moving across the sea more swiftly than a bird can fly. It is a boat with souls who are arriving at the Mount of Purgatory. At the stern stands an angel who is using his outstretched wings as sails. The souls on board are singing the 114th Psalm: "When Israel went out of Egypt." As soon as the boat grounds, they hurry ashore. They stand in the grass, rather at a loss, gazing round at the unfamiliar landscape. They are like emigrants in a strange land. Shyness and amazement are reflected in all they do. When they catch sight of Virgil and Dante they ask the way with heads humbly bent. This state of perplexity and doubt which marks the new arrivals sets the tone for the first eight cantos of *Purgatorio*. The souls are in a state of astonishment. They are like children standing in the window who think they see hideous creatures with threatening gestures approaching, only to discover the next moment that it was something harmless and familiar. Dante—in the third canto—is reminded of sheep coming out of a pen. One after the other they stop timidly in the gate, "casting eye and nose to earth," while the others huddle behind them, not knowing why (*Purgatorio*, III:79–84).

Among the newly arrived souls is the Florentine composer Casella, one of Dante's friends. Happy over this unexpected meeting in a strange land, they embrace each other, but Dante finds—as Ulysses did when he embraced his mother in Hades—that his arms clasp the empty air. His friend is dead, a mere shade who moves away with a smile.

Casella asks Dante, who is still in the first life, what he is doing here; and Dante replies that he is making the journey to return here once again—an excellent answer, as it is for the sake of his salvation that the pilgrim is traversing the realms of the dead and for the same reason that the poet is driving his poem forwards. Dante asks Casella to sing him a song, as he used to do in life. Casella sings one of Dante's own love poems which he has set to music: "Love that in my mind discourseth to me." The song is so melodious and sweet that all—Virgil, the dead who have arrived together with Casella, and Dante himself—listen delightedly, as though they had nothing else to do. Then Cato appears, his sense of duty no less strong in Purgatory than when he served the Roman republic. He upbraids them all, calling them "tardy spirits" (*spiriti lenti, Purgatorio,* II: 120), and reminds them that they have come to Purgatory in order to be cleansed and become worthy of beholding God's face. The poem goes on (*Purgatorio,* II: 124–133):

> Much as do the doves when—after gathering
> Wheat and corn and settling down to eat together,
> Noiseless, and without that pride of theirs—
> Something appears that frightens them, and
> They immediately abandon their repast,
> Because a greater urgency attacks them:
> So I saw that fresh band of wayfarers
> Stop singing and go towards the slope, like men
> Who walk without knowing where they may wind up.
> Nor was our own departure slower.

Even Virgil feels ashamed, for he has been unmindful of his duty to lead Dante towards greater perfection.

The world knows Dante as the man who loved Beatrice and sang her praises. But he is also a poet of friendship and his friends are present throughout the Comedy. In the twenty-sixth canto of *Purgatorio* the pilgrim meets and talks with Guido Guinizelli and the Provençal poet Arnaut Daniel. The pilgrim pays Guido handsome compliments, saying that he even loves the ink that his poems are written with. We are vividly aware of how much the friends enjoyed each other's company and of the love of language which finds such witty expression in Dante's prose work *De Vulgari Eloquentia.* But what compliment can be compared with that paid by Dante to the Provençal poet Arnaut? The latter goes up to the pilgrim, tells of his youthful follies and of his hope of Heaven. Dante the poet pays his tribute to Arnaut by letting him speak the Provençal tongue (*Purgatorio,* XXVI: 140–147):

> *"Tan m' abellis vostre cortes deman,*
> *qu' ieu no-m puesc, ni-m voill a vos cobrire.*

Ieu sui Arnaut, que plor, e vau cantan,
  consiros vei la passada folor,
  e vei jauzen lo jorn qu' esper, denan.
Ara vos prec per aquella valor,
  que vos guida al som de l' escalina,
  sovenha vos a temps de ma dolor."

"Your gracious question pleases me so much
That I neither can nor wish to hide from you.
I am Arnaut, who weep and sing while walking.
I look back in my mind on my past folly
And I foresee with joy the hoped-for day.
I beg of you now, by that blessedness
That leads you to the summit of the stairs,
Remember my suffering when the time comes."

Seen in this perspective, the Comedy is a race track where
the competitors seek fame through intellectual prowess,
through beautiful poems and fair language. We do not doubt
Boccaccio's word that in this circle of friends Dante longed
so eagerly for fame that he perhaps went farther than "be-
fitted his virtue."

In this circle one measures oneself at every turn with
the great dead. Virgil's shade is ever-present, like Rimbaud's
with young writers of today. The fabric of culture grows
longer and longer, woven with threads and patterns from the
past. All voices, living and dead, are contemporaneous. One
reaches out after a prize and says at the next moment to one's
chosen friend and rival: "What is the meaning of fame?
How swiftly it perishes! In a thousand years it will not matter
whether you died in your cradle or as a venerable sage. And
who achieves renown? The victor, while the vanquished are
forgotten." At the same instant one remembers with a pang
that Virgil is more than a thousand years old—and is alive.

An expression of this state of mind is to be found in the
eleventh canto of *Purgatorio,* where the pilgrim converses
with the famous miniature painter and book illuminator
Oderisi, who is being purged of pride, the sin which Dante
himself, not without a lingering arrogance, admits he has
yielded to. The honor man acquires in this world, Oderisi

says, is as shortlived as the green of the grass. He gives a number of examples of how one generation of artists ousts the other from the halls of fame. Not long since, Cimabue was all the rage, but now Giotto is in favor. Only yesterday Guido Guinicelli held pride of place, but now he has been pushed aside by Guido Cavalcanti. The poet is perchance already born who will drive "both eagles from the nest" (*Purgatorio,* XI:100–108):

> "Worldly fame is nothing more than a puff
> Of wind, which blows one way and then another,
> And changes names because it changes sides.
> What greater fame could you have, if old age
> Divested you of flesh, than if you died
> Before you gave up all your baby talk,
> A thousand years from now—which, to eternity,
> Is briefer than is the motion of an eyelash
> To Heaven's circle that revolves the slowest."

Several different readings have been put upon the Casella episode. It has been said that Dante here takes leave of troubadour poetry, that he chooses Cato's righteousness before pleasure, salvation before beauty. We see the pigeons pecking on the ground, the danger drawing near and the flock flying up. We see the souls, spellbound by the song, moving away from the music and the joy of fellowship in order to begin climbing the Mountain. Two images overlap; they express an attitude familiar to the mind. The pigeons vanish; the souls gathered round Casella on the shore vanish. What remains is the feeling that every experience bears within it the seeds of something else, that a leavetaking is natural for the soul, that in the sensory world of art everything points above itself. It is not wrong of the pigeons to eat seeds, any more than it is wrong for young people to listen to love poems. The wrong lies in becoming absorbed in something so deeply that we forget what is more important.

In Dante it is often a question of mental states and not of dogmas and doctrines. The Casella episode is the meeting between two friends. One of them is dead, the other is alive. The dead one lives on in his art. The meeting gives us a picture of the life the young Dante lived in the company of his friends, who, passionate like most southerners, express their affection in a way that is foreign to us, with embraces and kisses. Cato breaks into the circle, and a little world is burst asunder for a bigger one.

Thus at every moment the world in Purgatory expands in the same way as the world does in a young person's imagination. In childhood and youth we find one joy and behind that a greater one: beyond the lake, we glimpse the sea; beyond the advent star in the nursery window, the everlasting stars in the heavens; behind the one we love and dare not approach, a love which tears us apart; behind responsibility for our family, responsibility for all mankind.

The unique quality of the *Purgatorio* cantos is this *tendency,* this leap out of the confines of time and space. The first cantos might perhaps have too much innocence, romantic friendship, and alacrity to obey if everything in these cantos was not outlined against the background of Hell. We have just been rescued. A moment ago the light was a non-light which stabbed our eyes like a dagger. Now it is the warm, gentle sunlight which is shining on us. A moment ago hideous noises grated on our ears. Now the breeze is stirring, the waves are rippling, Casella is singing.

Those who live here have been saved from unheard-of perils, and they remind the reader that he too has been miraculously saved—from madness, petrification, death. As with Hell, so with Purgatory—we can refrain from an opinion about the court which has spared some and sentenced others to torment. And we can take no credit to ourselves for having been rescued from being worms in the ground or raving lunatics. We accept our escape and make no attempt to decide whether we should feel shame or gratitude for it. We say instead: This too is reality. Purgatory exists. There is a trust, not in Paradise and salvation and not in overcoming death, but a trust in an order of rank in the world of thought and feeling. In the search for the next plane, for a larger world and a wider perspective, for something more important than the pigeons pecking among the seeds, lies a meaning.

11

EXILE

i

DANTE LOVES FLORENCE with a passion usually felt
for a woman, not a city. This woman has cast him off, and
he reviles and curses her at the same time as the love is
spurting out of his eyes. To my knowledge, no poet has his
name so closely linked with a city as Dante does. For centuries the reader has been told on the flyleaf of the Comedy
that it was written by "Dante Alighieri, Florentine by birth
but not by custom."

In Dante's time Florence was in a period of violent expansion. At his birth the city had about forty thousand inhabitants. Thirty-five years later, when the fourteenth century
dawned, the population had almost doubled. Florence was a
medieval city enclosed within walls and moats, and a typical
feature of its skyline—as I mentioned in one of the *Inferno*
chapters—was the high towers which were built by the great
ruling families and which they shut themselves up in during
the constantly raging civil wars and family feuds. Florence
was also a free republic with contacts all over the world. "The
world's first modern city," Jakob Burckhardt has called it. Its
textile industry was famous. Its bankers represented the
strongest economic power of the age, and emperors, kings,
cities, princes, and the pope himself turned to them for
financial aid. Despite the ban on usury, the borrowers had to
pay extortionate interest. In defiance of the emperor's claim
to a monopoly in minting coins, since 1252 the city had
minted its own gold coin, the florin, with the likeness of John

the Baptist—the patron saint of Florence—on one side and a lily on the other, a lily which, according to a well-known line in the Comedy, was often stained red with party hatred. The florin was valuable wherever civilization extended, and it was copied and counterfeited. Just as Shakespeare seemed to draw much of his strength from England's development as a great power under Elizabeth I, and we seem to hear Drake's ship and the surge of the sea in *Henry IV* and *Julius Cæsar,* so do the vast claims in Dante seem to be bound up with Florence's ascent and the wealth and might of her townspeople.

Dante's family had lived in Florence for several generations. In Paradise Dante the pilgrim meets one of his ancestors, Cacciaguida (XV:88), who tells him that he was knighted by Emperor Conrad III—a member of the Hohenstaufen family and emperor from 1138 to 1152—and that he was killed during a crusade to the Holy Land. Death as a crusader evidently implied a distinction comparable in our day with having been a fighter pilot during the Battle of Britain in 1940 or having manned a Russian tank during the Battle of Stalingrad.

Several Dante scholars accept this hero ancestor of Dante's, even though what is said of him in the Comedy is all that is known about him. Much more doubt is attached to the statement by two of the early biographers—Boccaccio and Lionardi Bruni Aretino—that Dante's ancestors were supposed to be among the Romans who founded the town of Florence in the dim past. It was a convention of the age to attribute such ancestry to eminent men. Similar flights of fancy as to birth furnished every Italian city with a Roman or—still more distinguished—a Trojan past.

Pride of birth was part of the age, but in noble natures it never took the form of a magic password to pedigree and breeding; it was combined with the ability of the individual in thought and deed to attain equality with those who had gone before. On several occasions Dante has lashed out at pride of birth. In *Convivio* he writes: "We say of a horse that it is noble when it is of some use, and the same applies to a falcon or a pearl. Is a man to be considered well-born just because his forefathers were! Such brutish stupidity should be answered with a knife, not with words." This does not, however, stop Dante from vaunting his aristocratic past or from slipping into the Comedy discreet hints about Roman ancestry. Everything in Dante has grandeur and importance, but this does not mean that he lacks passions which are not usually accounted the most honorable. Giovanni Papini is right in saying that even if Dante is a Christian, he is seldom evangelical. The Gospels preach poverty, but in his own life Dante abhors poverty. The Gospels tell us to forgive our enemies, but Dante can rarely resist a chance of revenge. The Gospels advocate humility, but a prouder poet than Dante is hard to find. He fills his works with self-praise, and on his way past Limbo he allows himself to be elected into the company of the world's foremost writers. The rush of humility girds the pilgrim's head, but it is Apollo's laurel, which never withers, that his creator desires.

We have very few objective documents that shed any light on Dante's life. Nearly everything we know of Dante must be taken from his own works, all written during a life full of outside events and violent conflicts. There is not one extant line written in Dante's own hand. There was not even a signature to exhibit for the 700th anniversary in 1965; in fact, the anniversary itself was doubtful, for it is a mere supposition that Dante was born in 1265. The Comedy begins by telling us that the journey is undertaken in the middle of the pilgrim's life, and as we know that the Middle Ages reckoned the life span as seventy years, man has thus reached this middle point at the age of thirty-five. Since the journey is made in the year 1300—the arguments in favor of this are strong but not binding—Dante should therefore have been born thirty-five years earlier.

The Alighieri family does not appear to have played a very important part in the life of Florence. It belonged to the petty nobility which had been ruined by the rising class of bankers and industrial magnates. All his life Dante had a hatred of upstarts, jobbers, and usurers, of those who battened on others. There is no confirmation for a rumor that his father—of whom we know little more than his name, Alighieri de Bellincione—devoted himself to usury. Dante does not mention his parents in his writings, nor has he a word to say about his wife, Gemma Donati, and his five children. Two of his sons annotated the Comedy, but they reveal no sign of their father's genius. Dante's silence about his family has mystified the scholars and given rise to fanciful theories. We do know that both parents died early. When the pilgrim in the Comedy so often calls Virgil his father, and when his relationship to Beatrice on several occasions is illustrated with similes drawn from the relations between a mother and her child, it is possibly—as Papini has assumed—the reflection of an earlier need of parental affection.

Dante's family was traditionally Guelf, just as Florence can be called a Guelf city. The party names Guelf and Ghibelline had lost much of their original meaning by this time. In principle, to be a Guelf meant to be a supporter of autonomy and to side with the pope in the medieval struggle for power between pope and emperor. The middle class was Guelf, upheld freedom against all attempts at domination, and favored democratic tendencies in civic politics. "The town of Florence has never made concessions to an emperor, it has always been free," was the Florentines' answer to Rudolf of Hapsburg's representative in 1281. To be a Ghibelline was to recognize the supremacy of a world emperor and to see an ideal in an aristocratic and authoritarian form of government. The old nobility with castles and landed estates belonged almost entirely to this party. Such people were numerous in Dante's Florence, but they were being stripped of much of their power. In 1282 they were excluded from the government, and a "democracy" based on the trade guilds, but in reality dominated by bankers and industrialists, was introduced.

But an ideological frontier, guarded with theoretical arguments, no longer existed between Guelfs and Ghibellines.

The situation was much the same as between "Labour" and "Conservative" in our Western democracies.

With us, the ideological weakening has led to a milder political climate. Not so in Dante's Italy. During the whole of the thirteenth century a process of political demoralization was going on. With the death of Emperor Frederick II, the cause of the empire was as good as lost, and the field was open to Guelf strivings for independence. Europe was entering the long and painful period in which it still finds itself and which one day was to be characterized with the words "the national sovereignty." There was no longer a power with a claim to world dominion and enough strength to mediate between the up-and-coming nations. The disintegration led to constant wars. Dante learned to see Florence's and Italy's misfortunes as a result of the lack of a world emperor with power to make his word felt.

As the century went on, party passions in Florence grew increasingly violent. It became a rule that when one party came to power, the leaders of the other party were driven out, accused of heinous crimes, and sentenced to death or banishment. In addition, from time immemorial the city, like the whole of Italy, nurtured the tradition of the blood feud which passes its dagger from one generation to the next; in Hell Dante meets an ancestor who turns his back on him contemptuously because Dante has not avenged his death. These blood feuds got tangled up with the political struggle for power, so the harsh climate into which Dante was born is not difficult to imagine.

We are as ill-informed about Dante's youthful years in Florence as we are about everything else in his life. It is probable that he lived in relatively modest circumstances, but that he was well enough off to live the life of a free man and devote himself to studies and writing. He is a man of learning, and his knowledge extends over all the sciences of the age. For this reason it is unreasonable to think that his studies did not begin early. The thirteenth century was not a more culturally uniform period than any other age. It was known for its vast riches and versatility, and Dante had been borne in many directions. In following the path of his education it is important to remember that the ardor with which he gave himself up to poetry and philosophy during long periods of his life was exceeded by his political passion. His activity as a politician was his undoing, and it was to determine the course of his whole life.

During the thirteenth century, as in our day, art and politics were two paths which brought different strata of society in contact with each other. In Italy poetry was held in high esteem, and during the 1290's Dante was a poet who rose in the social scale because of his gifts and who acquired friends in the top circles. At the age of thirty or so Dante had apparently become more and more taken up with the political life of the city. Only those who belonged to a craft guild had the right to take an active part in this life. But in 1295 this rule was relaxed inasmuch as it sufficed to register with a guild in order to acquire right of participation. Dante registered with the apothecaries' and physicians' guild without—as far as is known—ever having grown a single medicinal herb or opened a vein. He had already served as a soldier in the Florentine army. According to Aretino, whose word is now generally accepted, he took part as a cavalryman in the Battle of Campaldino on June 11, 1289, at the age of twenty-four. In the Comedy there are allusions —see, for instance, the opening lines of the twenty-second canto of *Inferno*—to his having been in battle and seen horsemen riding to the attack. Eirik Hornborg, the Finnish patriot and historian—who would have made an admirable warden in a modern Purgatory, for he possessed to a marked degree Cato's social virtues—once said to me that the man who has never loved, fought in a war, and experienced old age knows nothing of life. Dante fulfilled these conditions. True, he only lived to be fifty-six, but life in those days was harder than it is now.

For several years Dante belonged to the Council of the Hundred in Florence, and for two months in 1300 he was made prior, one of the two men who wielded the executive power in the government of the city. After the middle of the

1290's the inner tension in Florence increased. The Guelf party broke into two factions, the whites and the blacks. Dante belonged to the former. The leader of the blacks was Corso Donati, a relation of Dante's wife. During this time the powerful Pope Boniface VIII tried to force Tuscany to submit to his suzerainty. Dante was one of the Florentines who were most violently opposed to the papal policy. His name was linked with numerous actions directed against the pope and the pope's bankers in Florence, some of whom were banished.

In the autumn of 1301, Dante was sent to Rome as one of the three leaders of an embassy to Boniface. The eternal city evidently made an overwhelming impression on him and in his works he alludes to its power and glory many times. But it was not so much papal Rome he saw, as the Rome of the emperors, Cæsar and Augustus. While he was there, Charles of Valois, the French king's brother, arrived in Florence, sent by the pope and in league with Corso Donati. He had been summoned in order to negotiate peace between the rival factions. The result of his intervention was the complete victory of the blacks. Civil war broke out and both sides showed cruelty and ruthlessness. When the blacks under Corso Donati had triumphed, the white leaders' houses and property were plundered and they themselves were, as usual, accused of foul play. Dante was one of those who were fined and sentenced to exile. Two years later the sentence was made more severe. Should Dante be found within the city walls, he was to be seized and burnt alive.

Dante was on his way back from Rome when he received news of the fate that had overtaken his party. The pope had detained him longer than the others on purpose, he suspected. He lets Boniface VIII ignominiously appear in the Comedy nine times. The other instigators of the black *coup* in 1301 are also well remembered. Charles of Valois is portrayed as a Judas who with his lance "makes the paunch of Florence to burst." The French royal house appears time and again under the same traitor's mark. In the twenty-fourth canto of *Purgatorio,* Corso Donati's brother Forese appears and prophesies that Corso will one day be dragged by wild horses to "the vale where sin is never cleansed," that is, Hell.

Dante's relationship to the Donatis is characteristic of his situation in the world. He was married to a woman belonging to this exalted family. One of his friends was Forese, with whom he exchanged frivolous sonnets in his youth. His mortal enemy in Florence was Forese's brother Corso. A sister to these brothers, Piccarda, whom Corso tore from the convent where she had sought peace and forced into a hateful marriage is in the Comedy. We meet Piccarda in Paradise (III:34 *et seq.*), and thus the sister and her two brothers have each been placed in a different realm of the dead.

ii

From the autumn of 1301 Dante lived in banishment. Millions of people in our day know what this means, for exile has again become a punishment with terrible consequences. In Dante's time there was, to be sure, a fellowship of values which made it possible for the exile to find friends and companions. There was a language, Latin, which was spoken by all men of culture, and a faith, Christianity, which manifested itself everywhere under the same forms. It is more difficult for the modern exile. Trotsky, cast out of the communist fellowship but retaining his communist convictions, became in the West—which saw in him a bloodstained hangman—a wandering Jew, a beggar, an outlaw driven from door to door, who was finally struck down by his mighty rival's revenge and died from wounds inflicted by an ice pick. But Dante was little better off. Like Trotsky, one of his severest torments was that he was vilified in his own country and everything he had done was distorted and misconstrued, while no one could or would defend him.

During twenty years of exile Dante was thrown upon the hospitality of different princes. He became a kind of strolling courtier, who paid for his board and lodging with the lustre—as yet not very bright—of his fame, his learning, and his rhymes. In *Paradiso* he asks his ancestor Cacciaguida,

who like all the dead can see into the future, what his fate
will be. The reader will remember that the pilgrim makes
his journey while he is still living in Florence. Cacciaguida
answers (*Paradiso,* XVII:46–69):

"As Hippolytus was driven out of Athens
By his pitiless and lying stepmother,
So will you be driven out of Florence.
This is willed, this is now being contrived,
And soon it will be brought about by him
Who weighs it where Christ is daily bartered.
As usual, the shouts of guilt will pursue
The injured party, but vengeance will be
Testimony of the truth dispensing it.
You shall leave behind everything you love
Most dearly, and this is the arrow
Which the bow of exile first discharges.
You shall find out for yourself how another's
Bread tastes of salt, and what a hard thing it is
To go up and down someone else's stairs.
But what will weigh heaviest on your shoulders
Will be the depraved and ill-willed company
Of those who fall into that valley with you.
Insane, irreverent, ungrateful, they will
All turn against you, but not long after
They, not you, will have reddened temples.
Of their beastliness their very movements
Shall be proof, so that it will be to your good
To have made yourself a party of your own."

These words summarize, with his customary superb concentration, Dante's situation in exile. Not without reason does
Cacciaguida refer to Hippolytus, for Florence is an ancient
as well as a medieval city. Modern scholarship—taking its cue
from Curtius—is more and more inclined to stress the unbroken unity in the tradition which unites antiquity, the
middle ages, and us. It is not primarily through so-called
renaissances, through new discoveries of classicism, that the
ancient heritage lives on. Antiquity has never died. The ancient institutions have gone on living, if under other names.
Dante may even have found solace in having been struck

down with the very weapon, ostracism, that was in constant use in the ancient cities.

Important parts of the Comedy are determined by this exile, which sets its mark in all Dante's works, except of course *Vita Nuova* and the youthful poems. In *Convivio* he writes:

> After it was the pleasure of the citizens of that fairest and most famous daughter of Rome, Florence, to cast me out of her dearest bosom (wherein I was born and brought up to the summit of my life, and wherein with their good leave I desire with all my heart to rest my weary mind, and to end my allotted span), I have wandered through almost every region to which this tongue of ours extends, a stranger, almost a beggar, exposing to view against my will the stroke of fortune which is often wont unjustly to be charged to the account of the stricken. Truly I have been a ship without sail and without rudder, wafted to divers havens and inlets and shores, by the parching wind which woeful poverty exhales. And I have seemed vile in the eyes of many, who crediting some report, perhaps had pictured me under another form; in whose eyes not only was my person held cheap, but every work of mine became of less esteem, both that which was already done, and that which was still to do.*

As the years pass, Dante becomes more and more obsessed with the thought of Florence. When writing about the Italian vernacular he seeks a sentence to illustrate a point of language and chooses this: "I entertain the greatest sympathy with all those who languish in exile and only in dreams can ever see their native land again." It is in exile that he plans and writes the Comedy which saves his name for posterity. Every line of it is influenced by his situation. In the seventeenth canto of *Paradiso* he calls Florence "the dearest place"; in the twenty-third canto of *Inferno* he mentions proudly "On Arno's beauteous river, in the great city I was born and grew"; in the fourteenth canto of *Purgatorio* he says that the

* Translation by William Walrond Jackson.

city is so wretched that it should not even be mentioned by name and compares it to a voracious wolf.

Hoping to reach Beatrice and the light eternal, Dante the pilgrim traverses the realms of the dead in the Comedy. Dante the banished poet, who links the pilgrim's destinies, roams from one Italian city to the next during his work on the poem. He stays with the princes of Verona and Can Grande della Scalla becomes his friend. He is the guest of the counts Guido at Lucca, of the Malaspina family at Sarzana. Perhaps he also visits Paris and its university. After his many wanderings he at last finds a haven with the princely family of Novello at Ravenna. During all these journeys, the hardships and humiliations of exile make him long for Florence. The pilgrim's and the storyteller's situation is the same. Reading the poem, we find that we cannot always distinguish them. We see the pilgrim in Hell and on the Mount of Purgatory. Beside walks the banished poet Dante. A moment ago we were in the realm of the dead. Suddenly we seem to be on the road between Lucca and Siena, approaching not the infernal city of Dis as in the eighth canto of *Inferno,* but a walled medieval town which closes its gates at dusk and leaves the stranger to stand in the darkness on the other side of the moat, anxious and alone, peering for signals from the top of the wall. We notice too that we do not meet spirits but other exiles, companions in distress, who —in this respect in the same situation as the dead—think of themselves as shades when they can no longer breathe the air of their native city.

We are on a journey in the realm of the dead but are passing at the same time through fourteenth-century Italy. On both planes we see Florentines who recognize each other by their dress, habits, and dialect. Jokes have been made about the number of Florentines Dante has placed in Hell. This is a mistake. Hell contains people from all quarters, but the pilgrim sees only those who are from his beloved and hated city. Wherever he is he asks for Florentines and looks right through all the others.

In a world without newspapers or public means of communication, one of the greatest pains of exile was to know nothing of those at home. That is why we see the pilgrim burning with eagerness to talk to Florentines. These, in their turn, are just as hungry for contact. "Stay thee, thou who by thy dress to us appearest to be some one from our perverse country" (lines 8–9) are words from the sixteenth canto of *Inferno*. When the pilgrim is passing the hypocrites in their gilded copes of lead he hears some words spoken in a Tuscan accent and stops. The Comedy is a novel of travel, on every page of which fellow-countrymen scattered by exile hasten towards each other, press each other's hands, tell each other news. The Comedy could also be called an anthology of meeting, in which every taste is satisfied. There are amiable, droll meetings such as the one in lower Purgatory with Belacqua, the maker of musical instruments, who brings a smile to Dante's lips because he is just as lazy in Purgatory as he was in life. There are the great meetings between friends, but there are also sudden encounters with countrymen who are enemies. Face to face with them, Dante feels the sympathy in his breast wrestling with his loathing and his desire for revenge.

The Comedy is a work to be read by those who have been cast out of their original fellowship. Throughout the poem we see Dante leap up as though bitten by an adder every time Florence is mentioned. It is Florentines who rouse the noblest but also the most savage impulses in his brain. In the desert of fire Virgil has to stop him from rushing down among the flames to embrace three highly deserving Florentine politicians. But when the fire is succeeded by the ice of Cocytus, it is a treacherous Florentine who makes Dante forget the claims of compassion and decency. In a frenzy he tears the hair from Bocca's head.

His love-hate finds expression in the strangest way of all in one of the last cantos of *Paradiso*. He has risen up through the heavens and the earth lies thousands of miles beneath him. He is above the fixed stars. His beloved is by his side. At such a moment what can the pitiful town by the Arno matter to him. He is about to depict the eternal light and he seeks images which will make it clear to the reader how his heart is uplifted and the power of divine love takes possession of him. He says he feels like the barbarian who has come from his bleak land to Rome with its glorious palaces and statues, and the simile reflects the deep impression the eternal city once made upon him. But not content with this image he takes another. He had come, he writes, to the divine from the human, to eternity from time, to a people just and sane from Florence (*Paradiso,* XXXI:37–39). This sublime taunt, flung in the face of his native city from the highest of the heavens, reveals the degree of the pain exile caused Dante.

The Comedy is about a man who journeys to gain the everlasting light in Paradise. One of the motives which drive him forward is the longing to come home, to have his good name restored, to listen to the ringing of well-loved bells. The Roman Catholic Church taught, and still teaches, that the prayers of those still alive can help the dead in Purgatory. Examples are given in the Comedy of the truth of this teaching. Forese Donati tells how the prayers of his wife, Nella, have lessened his sentence. But even the dead in Hell, who know that no hope is left, are anxious to be remembered by the living. "Tell the people about us when you return to the sweet light of day," says a tormented politician to Dante. "If any of you return to the world, strengthen the memory of me, which still lies prostrate from the blow that envy gave it" (*Inferno,* XIII:76–78), says Frederick II's unhappy chancellor Pier delle Vigne, who, like Dante in his relationship to Florence, is a faithful servant unjustly accused and banished. "When thou shalt be in the sweet world, I pray thee recall me to the memory of men" (*Inferno,* VI:88–89), cries the glutton Ciacco as he lies in the third circle of Hell with the storm of foul water and snow pouring down on him. Only the sinners farthest down in Hell do not wish to be remembered, and they try to keep their names secret from the pilgrim. We think that the worst punishment Dante can imagine is for a Florentine not to know who he is and even to desire such oblivion himself.

Behind the appeals to be remembered we hear the exiled

Dante's voice. It is not "the sweet sunlight" the sinners in Hell mean, but the streets and market-places of Florence. Behind the chancellor's plea that Dante shall speak well of him we hear Dante saying to fellow-countrymen he meets: "Speak to them at home, plead for me with those in power, contradict those who speak ill of me." In this way, what at first seems strange in Dante is changed into something which concerns us all. On the literal plane we do not think of the prayers as important, but in a figurative sense we are all in need of them.

iii

The greatest meeting between the pilgrim and a Florentine is in the tenth canto of *Inferno*. Dante and Virgil, with the aid of the archangel Michael, have penetrated into Hell proper, which, seen from without, looks like a medieval city. Nearest the city wall is "a spacious plain" which reminds Dante of the Roman necropolis at Arles, which is still in existence today. On every side are high stone tombs with the lids removed. Fires are burning in the sepulchers, which are glowing hot, and in them the spirits of the heretics are punished. The greater the heresy, the fiercer the flame. Out of one of the tombs a voice issues (*Inferno*, X:22–27):

> "O man of Tuscany, so true of speech,
> Who in this city of fire walk alive,
> May it be your pleasure to pause here.
> The language you are speaking proclaims you
> A native of that noble fatherland
> Which I, perhaps, molested far too much."

The pilgrim draws close to his guide in fear, not knowing where the voice comes from. As always, Virgil supports and encourages him. "Turn thee round," he says, "what art thou doing? lo there Farinata! who has raised himself erect; from the girdle upwards thou shalt see him all."

Farinata degli Uberti was one of Florence's great sons. For a long time his family was at the head of the Ghibelline faction. He was born at the beginning of the thirteenth century and died in 1264, the year before Dante's birth. He was a great patriot and an ardent partisan, who became head of his house in 1239. He probably stood out in Dante's imagination as Disraeli did in the young Churchill's. He was a mighty, semi-mystical figure in the past, yet not so distant that his footprints did not still reek of blood. Farinata was one of the leaders at the battle of Montaperti in 1260, when the Ghibellines routed the Florentine Guelfs, mainly because of Bocca's treachery. Farinata was thus an enemy of the party to which Dante's family belonged. The Ghibellines' hatred of Guelfic Florence was so strong that after the battle of Montaperti some of them demanded that the city be razed to the ground. This suggestion was opposed by Farinata. His love of Florence was greater than his party passion. By a vigorous protest he stopped the city from being destroyed.

On hearing Farinata's name, Dante turns round and catches sight of the Ghibelline chief, who has raised breast and head out of the fire in the tomb, thereby behaving "as if he entertained great scorn of Hell" (*come avesse lo inferno in gran dispitto,* line 36). Virgil guides the pilgrim between the sepulchers to Farinata. When they reach the foot of the tomb, Farinata looks almost contemptuously at Dante and asks him, "Who were thy ancestors?" Dante tells him. Farinata raises his brows and says: "Fiercely adverse were they to me, and to my progenitors, and to my party; so that twice I scattered them" (lines 46–48). "If they were driven forth, they returned from every quarter, both times," Dante retorts, "but yours have not rightly learnt that art" (*ma i vostri non appreser ben quell' arte,* line 51).

At this moment the conversation is interrupted. A shade appears beside Farinata in the sarcophagus, visible to the chin, a spirit which seems to have raised itself upon its knees. It looks around as though hoping to see someone in Dante's company; its hopes dashed, it says, weeping: "If through this blind prison thou goest by height of genius, where is my son and why is he not with thee?" (lines 58–60).

Dante has recognized the shade immediately and knows

whom he is looking for. The dead man is the old Florentine nobleman Cavalcante Cavalcanti, father of Dante's best friend and fellow poet, Guido Cavalcanti. Cavalcante is not in the same tomb as Farinata by a coincidence, for they were the same age and related by marriage. True, they belonged to different parties, as the Cavalcanti family was Guelfic, but in an attempt to reconcile the factions, Cavalcante had married his son Guido to Farinata's daughter Beatrice. The Comedy reflects a closed aristocratic society, and most of the people mentioned in it are connected by ties of family or friendship and by alliances of one kind or another.

The old Cavalcante Cavalcanti had a name as a free thinker and a non-believer in the immortality of the soul. Perhaps that is why we find him among the blasphemers. Down at the bottom of the tomb he has recognized Dante's voice, and he hoped to find his son in Dante's company. The surmise was natural for two reasons. Guido and Dante were close friends, and they had artistic aims in common. Guido's father alludes to this when he presumes that Dante has managed to descend to Hell alive thanks to his genius. Why, then, should my son not succeed in this, the father wonders with a stab of envy in his heart. His eyes rove round Dante in the same way as an ambitious father's eyes gaze round the platform of honor when his son's best friend is being presented with a prize.

Dante answers Cavalcante as gently and as modestly as he can. He says that he has not come to Hell of his own power but has been led by Virgil, whom Guido perhaps did not value as he should. Dante's reply is remarkable from many viewpoints. He takes quite for granted that he is writing about a journey to the underworld by virtue of his genius as a poet in Virgil's footsteps. At the same time he says that the aims he and Guido Cavalcanti once had in common are no longer sufficient for him.

Scholars have long puzzled over Guido's lack of appreciation of Virgil, but have not reached any definite conclusion. It is certain that Dante considers he has come farther than Guido, that Guido is a station he has left behind him, and that the journey he is now undertaking would never have been .possible if he had stayed on among his friends who were cultivating the new style. Virgil is a man of vision, who wrote of the golden age when all races would live in peace under a righteous ruler. Moreover, Virgil is the writer who—Statius testified to this—sensed the coming of Christ, who led to Christianity without himself being saved. Whatever Dante's mission, and it is likely that in this matter he often changed his point of view, whether it was a pilgrimage down into the hidden depths of the soul or the role of a prophet for a united Christianity and a new millennium, he was a man who served a great idea. Therein lay the difference between him and Guido.

But Guido's father has understood none of this. A moment ago his thoughts were all of his son's fame as a writer. But Dante's words have led them in another direction. Dante in his reply used the past tense: Guido "held [Virgil] in disdain" (*ebbe a disdegno,* line 63). Cavalcanti the elder is seized by a suspicion, more horrible than the one that in the arena of art his son might have had to give pride of place to Dante. "How saidst thou: he *had?*" he asks Dante. "Lives he not still? Does not the sweet light strike his eyes?"

For Dante this was a barbed question. As prior he had been heavily responsible when Guido was sentenced to banishment; during his exile Guido had fallen prey to a fatal disease. Dante could therefore be said to have caused his friend's death. But now, in the spring of 1300, when the Comedy is enacted, Guido is still alive. Dante could therefore instantly reassure the father, but he is not yet quite clear as to the conditions under which the dead live. Not long before, he had met the glutton Ciacco, who predicted the pilgrim's coming misfortunes. The dead thus knew what was to happen in the future, so they must also know conditions on earth at present. So how was it that Cavalcante did not know whether his son was alive or dead? Dante's bewilderment makes him delay his answer. The father thinks his awful suspicion is confirmed. He has risen to his full height in the tomb. Now he falls back and is seen no more.

During this scene Farinata has not changed his aspect. Unmoved, he resumes the conversation with Dante. The three chief actors in this *Inferno* canto are wrapped in wide mantles of solitude. They are so occupied with their own problems that the remarks they exchange have a different meaning for each one of them. While Cavalcante and Dante were talking, Farinata has been thinking of Dante's words that his, Farinata's, people had not learned the art of returning from exile.

"And if," he says, continuing his former words, "they have learnt that art badly, it more torments me than this bed. But the face of the Queen, who reigns here, shall not be fifty times rekindled ere thou shalt know the hardness of that art." Farinata uses as a timepiece Proserpina, who rules over the souls of the dead and whose face lights up at every new moon. Only fifty months are left until Dante shall be driven into exile. Farinata is mistaken, for in fact Dante will remain in Florence only two more years. For Farinata, thinking of the humiliations of exile was more bitter than being burned in everlasting fire. Now by prophesying his fate, he has given Dante something to think about. Dante's boast that his family has managed to return from exile is an empty one if he himself has not learned the art. We know that he never did.

Farinata goes on: "And so mayest thou once return to the sweet world, tell me why that people is so fierce against my kindred in all its laws?" The Ghibellines, as I mentioned, are still banished from Florence at this time, and the harsh laws against them are still in force. "The havoc, and the great slaughter, which dyed the Arbia red, causes such orations in our temple," Dante replies. He is referring to the battle of Montaperti; it was fought on a hill above the Tuscan river Arbia, which was stained with the blood of many a Florentine Guelf. Farinata sighs and shakes his head. "In that I was not single," he answers, meaning the bloodbath. "But I was single there, where all consented to extirpate Florence. I alone with open face defended her" (lines 91–92).

The meeting between the pilgrim and Farinata is a confrontation between two political opponents whose destinies are so similar that it is unreasonable to suppose that Dante the poet did not notice it. Since the death of Frederick II in 1250, the power of the Roman Empire had steadily declined. The Hapsburg emperors had found it hard to maintain their claims of sovereignty against the popes. In 1308 Albrecht of Hapsburg died, and his successor was Henry of Luxemburg, who was elected with the support of the French pope Clement V and in competition with the same Charles of Valois whom Dante called a Judas. This fact alone should have sufficed to make Dante Emperor Henry's man. At this time France was the strongest power in Europe. As a sign of this, the pope removed to Avignon. Emperor Henry went to Italy in 1310 to be crowned in Rome. The expedition, he hoped, would give him the prestige that he, having but little money or lands, needed so urgently. Upon his arrival in Italy many of the exiles were inspired with new hope. Dante was one of them. He threw himself passionately into the fight that blazed up; the issue was whether or not the Italian princes and cities would acknowledge the emperor's supremacy.

Dante was present at Henry's coronation with the iron crown in Milan. In the spring of 1311 he addressed an open letter to the princes and peoples of Italy, a letter so encumbered with rhetoric that it is difficult to recognize the stringent and concise author of the Comedy. But Dante was a pupil in the great school of rhetoric which had never closed its doors since antiquity and which in the Middle Ages was to be found chiefly in Latin literature.

> For a new day is beginning to break, revealing the dawn in the East, which even now is dispersing the darkness of our long tribulation," Dante writes. "Already the orient breeze is freshening, the face of the heavens grows rosy, and confirms the hopes of the peoples with an auspicious calm. And we too, who have kept vigil through the long night in the wilderness, shall behold the long-awaited joy. For the Sun of peace shall appear on high, and justice which, like the heliotrope, deprived of his light, had grown faint, so soon as he shall dart forth his rays,

once more shall revive. All they that hunger and thirst shall be satisfied in the light of his radiance, and they that delight in iniquity shall be put to confusion before the face of his splendor . . . Rejoice, therefore, O Italy, thou art now an object of pity even to the Saracens, for soon shalt thou be the envy of the whole world, seeing that thy bridegroom, the comfort of the nations, and the glory of thy people, even the most clement Henry, Elect of God and Augustus and Cæsar, is hastening to the wedding. Dry thy tears, and wipe away the stains of thy weeping, most beauteous one; for he is at hand who shall bring thee forth from the prison of the ungodly, and shall smite the workers of iniquity with the edge of the sword, and shall destroy them. And his vineyard shall he let out to other husbandmen, who shall render the fruit of justice in the time of harvest. . . .

It is unlikely that Henry of Luxemburg either personally came up to Dante's high expectations or shared his view of the loftiness of the imperial power. And indeed the hopes that Dante placed in him were soon to be dashed. The emperor found that the Italian princes by no means desired him as a peacemaker, but only as a court card in their own pack. With all the cynicism that belonged to the age he allowed himself to be exploited for such aims. But his indulgence was of little avail. He reached Rome and was crowned in June 1312. But by then an Italian conspiracy to drive him out of the country was already a fact. King Robert of Naples appeared as the leader of this conspiracy and took Rome. Behind the scenes Florentine diplomats and Florentine gold coins were unceasingly at work. Florence was shown to be the real organizer of the resistance to the emperor. The city had all the greater reason to adopt this attitude since the emperor wanted to restore his monopoly on the minting of gold coins, and this was gall and wormwood to the Florentines. In 1312 the pope, who in Henry had hoped for a counterweight to the French royal power, openly went over to the emperor's enemies. Henry's cause was as good as lost.

During these years Dante was in a distressed state of mind. The events taking place were a continuation, on a big historical scale, of the disaster that had overtaken him in 1302. In the spring of 1311 he remained near the border of Tuscany, waiting every day for the "God's anointed" whom he had called upon to make it possible for him to return to Florence. He took up his pen once more and sent a letter to his countrymen, donning the mantle of an Old Testament prophet. The Florentines, he writes, are opposing God's will in defying the emperor, who alone can give the world peace and justice. If they persist, a horrible fate is in store for them.

> The buildings which you have raised, not in prudence to serve your needs, but have recklessly altered to gratify your wantonness, these, encircled by no walls of a renovated Troy, to your grief you shall see crumble beneath the battering-ram, and devoured by the flames. The populace which now, divided against itself, rages indiscriminately, some for you, some against you, you shall then see united in their imprecations against you, for the starving mob knows nothing of fear. With remorse, too, you shall behold the spoliation of your temples, thronged daily by a concourse of matrons, and your children doomed in wonder and ignorance to suffer for the sins of their fathers. And if my prophetic soul be not deceived, which announces what it has been taught by infallible signs and incontrovertible arguments, your city, worn out with ceaseless mourning, shall be delivered at the last into the hands of the stranger, after the greatest part of you has been destroyed in death or captivity; and the few that shall be left to endure exile shall witness her downfall with tears and lamentation. Those sufferings, in short, which for liberty's sake the glorious city of Saguntum endured in her loyalty, you in your disloyalty must undergo with shame but to become slaves.

Dante here is predicting utter destruction. A month later he writes a letter to the emperor himself. He likens Henry to Augustus; he is to restore, to Italy and the world, the golden age of which Virgil once sang. He calls the emperor "the Lamb of God which taketh away the sins of the world." He reproaches him for not realizing that Florence is the chief opponent. The emperor must crush this evil city first. Hercules was unable to conquer the hydra, because for every head he struck off, new ones grew. He succeeded only when he went to the source of its power. In the same way the emperor, in his fight against the hydra of Italy, must learn that he should go to the root of the trouble. "Do you not notice, most excellent prince," Dante exclaims, having headed his letter "From beneath the springs of Arno," where "the stinking vixen is which mocks the hunters from her lair." The guilty one does not drink from the swiftly flowing Po, nor from the Tiber. No, this repulsive monster lowers its snout into the River Arno's waters and its name is Florence. It is an adder which buries its fangs in its mother's dugs. It is the sick sheep which passes the disease on to the whole flock. It is the unnatural Myrrha who lusts for the embrace of her own father.

Dante paints his own country to that country's mortal enemy as a hydra which must be crushed. One result of this letter was certain. As long as the régime then ruling in Florence remained in power, he could not return from exile. The city soon hit back. In September 1311, it issued a general amnesty for political exiles, but Dante's name was deliberately excluded. Dante was not as imbued with the principles of patriotic loyalty as we are, for he lived in an age when the ideas of universality had not yet gone under. For all that, his situation was a severe moral strain. He prophesied the downfall of Florence and tried to hasten it. The step between word and deed was short.

Farinata, who is in the tomb, and Dante the storyteller, who is writing the Comedy and shaping the dialogue between Farinata and the pilgrim, are thus in the same situation and have the same kind of tormenting memories. Farinata was accused in Florence of having been one of the leaders during the bloodbath that dyed the waters of the Arbia red. But he had no part in the plans to raze Florence. He had opposed the city's destruction. What about Dante? He had clamored for fire and the sword, but when Emperor

Henry finally set out for Florence after his coronation in Rome and the open breach with the pope, Dante, who had joined his army, refused to go with him. Apparently he could not bring himself to bear arms against his countrymen. But the murderous letters remained. Farinata, who defends himself in the Comedy, gives us a picture of Dante pleading for his cause while in exile. Behind Farinata, who raises himself up in the tomb surrounded by flames, we see Dante in exile, consumed by homesickness and pricked by his conscience. Farinata has only contempt for Hell; his good name in his native city is more important to him than the everlasting punishment. Dante, whose sufferings in exile were nothing compared with the torment of being pointed out as a dastardly wretch who wanted to bring about the annihilation of his ancestral city, feels the same way.

Farinata and Cavalcante are in Hell. They have been placed in a circle where blasphemers are punished, but as always we have not heard them refer to the sin they are supposd to be expiating. We are already accustomed not to confuse the external moral scheme with the internal and deeper guilt. Ulysses' sin was not the ruse with the horse, but his obsession for acquiring knowledge for its own sake. Farinata is so devoured by his political passion that he is indifferent to the horrors of Hell. Cavalcante in the heretics' fire is interested in his son's renown and not in the salvation of his own soul. They are both blasphemers in that they see life on earth and temporal aims as more important than Heaven and eternity. They appear on the scene together so that Dante the storyteller will have a chance to show that he has come farther along the road as regards both writing and politics.

Politics, internal politics in Florence, are a mania with Farinata. The loftiest idea, the brightest star that shines in his heaven, is that of patriotism. When this love of his native country conflicts with his party activities, he chooses his country. That is why he said no to his allies' plans to destroy the city. Within the sphere of party politics and patriotism, he is a man who has reached the limit of human capability.

When Dante allots him a place in Hell, it is because he thinks that he himself has progressed farther.

iv

Dante never gives up the thought of returning to Florence. But Emperor Henry's untimely death, the decline of the papal power, the increase in strength and pretentions of the national hegemonies, and the disruption in Italy were disastrous circumstances for Dante. He realized that a return brought about by political means was unlikely. When he dreams of a return in one of the last cantos of *Paradiso,* which was probably written only a year or so before his death, it is no longer a return in the capacity of a prophet calling for the fire and sword of a world ruler. Now he hopes instead that the huge poem on which he has been working for so many years and which has already brought him fame— for as the cantos are written, copies are made and distributed —will be the battering-ram that breaks down the opposition. "Should it e'er come to pass," he writes at the beginning of the twenty-fifth canto, "that this sacred poem" (*il poema sacro*) "to which heaven and earth have set hand so that for many years it has made me lean, should conquer the hatred which shuts me out of the sheepfold where I slept as a lamb, then shall I with whitened hair and changed voice receive the poet's laurel wreath at the font in the Baptistry where I was once received into the Christian faith."

A discussion, in which nearly all leading Dante scholars have taken part, has been carried on as to the extent and manner of Dante's development as a political thinker. Does he see the world's affairs with a different eye during the years he takes an active part in world politics and during the period when he is writing the Comedy? An essential condition for such a discussion is, of course, the ability to date Dante's works with any certainty. It is generally agreed that the book on the vernacular, *De Vulgari Eloquentia,* and *Convivio* were written before *De Monarchia* and that this last work was completed during Emperor Henry's sojourn in Italy, probably in

1312. It is just possible, however, that *De Monarchia* was finished after the emperor's death in 1313. The Comedy is then allotted the part of Dante's life that remained—roughly eight years. Bearing in mind the vast size, external and internal, of the Comedy and the fact that in *Vita Nuova*—a work presumed to have been written in the 1290's when Dante still lived in Florence—Dante announces a great work with Beatrice as the leading character, we must surely wonder whether the Comedy took only eight or ten years to write. No definite statements are possible. The material is too vague. The attempts made to date various sections of the Comedy on internal grounds seem a waste of time to me.

But even if we dare to rely on this generally accepted chronology, the difficulties in following Dante's course of development are great. *De Monarchia* is a political tract. In it Dante appears as a vigorous reformer and logical, stringent reasoner. He drives his argument forward as resolutely and skillfully as a jockey does his horse on the racecourse. He argues against the political ideologies of past and present ages, and his views can be established with the greatest exactitude. The Comedy, on the other hand, is a poetic work with an intricate symbolic and allegorical apparatus. It is a living organism and not an abstract line of argument. To sum up and compare the thoughts that Dante expresses in *De Monarchia* and in the letters with corresponding ideas in the Comedy is like introducing a live plant or a flying bird into a mathematical equation. One scholar, Professor A. P. d'Entrèves, who has written an ingenious book about Dante as a political thinker, holds that Dante changed so radically between *De Monarchia* and the Comedy that on one essential point the Comedy should be regarded as a repentant sinner's work of expiation. In the Comedy Dante is supposed to regret having championed Emperor Henry, and above all to feel remorse at having likened the emperor to Christ. Christianity maintains that mankind is to be saved from within, through the salvation of the individual, and not through an external liberation. Dante, so d'Entrèves says, wanted to see the universal empire as a power just as God-inspired as the universal church. Beatrice reproaches Dante because of this blasphemy when the two lovers meet at last in the thirtieth canto of *Paradiso.*

D'Entrèves' theory has not gone unchallenged. Charles Till Davis points out quietly in his work *Dante and the Idea of Rome* that it was part of the traditional ceremonial during the Middle Ages to liken the emperor to Christ. It can be added that Dante in Paradise indicates the place in Heaven which Emperor Henry is to occupy when he dies, and that this place is one of the most exalted. There is nothing to show that he changed his mind on this point. But in my view it is not necessary to construct a course of development. Dante was obsessed by his love of Florence, but this love had its complement in a universalism which went through his life like an inciting *leitmotif.* Most people would agree with d'Entrèves that Dante in exile was forced to become a world citizen. It was said that Cato felt he was living not for his own sake, but for the sake of all mankind. The same is true of the aging Dante Alighieri from Florence. But it is not hard to find evidence from every period of his life for his universal turn of mind, which was an inheritance from the universal Roman empire and the universal ancient culture which he tried to restore. Even in his book on the vernacular he writes controversially against those who in all things put their own land first: "But I, who have the whole world for my native land, just as the fishes have the sea, would rather. . . ." The words are borrowed from Brunetto Latini's work *Trésor,* the very work which Brunetto particularly commends to Dante when he meets him in Hell. Perhaps this was what Dante was thinking of when he said that Brunetto had taught him how to become immortal.

For Dante, one way to immortality was to fight his way out of Florentine nationalism and to write with the good of all mankind, not Florence's, as his aim. This path was not merely duty but also consolation. The writer and thinker has no native land. He is at home wherever he can write and think in freedom, and in exile wherever this freedom is denied him. He finds fellow countrymen where free thoughts are exchanged. Or, as Dante wrote to a friend in Florence in 1315, after having heard that he could return to his home town on certain humiliating conditions: "Have I not the same sun and stars above me wherever I am? Can I not ponder the same great truths under whatever sky I am living, without having to return and let the people of Florence take honour and dignity away from me?"

The Comedy is a work about fellowship outside time and space, and Dante meets mostly writers and thinkers in the realms of the dead, people who live under the sign of universalism and have a sense of responsibility for humanity. Of none is this so true as of Virgil, who wrote the *Aeneid* for the sake of the golden age that was to result from all people living united under a just rule.

In the letter to Emperor Henry in the spring of 1311, Dante quotes words taken from a work by the Roman poet Lucan, one of those he met in Limbo. Lucan wrote about the Roman Curio, who made his mark in history by energetically exhorting Cæsar to cross the Rubicon, and in this way decide the issue of power. "Strike hard!" Curio shouted to Cæsar, according to Lucan. Now is the right moment, while the various factions are weak and vacillating. Dante applies these words to Emperor Henry's situation. He should press on to Florence without delay, just as Cæsar moved on towards Rome. Like Dante, Curio was a man who lived in exile, and he had personal reasons for wishing Cæsar in power. The advice he gave Cæsar helped to increase the dissension in the Roman empire. Oddly enough, in the Comedy, Dante has placed Curio in Hell among the sowers of discord (*Inferno,* XXVIII:94 *et seq.*). Dante shows us Curio "with tongue slit in his gorge," struck dumb because he spoke too much at the Rubicon. He is eaten by remorse at the thought of the advice he gave.

Does this mean that Dante changed his political views? In 1311 Curio was a good counselor, and his advice to Cæsar agreed with Dante's advice to Emperor Henry. But in the Comedy Curio is remembered only because he sowed discord among his countrymen. D'Entrèves draws the conclusion that Dante regrets having tried to persuade Henry to march on Florence. Curio in Hell does penance for Dante himself. This idea is warmly endorsed by Colin Hardie, a scholar who, more firmly than anyone else, holds that the Comedy should be seen as a self-analysis. Even here Charles Till Davis is sceptical. If Dante condemns his advice to Emperor Henry in 1311, it would mean that he also condemns his view of the imperial power as the only one that could guarantee peace. This is absurd. In the Comedy none is more severely punished than Cassius and Brutus, who betrayed the emperorship.

But does it really matter if Dante has placed Curio in Hell before or after the letter to Emperor Henry? In the Comedy Curio is punished for being one of those who sowed discord among his fellow men. Dante must have accused himself in the same way for having urged the emperor to crush Florence. In the mute and plague-stricken Curio, we can see a picture of Dante himself, an exile like Curio, tormented by the boils of his conscience. But the Curio-Dante who intervened, or tried to intervene, in world history by urging Cæsar to cross the Rubicon and Henry to march on Florence, is also present in the Comedy. On the moral plane Curio is perhaps a figure who foreshadows the greatest sower of dissension of all, Lucifer, who caused strife in Heaven. But the Comedy is not merely a moral argument, nor is it merely a poetic work. It is also a political thesis. It advocates a world emperorship, which derives its authority not from the pope but directly from God. As the enemies of this idea, and thereby of God, the Comedy points to the powers that were against universal monarchy: Florence, France, and Pope Boniface VIII. It is unreasonable to think that Curio is placed in Hell because he supported this universal monarchy.

v

In the sixth canto of *Purgatorio* Dante and Virgil meet the Italian poet Sordello, a troubadour from the beginning of the thirteenth century, who was known for his political ambitions. Sordello is sitting by himself on the ground, and he gives the two friends a mute glance as they pass. He is like a lion at rest.

Virgil goes up to Sordello to ask the way and receives another question in reply: Sordello wants to know his name. It is Virgil's custom to introduce himself with the sentence said to have been engraved over his tomb and which began with the name of his birthplace, Mantua. At the instant the city's name passes Virgil's lips Sordello leaps up, interrupts him with a shout of joy, and embraces him: He too was born in Mantua. Overcome by the feelings evoked by the city of his birth, he forgets that it was Virgil's name he was asking.

The scene gives a vivid picture of Dante in his relationship to Florence. It also brings true his dream of a just citizenship that contrasts with the bitter schism that dominated public life in the fourteenth century. Dante the storyteller improves the occasion and steps out of the framework of his poetical work with a lament over the state of affairs in Italy, over his native land which has become a "hostel of woe" and a "vessel without pilot in a mighty storm." The country which should be mistress of provinces has become a brothel. Sordello and Virgil rush into each other's arms at the mere mention of their native soil, but "now in civil tumult are distraught thy living citizens, at daggers drawn those whom one wall incloses." Rome is widowed and alone, mourning her husband, the emperor. Florence is like a sick woman tossing on her couch to ward away her pain.

Day is declining. In Purgatory no one can ascend the Mountain once darkness has fallen, for evil is not fully overcome and has greater power after sunset. Sordello leads Dante and Virgil to a valley full of scented flowers. Seated on the grass are dead princes. The twilight deepens and sadness, homesickness, and a foreboding of danger fill the air. The princes, who have been singing a song to the Virgin Mary, fall silent and gaze up at the sky. Two angels fly in over the valley. Their raiment is green, "as tender leaves just born," and they have flaming swords with broken points. They alight one on each side of the valley to guard it against evil.

When night comes, Dante carries on a political discourse with the dead princes, and Virgil instructs him in the stars blazing above them. Suddenly Sordello points to the head of the valley. The sense of danger turns out to be well-founded. A snake is sliding towards them through the grass and flowers, turning its head round now and again and licking itself. At the same moment the two angels, "the celestial falcons," have flown up, cleaving the air with their green wings. The serpent flees back to the abyss from which it came. The angels, "both wheeling up as one," return to their posts, and it is quiet once more in the valley of the princes.

These "negligent rulers" have allowed themselves to become far too taken up with earthly worries. They are now doing penance. As a gentle lesson the thousands of flowers spread their beauty and their scent. They have neither toiled nor spun, yet even Solomon in all his glory was not arrayed like one of these. The princes in the valley are one of the many visions of a just world rule and a right universal fellowship that are presented in the Comedy. The farther we come in the poem, the more glorious the colors in which this kingdom of righteousness shines.

Augustine distinguished between God's city and the world's city. He called the fellowship of the chosen Jerusalem, and that of the lost and the damned, Babylon. But for Augustine both Jerusalem and Babylon are spiritual cities and should not be confused with any earthly fellowships. The Church may resemble Jerusalem, and the state may resemble Babylon; but the frontier between the two kingdoms passes through every state and through every man's heart. During the centuries after Augustine, Christian thinkers developed the idea of the God-state. Jerusalem as an invisible fellowship, as a city which has its foundation only in men's souls, is changed more and more into a power which is tangible in the world of the senses. The Church claims to *be* Jerusalem, and its highest representative, the pope, is not only a leader

of souls, but also a ruler over members of society. In the last
resort, too, the pope has authority over the rulers of the
people and over the emperor. If the emperor is given sanction
by God's representative on earth, then the empire he governs
will also be holy. Babylon disappears, and a kingdom of
righteousness with the pope as head emerges in its place.

Dante opposed this political theory with all his might. *De
Monarchia* is a pamphlet which sets out to show, among other
things, that the emperor derives his power directly from
God and not through the mediation of a pope. Dante maintains that humanity has a common goal here on earth and
that this goal consists of making use of everybody's full
intellectual power. He is the first to think of humanity as
a unit which has a meaning in itself. To the theologians, man
exists for the sake of God. The whole point of humanity
was that it should be saved. The consequence of all power
on earth converging in the pope's person was that conditions
here on earth were of very little importance. In *De Monarchia*
Dante shows that the individual best acquires wisdom and
virtue if he is left in peace. Therefore, for all mankind, peace
must be the most important thing, for people are only
capable of gaining their objectives if they are at peace. Only
the universal empire, extending all over the earth, having
its foundation in justice and drawing its strength from compassion and love, can give mankind the peace it needs.

Dante's endowment of human life on earth with a meaning which has nothing to do with salvation and the life everlasting is a vital stage in mankind's development. It is easy
for us to share Dante's evaluations. We are well aware that it
is essential to overcome the dissension on earth and that this
can come about under the guidance of an international organization. We realize that a war can obliterate our civilization and that peace is the most vital task of our century.
Moreover, we think that the meaning of humanity is that
each one of us shall be allowed to develop in accord with
our talents and that this is possible only if peace can be kept
and prosperity increased.

Dante abhorred and feared the dishonesty which results from the confusion of the Augustinian God-state with a worldly fellowship. It was therefore necessary for him to show that the emperor, who was first and foremost a guarantee for peace and who was the highest representative of earthly justice, should receive his sanction directly from God. During one period of his life he strove to get an emperor recognized as world ruler. But when the Comedy is written, it is not an immediate political aim which he has in mind. Instead, the poem becomes a vision of a fellowship in which the princes' striving for righteousness and justice exists side by side with the saints' longing for salvation and eternity. In Paradise the righteous princes together form an eagle, which speaks to Dante. But the eagle, at the same time as it represents the Roman imperial power, is a bird of God. The kingdom of Heaven, imagined by Augustine as a fellowship of souls, merges with the earthly kingdom of peace.

Let us return to Farinata for a moment. The pilgrim continues his discourse with the Ghibelline chief. He is worried because old Cavalcante has misunderstood him. He asks Farinata to tell Cavalcante down in the tomb that his son is still alive. He wants to go on talking to Farinata, but Virgil grows impatient, and the pilgrim only has time to ask which spirits are being tormented with Farinata. The latter replies: "With more than a thousand lie I here; the second Frederick is here within, and the Cardinal; and of the rest I speak not." Then he disappears and the pilgrim continues his journey at Virgil's side. His worried looks cause the Roman poet to ask: "Why art thou so bewildered?" We are not told what the pilgrim replies. Virgil goes on (*Inferno,* X: 127–132):

> "Let your memory preserve what you have heard
> Against you," that sage commanded. "And now
> Pay close attention"; and he raised a finger.
> "When you are standing in the sweet ray
> Of her whose lovely eyes see everything,
> You will learn from her the voyage of your life."

In this way Dante the storyteller has stressed the importance of the conversation between Farinata and the pilgrim. It is a key passage for those who want to understand the development the pilgrim undergoes. Farinata, despite his moral greatness, stays on in Hell because Dante finds his lodestars insufficient. In the design of the poem Farinata is indeed a blasphemer, just as old Cavalcante is, because they have not gained the understanding that humanity, by bringing about the earthly kingdom of peace, prepares itself for the eternal one. This is what Beatrice in Paradise will enlighten the pilgrim about.

Frederick II, the most brilliant of the Hohenstaufens, and the Cardinal, the only ones of his "fellow criminals" whom Farinata considers it worth mentioning, were both ambitious men who saw a final goal in the personal might of the emperor. Like Farinata, their goal lay within time. That is why they are in Hell.

12

BEATRICE

AT THE TOP of the steep Mount of Purgatory lies the Earthly Paradise where Adam and Eve once lived in perfect bliss. On the pilgrim's journey, it is identical with the sunlit heights which he glimpsed in the first canto of *Inferno* and which he was stopped from climbing by the leopard, the lion, and the she-wolf. Now, in the twenty-eighth canto of *Purgatorio*, he has arrived there.

The Earthly Paradise is a forest. The sunlight filters through the leaves, the scent of flowers fills the air, the birds are singing. The divine forest (*la divina foresta*) is a counterpoint to the wild and dark wood in which the pilgrim went astray. Dante the poet does liken it to the pine wood on the bank of the River Chiassi near Ravenna, but it is not subject to the earthly laws of nature. The Garden of Eden is created spontaneously by God. What takes place there flows directly from His will.

Before the pilgrim enters the forest, Virgil tells him that his trials are over. He no longer needs Virgil's guidance. "Wherefore," Virgil says—and it is the last time we hear him speak in the Comedy—"I do crown and mitre thee over thyself" (XXVII:142).

These last cantos of *Purgatorio* are more teeming with ideas than usual. I approach them with diffidence. When I try to formulate something about their contents, I am more aware than ever of my inadequacy. I know that this feeling will be intensified with every step forward in the Comedy and reach its painful climax in Paradise proper. More resolutely than before, I must choose one way and leave the others. Among much else, therefore, I must pass by the woman picking flowers whom the pilgrim first meets in the fragrant woodland and their conversation on the nature of Paradise and innocence and concentrate on the woman that the flower-gatherer presages—Beatrice.

At one time Beatrice was Dante's beloved on earth. She has been dead for ten years, and her soul lives in Heaven. She went down into the underworld to ask Virgil to save her friend from the Dark Wood. Now she has left Paradise proper for the second time in order to meet the man she loves in the Earthly Paradise and be his guide through the ten heavens. During his pilgrimage her lover has looked forward to this moment. The thought has spurred him on. At moments of peril Virgil has only had to mention her name for Dante to conquer his faintheartedness. Just before entering the Earthly Paradise—in the twenty-seventh canto —the pilgrim is compelled to go through the fire that purges those who have been too prone to earthly love. He quails before the ordeal. Virgil induces him to pluck up courage by saying that Beatrice is waiting for him on the other side. Then, Dante says (*Purgatorio,* XXVII: 37–42):

> Just as Pyramus, when dying, opened his eyes
> At the name of Thisbe and looked at her,
> And the color of the mulberry turned to red;
> So I, on hearing the name that always
> Shoots up in my mind, lessened my resistance,
> And turned to face my learned leader.

Love opened Pyramus' eyes even though death had already dug its claws into him. The love that Beatrice inspires in the pilgrim has the same power.

The pilgrim wanders on through the Garden of Eden along the bank of a river, Lethe; by drinking of its waters the souls forget all the sin from which they have been re-deemed. On the other side of the river, the air seems aflame. The pilgrim is aware of seven huge lighted candlesticks advancing towards him to the shouts of "Hosanna!" After the candlesticks come twenty-four elders clad in white raiment and crowned with lilies. They are followed by four beasts crowned with green leaves. The beasts have six wings and these, like Argus, are studded with eyes. Dante the poet states that he will refrain from depicting them in detail. He has no time. He refers the reader who wishes to know more to Ezekiel, where the beasts are described.

The four beasts are followed by a two-wheeled chariot of the type used by the Romans in their triumphs. It is drawn by a griffon, whose limbs are of gold. Three women are dancing at one wheel, four at the other. Behind them are two aged men with grave and dignified bearing. They in turn are followed by four men of humble mien, and last of all comes an old man alone, walking in a trance but with a keen visage. These last seven male figures, instead of being crowned with white lilies like the twenty-four elders, are wearing chaplets of roses and other red flowers. Viewed from a short distance, they all look as if they were aflame above the brows.

On the main points, commentators are agreed on the meaning of this procession. The candlesticks symbolize the seven gifts of the Holy Spirit. The twenty-four lily-crowned elders are the twenty-four books of the Old Testament. The four beasts with the Argus eyes represent the four Gospels. The chariot is the Church and the griffon is Christ. At the right wheel dance the three theological virtues of faith, hope, and love, and at the left wheel the four cardinal virtues of temperance, justice, fortitude, and prudence. The old men that follow are the remaining books of the New Testament, and the old man of acumen who walks in his sleep is of course John, who wrote the Revelation in a state of God-given trance. As anyone familiar with the Bible will have realized, most of the phenomena in the procession—the candlesticks, the twenty-four elders, the beasts with the eye-studded wings—are taken from Revelation as well as from Ezekiel. It is Holy Writ which the pilgrim in a vision sees proceeding through the forest of Paradise. It is also time itself which is passing by, the whole history of mankind from the creation to doomsday.

There is much in the Comedy which is fantastic and bizarre, but Dante the storyteller makes an effort to give it all an air of credibility. Even the monster Geryon with human face and dragon's body convinced us of his existence. Now, with the procession, it seems as if Dante were offering us merely an allegory. Without the key, the scene in the forest means nothing. Or is this perhaps a biased statement? We can of course view the procession as a spectacle, as a play with the performers in masks and costly dresses. We are sitting in the stalls and gazing in wonder at the brilliantly lit stage. We are glad that there is a world so far away from everyday life. But it is not a game we are watching. Dante the poet has never yet been so serious as he is here.

A host of angels is hovering round the chariot. One of them, "as if sent from heaven" (*quasi da ciel messo, Purgatorio,* XXX:10), thrice sings the words from the Song of Songs: "Come with me from Lebanon, my spouse." Other angels strew flowers and all cry: "Blessed be thou that comest! O give ye lilies all with liberal hand!" Note that these words are said in Latin, the language of the Church, and not in Italian: *"Benedictus qui venis, manibus o date lilia plenis."* Among the angels in the chariot, the pilgrim sees a woman in a green mantle and snow-white veil with olive fillet. Under the mantle she wears a dress the color of living flame. Although the woman is veiled, he knows at once who she is (*Purgatorio,* XXX:34–48):

> And in my spirit—which for so long a time
> Had not been overwhelmed with awe
> Nor trembled violently in her presence—
> And even before my eyes could gather more,
> Through some secret power coming from her,
> I felt the tremendous force of an old love.
> No sooner were my eyes assailed by that
> Supreme force, which had pervaded me even
> Before my boyhood years were behind me,
> Than I turned to the left, with that reliance
> That makes a little child run to its mother
> When it is afraid or has been injured,

William Blake: The ledge of the proud in Purgatory. An angel is descending. *Purgatorio* XII. Notice the urgent, inspired movement, which characterizes Dante's presentation and which Blake has so brilliantly captured. We see unmistakably that this angel is eager to help. *British Museum, London.*

Beatrice as Dante Gabriel Rossetti (1828-1882) saw her. This romanticized young Florentine woman has usually been displaced in our age by a somewhat harsher conception.

A primitive picture by Marziana, who lived in Venice from about the year 1400, shows Beatrice in the triumphal car speaking sternly to Dante. The gryphon drawing the car symbolizes Christ.

Sandro Botticelli: The triumphal procession in the Earthly Paradise. See *Purgatorio* XXIX *et seq.* At the head of the procession can be seen the seven holy candlesticks. The Christ-gryphon's wings reach up to heaven. Beatrice stands on the triumphal car. *Duke of Hamilton Collection, Print Room, New Museum, Berlin.*

And said to Virgil: "There is not a dram
Of blood left in me that is not throbbing.
I recognize the signs of my old passion."

At this moment the pilgrim discovers that Virgil is no longer
beside him. Virgil's words to Dante about the crown and
mitre hinted that his role as guide and teacher was played
out. But the pilgrim had not grasped that he was to be left
alone and that the poetic art he had hitherto practiced was
no longer adequate. Virgil had returned to Limbo. The
memory of how, when they arrived at the Mount of Purgatory, his friend washed his, Dante's, stained face with dew
flashes through him. Three times, with mounting anguish, he
calls out Virgil's name. His threefold cry is in itself a compliment to Virgil, who at moments of great feeling liked to
use this figure of speech. Dante the pilgrim says, "My dew-
washed cheeks" (*guance nette di rugiada,* line 53) turned
dark again with tears, and these words are all the poet needs
to revive the cleansing ceremony on the shore.

Beatrice regards him from the chariot, displeased at his
grief for a dead friend at this crucial moment of his life.
She says: "Dante, for that Virgil goeth away, weep not yet,
weep not yet, for thou must weep for other sword." The first
word Beatrice speaks to the pilgrim is his name. It is the
only time the name is mentioned in the Comedy. It is charged
with reproach. There is perhaps a tinge of jealousy.

Who is Beatrice? According to St. Luke's Gospel, Jesus'
disciples shouted as he entered Jerusalem: "Blessed be he that
cometh in the name of the Lord." These words from the 118th
Psalm referred to the coming Messiah, the saviour of mankind. Beatrice thus comes towards the pilgrim as if she were
Christ. We also know that Beatrice is the young woman
whom Dante loved when he was a young man in Florence.
He had seen the red dress she is now wearing before. It
reminds him of their first meeting "ere I was out of my boy-
hood." He had told of this in the first of his books, the
autobiographical *Vita Nuova.* In one of the very first lines
he says that he met Beatrice when he was nine years old and

she a few months younger. "She appeared to me clothed in most noble hue, a subdued and modest crimson, cinctured and adorned after the fashion that was becoming to her most tender age. At that point I verily declare that the vital spirit which dwelleth in the most secret chamber of the heart began to tremble so mightily that it was horribly apparent in the least of my pulses."

The crimson dress is only one of the many links between *Vita Nuova* and the Comedy. Even the vision with Beatrice in the midst of the angels is foreshadowed in the twenty-third chapter of the earlier work, where Dante tells how he experiences Beatrice's death in a dream: The sun is eclipsed, birds fall dead in flight, and there is an earthquake. Beatrice is dead, and when the poet gazes up to Heaven he sees a host of angels ascending, with a dazzling cloud in front of them and singing "Hosanna in the highest!" The white cloud is Beatrice rising to Heaven. Now she returns in the Comedy in the company of the same angels and acclaimed by the same shouts of "Hosanna!"

A voice from the chariot sang of the bride in the Song of Songs. She was a real woman with "doves' eyes" and "hair as a flock of goats that appear from Mount Gilead." But she was also an image of the Christian united with the Saviour-bridegroom. We need not be surprised, therefore, that Beatrice is at once the beloved from Florence and a sign of something higher.

Love poetry of a chivalrous nature had existed for a long time in southern Europe. The troubadours sang of a woman whose beauty and charms aroused the noblest feelings of the soul. In her they did not seek sensual pleasure and the act of possession—that need was met by wives and harlots. The beloved of the troubadours was a mistress, a *domina,* to serve and obey. The relations between her and the poet-lover were rather like those between a feudal lord and his knight. On a higher plane the resulting poetry was, it has been said, the first since antiquity which dared to imply that love for an earthly woman carried the same obligations as the thought of the soul's salvation. He who followed a *domina* was in fact a heretic, for among women on earth only the Holy Virgin was worthy of worship such as this. Many of the troubadours ended their lives in a monastery, where they did penance for having given themselves up to an earthly love. We meet one of them, a man by the name of Folco, in Paradise where, in the heaven of Venus, he represents those who devoted their life to earthly love but had the sense to turn to higher things in time.

We cannot say with certainty whether or not Beatrice existed. The generally accepted view is that her original in real life was a Florentine lady whose name, Boccaccio tells us, was Bice and who was the daughter of one Folco Portinari. There are scholars willing to stake their lives on the belief that she is only an allegorical figure, a personification of the divine grace or of theology. There are others who, like Etienne Gilson, go to extravagant lengths to show that she is not *only* an allegory. But whatever we may think and write about Beatrice, the only material we have at our disposal is what Dante himself has given us. The name that Boccaccio mentions, like the name of the Simone di Bardi whom she is supposed to have married in 1277, is of little help to us. There is no doubt that Dante's relationship to Beatrice has something of the troubadour's love. Beatrice has certainly been a woman who inspired the noblest thoughts and feelings in her admirer. She is equipped with the attributes the troubadours gave their beloved. But both in *Vita Nuova* and the Comedy she is just as often a symbol of humble service as a mistress. In *Vita Nuova* she cuts her lover in the street because she has heard that he has been paying court to another. In this she behaves in accord with the familiar rules of the game of earthly love. But she differs radically from other women in literature who are in love. As far as characters in literature can, Isolde, Juliet, Anna Karenina, and Madame Bovary exist as independent personalities in their respective works. For them, love is a passion which devours them whole. Love is their fate, and they live as captives within its flame. For the sake of love they defy the gods. Francesca in the fifth canto of *Inferno* is one of them. They are present in the dramas they are acting in at every moment, and it would never occur to their lovers not to regard them as the sweet object of their passion. Beatrice, on the other hand, serves something greater than herself.

Eliot has said that when Dante in *Vita Nuova* depicts Beatrice, he does not tell us what he consciously felt for her while she lived on earth. He describes instead what love for her meant to him when he viewed it in the light of mature reflection. Dante saw her when she was a little girl and her beauty aroused inexplicable feelings. When he grew up he sensed that his love for her contained something greater than the longing to possess her. He saw in her the sum of all earthly delights, but also a sign which pointed beyond herself. When she died this sign remained. She appeared to him as a guide to a more sublime beauty and a greater happiness than any that life on earth can offer. She was a decoy which enticed him not to herself but to another.

But this is only partly true. Beatrice is not merely a decoy. In the poem she is not as concrete as the bride in the Song of Songs, but neither is she purely abstract. Dante ends *Vita Nuova* with the promise that one day he will write of Beatrice "as no one has ever sung of a woman." The words do not refer, as is generally thought, to the degree of his passion and the beauty of his song. They refer to the *nature* of his feeling. He did not mean that in the arena where the loved ones of all the troubadours competed, his beloved was to be awarded the prize. Dante did not imagine that his greater poetic gifts would place Beatrice foremost among all celebrated women. His beloved was at once an earthly woman and a saint, at once the bride in the Song of Songs and the same woman interpreted on the three mystical planes of meaning. The contest as to whether she is an allegory or a real woman can be called off. Beatrice was meant to be both simultaneously.

Beatrice already plays her dual role in *Vita Nuova*. In the twenty-third chapter, when Dante dreams that she is dying, he draws a parallel with Christ. In the twenty-fourth chapter the comparison, it seems to us, exceeds the bounds of blasphemy. Dante sees a woman coming towards him. Her name is Johanna. It was John, he recalls, who preceded the true light (*la verace Luce*) and of whom it was said: "The voice of one crying in the wilderness, Prepare ye the way of the Lord." Sure enough, after Johanna comes the young Beatrice. When it says in *Vita Nuova* that Beatrice is a wonder, when many say of her as she passes by: "She is not a woman but one of Heaven's sweet angels," this is not, as Professor Singleton in particular has stressed, to be regarded as a compliment but as a statement of fact. As proof of this, Dante discusses in detail in the twenty-ninth and thirtieth chapters Beatrice's relationship to the sacred number three. The whole of this little work has a numerical mysticism which seems strange to us. Dante sees Beatrice for the first time when he is nine years old. It is at the ninth hour that vital matters take place. And nine is three times three. "Thinking more subtly," Dante says, "and according to infallible truth, this number was her very self . . . Therefore if three is the sole factor of nine and the sole factor of miracles is three, namely Father, Son, and Holy Ghost, who are three and one, this lady was accompanied by the number nine to give to understand that she was a nine, that is, a miracle whose root is the wondrous Trinity alone."

When the two lovers meet in the Earthly Paradise the pilgrim weeps not only because he has lost a friend. It is naturally painful to him to know that a good and just man like Virgil has been forced to return to Hell. But the meeting with Beatrice is also painful. She is wearing the same crimson dress she had as a child, and he feels within him signs of the former flame. At the same time he hears the angels sing "Blessed be thou." Therefore, the meeting with Beatrice after so many years also means a farewell.

Virgil, who now disappears, is not only a friend who has accompanied the pilgrim on his journey. He also represents friendship, the ancient poetry that Dante loved, knowledge, the free world of beauty. Virgil is an incarnate image of Purgatory, of a rich and meaningful life. Since leaving Hell, where the doomed live in an eternal vicious circle, the pilgrim in Purgatory has relived his life on earth and is at this moment about to enter another kind of eternity, that of divine light. What we witness in the Earthly Paradise, therefore, is the end of time, a finish to life.

The meeting takes place in the Earthly Paradise, the symbol of blissful sensuousness and complete earthly happiness, and both the pilgrim and the reader are mindful of this. It is when Dante feels the old fire kindling within him that he turns to Virgil for help. He knows suddenly that Beatrice is dead, that his having chosen to depict her as a saint meant a sacrifice for the sake of poetry and for the salvation of his soul. Beatrice is not the goal of his journey. He has known this all along. But the pilgrim is living in life, not in an arithmetical example. Now he realizes that he will never see her again. Once she stirred up indescribable feelings inside him. She was an instrument which led him towards a higher and richer life. Her eyes and her mouth were balconies from which he could peep into her soul, and her soul bore witness of her origin in God. This platonic thought, which permeates all medieval philosophy, is natural to all who love and who always will think they glimpse in the beloved's face something which is superior to herself.

But Beatrice was also the sweet being who was the crown of all created things. Now, in the earthly paradise, it dawns on the pilgrim that henceforth Beatrice will be merely a sign, a memory from his life on earth and in Florence as a young man. For the last time Beatrice is near the pilgrim and the storyteller, as though she were still living, as though an Earthly Paradise existed. During the meeting in the celestial forest the four planes of meaning all try to take the stage at once; all four assail the poet with tears and cries to give his whole attention to each one of them. This fourfold attack overwhelms the pilgrim and makes him weep. Beatrice must speak his name and recall him to awareness of the eternal light which is the aim of his pilgrimage. Now that Beatrice and not Virgil is the pilgrim's guide, we can no longer call her woman; the literal plane of meaning has receded, even if it never entirely disappears. In the whole of *Paradiso,* which, more than the other parts of the Comedy, should be Beatrice's because she plays the leading part in almost all the cantos, she is in fact only a mirror which reflects the light, a sign without earthly personality who points beyond herself.

But before the pilgrim and the reader are led into the greatest canto of the Comedy, that which deals with Paradise proper, they witness a dramatic continuation of the procession in the forest that is resounding with celestial harmony. Beatrice has called Dante by his Christian name—everyone in the three realms of the dead is called by the Christian name as a sign that the important thing here is the individual and his moral and religious conduct, not official and family matters and social position. Beatrice reproaches Dante and, having twice affirmed that she really is Beatrice, asks him how he has dared to draw nigh the Mount. "Knewest thou not that here man is happy?" (*non sapei tu che qui è l'uom felice?, Purgatorio,* XXX:75). Full of shame, Dante bows his head. The angels sing another song, an appeal to Beatrice to show compassion to the penitent. He stands for a while in mute distress, then, sensing this pity, finds relief in tears. We wonder whether Dante's grief for his lost friend makes Beatrice remind him that in the presence of God man is happy and should not think of anything else.

Beatrice speaks again. "He who stands there weeping," she says, showing by her use of the third person that any intimacy in their relationship is now out of the question, "had been furnished by nature with great gifts. For a time he gave signs of promise when I led him towards the right goal. But when I died, I ceased to mean anything to him. He strayed along devious paths and pursued false visions of happiness. He fell so low that only one thing availed—to show him the lost people (*le perdute genti*). That is why I went down into the underworld and persuaded Virgil to guide him." She asks Dante if he confesses his erring ways. Confused and stammering, he says yes.

Here we have confirmation that Hell was shown to Dante

for the sake of his salvation, that images of sin and sinners were held up before him so that he would become aware of his own sins. Beatrice continues her questioning of Dante while the procession stands still and the angels listen. Asked why he transgressed, Dante replies, still weeping, that "present things with their false pleasure" (*le presenti cose col falso lor piacer, Purgatorio,* XXXI: 34–35) turned away his steps. Beatrice answers that remorse whirls back the grindstone and blunts the edge; he should therefore stem the flow of his tears. She adds that neither nature nor art ever gave him such pleasure as the beauty bestowed on her in life; if her death robbed him of this supreme joy, no mortal thing should have allured him. Dante realizes that what she says is true. He sees that her present beauty exceeds her beauty on earth just as much as her beauty in life exceeded that of other women. He is so overcome by remorse that he falls senseless to the ground. The reader will recall that the pilgrim swooned before another woman, Francesca, in the fifth canto of *Inferno.* Then too he fell down as though dead. Francesca is present at this moment as the memory of a woman who was her lover's earthly goal. It is now clear to Dante that, from the very first, Beatrice was meant as an apparition of the highest good, that she was not his beloved but a saviour, that she was Christ in *his* life.

When Dante comes to his senses he is led up to Beatrice, who is standing near the golden griffon which represents Christ. He sees the griffon reflected in her eyes and sees it change form inside her pupils. Now it is an eagle and now a lion, as a sign that Christ is both God and man. It cannot be said more plainly what Beatrice's eyes are. They are the two springs in whose water the celestial light is reflected. As a further sign, the angels now beg Beatrice to let her lover see her mouth and its smile. The veil falls, and Dante sees that which can never be described: "O glory of living light eternal" (*Purgatorio,* XXXI: 139). He sees the holy smile (*lo santo riso*) which on earth made him fall into the old toils. For an instant he is dazzled as though he had looked into the sun.

The procession moves on. Dante walks by the right wheel of the chariot. He sees a tree bare of leaves or flowers. The griffon draws the chariot up to it and binds the pole to the trunk, and at once the tree burgeons. Beatrice sits down under it. Everything happens as swiftly, inevitably, and fantastically as in a dream. An eagle swoops down from the sky and rends the tree, which smites the chariot, making it reel like a ship in a storm. A fox leaps into the chariot and a dragon thrusts its tail up through it and wrenches out part of the bottom. The chariot is transformed into a monster which a harlot rides. Beside her is a giant, and they exchange lustful kisses.

Beatrice stands up and speaks as though at this moment she were Christ Himself, for she uses Jesus' own words to His disciples as they are expressed in the Vulgate in the Latin inspired by God Himself: *"Modicum, et non videbitis me, et iterum,* my beloved sisters, *modicum, et vos videbitis me* —A little while, and ye shall not see me: and again, a little while, and ye shall see me." Beatrice tells Dante that the chariot which the dragon broke "was, and is not," that someone sent by God with the figure 515 will come and kill the harlot. She says that her words are obscure but that events themselves will solve the riddle, and she begs Dante bear in mind what he has seen and write it down in his poem. "I also will," she says, "that thou bear it away within thee, and if not written at least outlined, for the reason that the pilgrim's staff is brought back wreathed with palm" (*Purgatorio,* XXXIII:76–78). Beatrice is alluding to the way the pilgrims to the Holy Land twined a palm leaf round their staff so that all could see where they had been. She charges Dante with the task of writing the great poem.

What does all this mean? Commentators do not leave us in the dark. The triumphal car is, as I have already said, the Church. The harlot is the papal see under Boniface VIII. The giant is France, which enters into a shameful union with the pope and is soon to drag the papal chair in abasement to Avignon. The figure 515 is perhaps the same liberator as the greyhound Virgil foresaw in the first canto of *Inferno,* and

so on. But we cannot be quite convinced that it *is* an allegory
we see, an allegory that can be explained. It is very possible,
as the English scholar Hardie has suggested, that the procession and the scene with the eagle, the fox, and the dragon,
are pictures which symbolize Dante's own spiritual development.

Let us put the question aside for a moment and ask ourselves instead: What was the sin Dante had committed,
which Beatrice now reproaches him for? There is no lack
of theories. Scholars have sought to base their opinions on
the length of time the pilgrim spends on the different ledges
in Purgatory and the degree of interest he shows in various
sins. He confesses that one day he will stay for a long time
on the ledge of the Mount where the wrathful are purged.
But that he need spend only a short time among the envious.
He will be burned in the fire of the love-sinners and bear
grievous burdens among the proud. Some think that his sin
was to love other women after Beatrice's death—proof of
this can be found in his love poems. Others say that Dante
deserted Beatrice, the representative of theological wisdom,
for philosophy, and that this is borne out in *Convivio*. Professor d'Entrèves, as I mentioned before, has put forward the
thought that Dante in the Earthly Paradise regrets having
seen a Christ in Henry VII and having set man's temporal
happiness as a goal in itself, thus making himself guilty of
blasphemy.

It seems to me to matter very little whether we can de-
fine Dante's sin or not. He says himself that it was the
present things (*le presenti cose*) which led him astray. These
words can apply to almost anything. What does matter to us
is that, having reached the meeting between Beatrice and
Dante, we are at the great turning point of the poem; that at
this moment all the present things—life with its joys and
pains and ambitions—must yield to something greater and
more essential. Dante has said in his fine and dignified letter
to Can Grande della Scala that the aim of the Comedy is to
lead man from tribulation and confusion to happiness. The
pilgrim in the poem represents all humanity. Without ad-

mitting that everything must be subordinate to the great goal, we can never carry out our pilgrimage towards the happiness that is contemplation and mysticism in Paradise proper. Everything else—women, sensual pleasures, political ambitions, homesickness, longing for wife, children, and friends—must be put aside, must be acknowledged, not only in theory and with the lips, but also in practice and with the heart, as merely *le presenti cose* which have no real value. It need not, therefore, be any particular sin which Dante confesses to Beatrice. The question here is the concentration of the personality on one vital thing. The meeting denotes the actual moment of creation for the poet Dante Alighieri. The fault Dante confesses is that he did not understand the nature of Beatrice's smile, did not understand that she was Christ for him. Now, at the behest of the angels, she lets her veil fall and he sees who she is.

It is difficult to follow Dante's thought and feeling when, in both *Vita Nuova* and the Comedy, he outlines Beatrice in analogy with Christ. When *Vita Nuova* was to be printed for the first time in the sixteenth century and permission was sought from the censorship authorities of the Church, they had grave misgivings when they read that the lover hears shouts of "Hosanna!" in his dream when Beatrice dies. They also found it unseemly that her friend should be portrayed as a John the Baptist. Therefore, they decreed that these passages should be cut. Since then most people, rather than accuse Dante of blasphemy, have preferred to regard Beatrice's Christly attributes as a kind of poetical adornment. In the scenes in the Garden of Eden, however, such an interpretation is absurd. Beatrice is at once God and man, in the same way as the griffon reflected in her eyes. Dante has furnished her with a Christlike dimension and it bursts the earthly frame that once enclosed her. But we are never *quite* sure where we are. The crimson dress is glimpsed the whole time, and the heart begins to thump. All three realms of the dead are present at the great meeting in the Earthly Paradise.

Paradiso
Paradise

13

THE LIGHT ETERNAL

IN CHARLIE CHAPLIN'S FILM *The Kid,* Chaplin the tramp falls asleep on the steps of the hovel where he lives. His boy has been kidnapped, but Charlie is compensated in his sleep. He dreams that he has come to Paradise. There, the blest flap about like white hens. Even the dogs have wings. Former enemies give each other sanctimonious looks. The tramp is one of the actors in an Elysian farce, which true to style ends in a fight with all feathers flying.

Just as the Greek gods have fallen from their Olympian splendor and become farcical characters in Offenbach or advertising agents for cosmetics, so have the symbolic figures of the Christian fantasy been transformed and debased. The devil is a clown in comic papers and revues, and the angels, who once bore flaming swords and touched the hollow of Jacob's thigh when he ventured to wrestle with one of them, have been remolded by our modern devotional industry into repulsive boy-girls for Christmas decorations.

Chaplin's dream of Paradise is a satire upon existence in Heaven such as it is conceived in the popular mind. Paradise is a sickly-sweet eternity of Sundays with the bleating of saved sheep, with white nightshirts, and with palm-leaves waving. It is a Paradise so de-sexed and dull that it frightens young people far more effectively than the torments of Hell.

Dante's Paradise has the same relation to this mawkish Heaven as Bach's fugues have to pop-music, as the oak to crepe paper flowers, as the ocean to a glass of tepid water. But in many countries, not least in Scandinavia, there is a prevalent convention, tenderly nurtured by generation after generation of expert literary historians, that this part of *The Divine Comedy* is the least important, artistically and humanly. It would be most discourteous to presume that the learned gentlemen had tired before they got as far as the *Paradiso*. Perhaps they have been beguiled into confusing the Paradise that has been dragged down to the world of triviality and comedy with Dante's vision. It is high time for a critical revision. Dante himself says again and again in the *Paradiso* cantos that his strength is not equal to the mighty task he has set himself. In the thirtieth canto, at the sight of Beatrice's renewed beauty, he says he has been vanquished more than any comic or tragic poet ever was by his theme (lines 22-24). He declares he will be content if in his poem he can preserve the merest spark of the eternal light in Paradise. On several occasions he uses the simile of a man who awakes from a wonderful dream and tries in vain to recall what he has seen. Only the feeling of a superhuman bliss remains, while his memory fails him when he attempts a reconstruction. Those who accompany Dante in this his greatest song must think and say the same. To give a true idea of even a fraction of what the *Paradiso* cantos offer is beyond me.

What is Paradise for Dante? On the literal plane, it is the place where the saved go after death, once they have been purified for a varying period of time in Purgatory. The pilgrim, at Beatrice's side, passes through the heavenly spheres. As in Hell and in Purgatory, he finds that a perfect mathematical order prevails. Like Hell, Paradise consists of nine circles, nine heavens which arch above the earth, one beyond the other. Outside these nine rings is the Empyrean where God dwells and which lies outside time and space. The whole world is enclosed in this divine timeless and spaceless existence. Everything that has emanated from God strives to unite with the Empyrean and this longing has the greatest effect in the ninth heaven, the crystalline heaven, also called *Primum Mobile,* which moves with incomprehensible speed. Each heavenly sphere derives its power and its movement from the one above it. That is why each heaven arches round, and the nearer to earth the slower the movement. Within each heaven stars and planets move in the same way as ants which creep on a moving wheel. In *Convivio* Dante has described the heavens in detail and also given their symbolic meaning. The seven heavens that are nearest us—those of the Moon, Mercury, Venus, the Sun, Mars, Jupiter, and Saturn—correspond to the seven fine arts: grammar, dialectics, rhetoric, arithmetic, music, geometry, and astronomy. To the eighth heaven, that of the fixed stars, belongs natural science and to the ninth, *Primum Mobile,* metaphysics. Finally the Empyrean, where God's love dwells, is the abode of theology.

We therefore find ourselves not only in the blessedness of salvation, but also in a huge celestial university, where we are moved up into a higher class and a higher wisdom every time we leave one heaven for another. In each heaven the pilgrim meets blest souls with whom he converses as is his wont. The blest have been placed according to a moral system which, on the whole, is that of contemporary theology. In the heaven of the moon, which is nearest the earth, live souls who have been inconstant in a promise. In the heaven of Mercury are spirits who have aspired to fame in the world and for that reason have been spurred to noble deeds. Yet they have thought too much of their own glory to deserve a still higher placing. In the third heaven, that of Venus, are found those who have devoted their life to love but have seen in time that love of God is more important than all else. In the heaven of the sun the great scientists and philosophers converse with each other. In the heaven of Mars the crusaders are gathered, in the heaven of Jupiter live righteous princes, in that of Saturn theologians and fathers of the Church. Finally, in the crystalline heaven only the angels are able to bear the immediate proximity of the divine presence.

As in Hell and Purgatory, the people in Paradise are separated from each other, divided up into grades and orders in the realm of virtue. But there is one big difference. Paradise is a purely spiritual kingdom and those who live here are not subject to the laws of time and space. Therefore Piccarda Donati, the young woman who entered a nunnery to find peace and was torn away from it and forced into a hateful marriage, does not really live in the heaven of the moon, where Dante meets her. Nor does the holy St. Thomas Aquinas live in the heaven of the sun, though that is where he offers Dante his instruction. People *show* themselves to Dante in the various celestial spheres. But they all *live* in the tenth heaven in immediate fellowship with God. When they appear to Dante in one heaven or another, therefore, it is not because they dwell there. In Hell and Purgatory the souls are captive in the different circles. In Paradise they reveal themselves in order to show the pilgrim the degree of their bliss, and then they return to the divine light. Without these dramatizations the pilgrim would not be able to grasp the world of pure ideas to which he comes.

On one level of significance it is not difficult to understand this double life of the blest. Those who live in Paradise are souls who have been saved, yes, but the measure of their happiness is that their chances of happiness have been realized. Just as we could conceive of the torments of Hell not as punishment but as a state, we must in Paradise understand that those we meet are not rewarded but are living in a state of grace. They are people who have been made use of. They have been exploited by life to the utmost limit of their potentialities, and they are all equally happy. But at the same time they know quite well that there are different degrees of capability, that nature, or God if we like, has set a limit to what they can feel, think, and do, that in the world of the spirit there is a hierarchy as implacable as the table of atomic valences. They are content with what they themselves have received and would think it a sin to expect more. The measure of bliss is in accord with their nature.

We readily understand that it must be so in Paradise, if we take examples from the world of poetry. Bellman is a great poet. In the divine ecstasy of his poems, in Fredman's, Movitz's, and Ulla's frolics, laughter, and tears, in the shimmer and movement of the Stockholm pictures, he found an outlet for his genius. He is an inimitable poet who need stand aside for none and his happiness at the moment of inspiration is such that it belongs to the tenth heaven. But when he appears to us—in our imagination, that is—he does so in a celestial sphere which is lower than Shakespeare's and Dante's. The vaults they stretch are higher than Bellman's. The register of their feelings is bigger, and they represent a wider section of the human world. In our mental paradise we see them in a higher celestial sphere.

Or perhaps a simile drawn from chess, which was well-known to Dante and which he alludes to in the Comedy, is more precise. The chess-player knows his limitations, how many moves he can work out ahead at a given moment of the game. In the heaven of sixty-four squares he takes without protest the place to which his ability entitles him. But when it comes to concentration on the game and awareness of the rules to be followed, rules which preclude all fraud and cheating, the expert and the novice are equal.

It is the same with every human being. Those who love are happy if they can offer all they are capable of in love. But the capacity to love varies.

As I said before, the prejudices with which an Elysian life is encumbered put certain difficulties in our path when we first arrive in Dante's Paradise. We have still another obstacle to surmount. When Dante wrote about Hell and Purgatory, he was a poet belonging to a proud tradition. Virgil, like Homer, had let Aeneas descend into the underworld. Dante probably knew the *Aeneid* by heart, and he borrows from his master unabashed. Those who want assurance on this point should read Edward Moore's well-known work. When Dante ascended into Purgatory he also had a number of predecessors. He sang of nature on earth, love, friendship, the Church. He set out on a vast journey in thought, but he was not alone.

When he goes up into Paradise, on the other hand, he is exploring an unknown way, even if he does receive an impulse or two from the Arabian ascension into heaven which caused so much talk among scholars a few years ago. Only now does he really become like Ulysses, who went in search of the undiscovered lands on the other side of the globe. Now the great mystics, philosophers, and theologians are his teachers, and they were not poets. Dante has to create his own world of symbols. In the introduction to the second canto of *Paradiso,* Dante the poet addresses himself to the reader (*Paradiso,* II: 1–15):

> O you who, desiring to listen,
> Have followed in your little barks behind
> My vessel that goes singing while it sails,
> Turn back to see your own shores once again;
> Do not put out to sea, for it may be
> That, losing me, you lose your own bearings.
> No one before me ever cruised these waters.
> Minerva blows her breath, Apollo guides me,
> And the nine Muses show me where the Bears are.
> You other few who stretched your necks in time
> Towards the bread of angels on which we live here,
> But of which no one ever has his fill,
> Well might you launch your ships on the deep brine,
> And use the furrow that I made
> Before the water levels out again.

The feeling of being on an uncharted sea is present throughout all the *Paradiso* cantos. In *Inferno* Dante drew material for the building of his poem from the narrow alleys of medieval cities, from places of execution and torture chambers, from hospitals and madhouses, and from the unsafe highways he walked as an exile. In *Purgatorio* he built with impressions of the vernal Italian countryside, of churches during divine service, of meetings with friends, and of nostalgic talks about his native town, and the Paradise perhaps awaiting him.

In Paradise he had to find a world of form suitable for depicting the realm of pure spirituality. He builds Paradise of light and reflections of light. On arriving in Paradise, therefore, we are dazzled. It is like emerging from a long confinement in a dark room into the bright sunshine of an

April day. The light glitters in a million drops of water, in the pools on the road, in the swift white clouds. Sparks flash in front of us, and at first we see nothing. Our eyes must get used to it. I think many people fail to give themselves time for this process of adjustment and therefore never feel at ease in Dante's Paradise.

When the pilgrim enters the lunar heaven, his first stop, he sees faces around about him as one sees one's own face in a window pane or in still, shallow waters where the bottom is glimpsed beneath the reflection (*Paradiso,* III: 10–12). The pilgrim thinks they really are reflected images and turns around in the hope of seeing the people who he thinks are standing behind him. Beatrice smiles at his mistake, a counter-error to the mistake Narcissus was guilty of. For it is not reflections he sees but the blest themselves who appear in these faint, glimmering images. But it is only in the lower heavens that the souls are visible. Higher up they are entirely wrapped in light and the pilgrim sees neither their features nor their bodies. As he rises through the heavens he sees the blest as stars, flames, wheels, and live coals. They move like birds that pass in flocks over the fields. They form now a cross, where single blessed ones hover like specks of dust in a sunbeam, now a crown, now a holy letter, now the head of an eagle. It takes place with the same naturalness as migrating birds make patterns on the sky. At other times they emerge like stars in the dusk, so faint that one is not sure whether or not they are there. The next moment they blaze up, blinding the pilgrim with a radiance as strong as that of a ruby in the sunlight.

Dante presents a lyrical spectacle, a celestial ballet, which is firmly balanced and held together though it seems to move in endless space. The blest in the solar heaven, who appear only as flames, arrange themselves in rings and circles singing round Beatrice and the pilgrim. Suddenly they fall silent, resembling young women who stand still in the middle of the dance, wondering whether the music is going to begin again. But lest this image force itself too strongly on the reader, Dante lets it soon be pushed aside by another, and he calls the encircling flames a holy millstone that revolves round its axle.

Dante uses phenomena on the verge of tangibility in his celestial building. They are moments of repose in nature or in the world of men. The boat moves forward with the even stroke of the oars, and suddenly at an order the oars are still and the boat glides on in silence. The souls gather round the pilgrim as fish dart up when something is thrown to them in the water. Piccarda Donati in the lunar heaven tells the pilgrim how she was taken from the convent where she had sought peace and was forced into marriage. When her speech is ended she vanishes, it says, like a weight sinking down through the water. Dante follows her with his eyes as long as he can. In the twenty-fifth canto the apostle James approaches Peter as a dove approaches his mate, circling ever nearer and cooing to the object of his love. The souls move like a spark inside a flame or like the notes of a flute within the accompaniment of a guitar.

What then does this play of light and music express? Happiness in Paradise is a reflection of the eternal light. Therefore all who appear in the ten heavens must also bear witness to the light. Light is the very stuff of Paradise. The blest are so filled with light that the pilgrim has difficulty in grasping it. He undergoes a hardening process and learns to bear more and more light. The blest, who all live in the highest heaven, show themselves to him in the various spheres clad in lower forms of light in order to shield his eyes. Hour by hour the pilgrim's capacity increases, and in this growth Paradise displays one of its most vital components. Paradise in Dante is the instant of enlightenment, when after long searching we see in a flash that we have been offered a higher truth, which shines with a brighter light than the lower truth that we grasped a moment ago. Paradise is the second when the soul understands. Paradise is the opposite of the stationary. Paradise is movement everlasting, and that is why Dante sometimes arranges the souls as in a dance, just as the heavens themselves move. And the movement never comes to a stop. Everything is in a state of expansion; everyone knows that happiness will one day be much greater.

In Paradise the pilgrim attains the knowledge he is striving for. The heavens do not symbolize the seven fine arts, as well as physics and metaphysics, for nothing. Everything that humanity has garnered of insight and wisdom is offered in Paradise, and this feast of knowledge can only be rightly enjoyed by those who have learned that superficiality, ignorance, and witless stagnation are the truly hellish state, affording an existence without hope.

The pilgrim is offered the highest knowledge of the relationship of free will to grace, of a just form of government, of God's nature. He is instructed in much that has little interest for a modern reader. He meets Adam, and is concerned chiefly with what language was spoken in Paradise. He is taught the nature of the moon and the cause of the moon spots. He finds out why it can rightly be said that Titus, in destroying Jerusalem, avenged the death of Christ, although the crucifixion took place at God's own wish. Faced with the possibility of receiving answers to the highest questions, we perhaps would have preferred to ask other ones. But even if the content of the wisdom offered to the pilgrim should not be overlooked and will soon be made the subject of an analysis, Paradise has this powerful effect not only because of what it contains but because of the kind of conditions that prevail there. It is not the results that we notice first, but the inner movement, the actual principle. To be in Paradise is to gain knowledge and to possess this knowledge simply and without question as our natural heritage. To be in Paradise is to listen to the life stories of great men and women and to be fired by the passion that led them on in their lives and deeds. For Dante, St. Francis of Assisi and St. Dominic stand out above all others as incomparable examples. To be in Paradise is to find that we are at home, that hitherto we have loved transitory things and are now offered the things that endure.

14

LIFE WITH GOD

THERE IS A DIFFERENCE, says Augustine, between using a thing and taking pleasure in it for its own sake. Let us suppose we are living in a strange land and that we shall not be happy until we get home. One day we can stand it no longer. We lift ourselves out of our misery and prepare to return to our native land. We have to use some means of transport in order to reach this country where our happiness lies. But the landscape through which we pass is beautiful and the journey itself pleasant. One day we find ourselves enjoying these things, which we should be using only as a means of getting home. We have no wish to hurry and become more and more taken up with these temporary pleasures, gradually forgetting all about our destination, which alone can make us really happy.

In this earthly life we are all in the same situation as the exile. We are pilgrims who have strayed far from God, and if we desire to return to His kingdom we must *use* the world, not enjoy it. The world is only a means. We proceed towards the spiritual and eternal by way of the physical and temporal.

This Augustinian concept of pilgrimage permeates *The Divine Comedy* from the first line to the last. During these centuries the imagination was caught not only by the soul's journeying—which has always been a central ingredient in Christianity—but also by a pilgrim's progress of a more concrete kind. Every year thousands of pilgrims from all countries in Europe streamed to Santiago de Compostela, where the apostle James was said to be buried, and to the holy tomb in Jerusalem. As in our day, religious, cultural, and political aspects were woven into these travels together with pleasure-seeking and curiosity, and a tourist industry arose which was a typical feature of the Middle Ages. When Dante depicts how he and Virgil proceed through the realms of the dead, he likes to use images from this life of pilgrimage. He says that the penitent gluttons on the sixth terrace of Purgatory are like pilgrims sunk in thought who, meeting strangers on the way, turn around but do not stop. "Like as a pilgrim whose will is to return" (*pur come peregrin che tornar vuole*) he says in the first canto of *Paradiso* (line 51). In the chapter on Beatrice I mentioned that she instructs Dante with the aid of a simile- the palm-decked staff of the traveler to Jerusalem.

Behind the individual pilgrimages was a greater journey with the same goal. Dante lived in the age of the crusades. He was twenty-six years old when the last Christian possession in the Holy Land was lost and the pilgrims could no longer reach Jerusalem. One of the accusations he levels at Boniface VIII, whom he calls "prince of the new Pharisees," is that the pope makes war upon other Christians instead of upon the Saracens (*Inferno*, XXVII:85 *et seq.*). With pride Dante lets his ancestor Cacciaguida in Paradise tell that he took part in a crusade, during which he met his death.

The goal of these armed pilgrimages was Jerusalem, the city of God. But—the reader who wishes to know more about these things is referred to Johan Chydenius—the Jews' capital city was not the final goal of the crusaders. The earthly city of Jerusalem was a symbol of a celestial Jerusalem, to which the Christian ultimately aspired. Those who undertook the long journey to Jerusalem prepared themselves for the second journey, the life pilgrimage to the city of God. On the literal plane, Jerusalem was the Jews' capital, and, with the taking of the city by the crusaders on July 15, 1099, became the Kingdom of Jerusalem. On the allegorical plane it was a symbol of the Church, on the moral plane an image of the soul, and on the anagogic, God's city in Paradise.

One remarkable result of the crusades was that the literal meaning was accentuated. For centuries Jerusalem had been held by the Arabs. The city was outlined in the far distance, and its symbolic meaning became all important to Christendom. The crusades restored the balance between the literal plane and the mystical planes. When Dante's Comedy triumphs even on the first, the literal plane, it is perhaps because the poet has drawn strength from the crusades and from a re-established historical Jerusalem.

In the poem Dante is on a pilgrim's progress towards his paradisal native land. The characteristic feature of the people he meets in Hell is that they have forgotten that they too are on a pilgrimage. Believing that they can be happy in the foreign country that life on earth represents, they have become petrified in selfish desires. Francesca saw an end and not a means in the man she loved. Ulysses sought knowledge for its own sake. Farinata was so devoured by his political passion that he was indifferent to the eternal things. His final goal was Florence in the same way as that of the Jews—from the Christian viewpoint—was Jerusalem. The right attitude was to understand that Florence, like Jerusalem, was the symbol of a heavenly city which, without detracting from the importance of the earthly one, imposed a greater claim and opened a wider perspective.

Even in Purgatory the souls forget they are pilgrims. The beautiful landscape and the meeting with friends tempt them to linger. Dante says in the second canto, when Casella sings (*Purgatorio,* II:115–117): "My Master and I, and all those people standing there with him, seemed so delighted that nothing else appeared to touch our mind." It is then that Cato interrupts the song and rebukes them for their tarrying. Dante has forgotten his pilgrimage, just as during his life he may often have set his own writing before his soul's salvation. Note that Casella sings one of Dante's own poems.

But in Purgatory the aberrations are only brief. The souls *know* that they are strangers so long as they have not come to God's city in Heaven. That is why, as they arrive at the Mount in the boat piloted by the angel, we hear them singing the 114th Psalm, "When Israel went out of Egypt," the real significance of which, in Dante's own words, is the soul's homecoming to God. The underlying theme of the *Purgatorio* cantos is this return. The eighth canto begins with two verses which echo throughout the whole of *Purgatorio*. It is evening and the pilgrim is about to go down into the valley of the princes (*Purgatorio,* VIII: 1–6):

> It was the hour now that turns back sailors'
> Longings, and fills the heart with tenderness
> The day they say good-bye to their sweet friends;
> The hour that pervades with love new pilgrims
> When, from a distance, they hear bells tolling,
> As if in mourning for the dying day.

When the sun has set in the valley which the sword-bearing angels guard against the serpent, the princes sing the Latin hymn *Salve Regina* (*Purgatorio,* VII:82), which in translation runs: "Hail, O Queen, mother of pity, our life, our joy, our hope. To thee we call, Eve's banished children, to thee we sigh, weeping and lamenting in this vale of tears. Thou our advocate, turn thy loving eyes to us and show us after this our exile Jesus, thy blessed Child."

When Dante meets the envious, whose eyelids have been sewn together, and asks if any soul among them is from Italy, he receives the reply (*Purgatorio,* XIII:94–96): "O brother mine, each one is a citizen of a true city [i.e., *Paradise*]; but thou wouldest say, that lived a pilgrim in Italy."

In Paradise there is not even the temptation to forget one's pilgrimship. Dante, at Beatrice's side, has attained a purely spiritual kingdom, and as a sign of this the journey itself comes to an end. In Hell progress was difficult partly because of the wild nature of the place and partly because, on an inner plane, the pilgrim sought to ward off the knowledge of himself that Hell offered. In Purgatory it was arduous to go forward at first, and Dante quailed at the ordeals and purification imposed upon him. Resistance did not cease until he neared the end. In Paradise Dante needs only *imagine* a new sphere of heaven, and he is there. If Purgatory is a school for thought and feeling where one has to muster all one's strength, then Paradise is an academy where the preparatory studies are completed. The moment the teacher enters and the discussion begins, all have reached the great subject itself. The greatest sacrifice now would be to refrain from taking part.

Even when the pilgrim arrives at the lowest of the celestial spheres, the heaven of the moon, he feels a happiness as great as that vouchsafed the poor Boeotian fisherman Glaucus, who found an herb which turned him into a sea god (*Paradiso,* I:68–69). While Dante rises from heaven to heaven, Beatrice grows more and more beautiful and her smile more and more radiant. The twenty-third canto—by then the pilgrim has entered the heaven of the fixed stars—begins with the simile of a bird which, having spent the night peacefully in its nest among the leaves, alights on the open spray to await the sunrise, when it will see its young ones again and seek food for them. In the same way Beatrice waits to see the triumphal procession in which Christ himself, Mary, and all the saints take part. Dante says that his eyes could not bear to look on Beatrice's beauty at this moment. He feels like a man who, himself in shadow, sees a flowery meadow suddenly lit up by sunlight that streams through a rift in the clouds. He doubts whether he can endure the light itself. On another occasion he, like Paul on the road to Damascus, is so dazzled that he is blinded until Beatrice heals him with her eyes, which have the same "power that was in Ananias' hand" (*Paradiso,* XXVI:12). Dante is undergoing the process of purging. Earlier, he had to steel his will and press on. Now, he wants to rush forward and must learn that he is not yet ready for the highest sphere of heaven.

When Christianity first appeared it was only one of many religions in the Roman empire. As the centuries passed, it absorbed ideas from the ancient culture and from the oriental religions with their mysteries. During the thirteenth century, the most vital element in Christian thought was the Platonic philosophy. Even if Plato was not known through his own writings, his thinking leavened all profane and theological speculation. A cornerstone of this school of thought was the idea that everything created seeks its home. Fire rises towards its origin in the fiery sphere. The stone falls, since its home is the earth. Man's soul is created by God and retains a vague memory of the bliss he knew and the light he saw when, at the moment of his creation, he issued from God's hand.

In *Convivio* Dante writes that all things long to return to their origin and therefore the soul longs to return to God.

> And just as a pilgrim who travels by a road on which he never went before thinks that every house which he sees from afar is an inn, and on finding that it is not fixes his trust on some other, and so from house to house until he comes to the inn; so our soul as soon as ever she enters on this new and hitherto untrodden path of life bends her gaze on the highest good as the goal, and therefore believes that everything she sees which appears to contain some good in itself is that highest good. And because her knowledge is at first imperfect through inexperience and lack of instruction, small goods appear great to her, and therefore her desires are first directed to these. So we see little children fixing their chief desire on an apple; then as they go farther they desire a small bird; then going farther still, fine clothes; after this a horse, then a mistress; after this moderate riches, then great, and afterwards the greatest wealth.

Dante is instructed concerning the same pilgrimage of thought and heart by Marco Lombardo on the terrace of the wrathful in Purgatory. Lombardo says (*Purgatorio,* XVI:85–94):

> "From the hand of him who loves her before
> She is, there issues, like a tiny girl
> Who romps about, now laughing and now crying,
> The simple little soul that knows nothing
> Except that, moved by a happy maker,
> It gladly turns to whatever it enjoys.
> It has a taste of meager things at first,
> Becomes deluded by them, and pursues them,
> If neither guide nor rein divert its fondness.
> For that reason the law is imposed as curb"

Therefore, Lombardo goes on, man needs law and a just form of government. But because in the depths of his heart he remembers the moment of his creation, he shall strive to turn back to God once he has awakened to a proper realization. At every moment he intends to break away from the strange country. But every human being has part in the sinfulness that came into the world through Eve's transgression. That is why humans confuse ends and means and set their hearts on things of little value. If man's will were free, he would rush into God's arms, but his will can be made really free only through God's grace. This grace takes effect in two ways simultaneously. In Christ, God has taken human form and thus expiated the sin that mankind has committed, a sin which man could never wipe out by himself. But God's grace is also effective in the individual's life as a living power, for every man has an insight which is a ray of the highest intelligence and which is the primordial power from which everything was created.

Dante the pilgrim undertakes his journey through the realms of the dead in order to attain freedom of the will, to become conscious of his origin. Now, in Paradise, he has reached his goal with the help of Beatrice, representative of the divine grace. She says to him (*Paradiso*, I:136–138): "Thou shouldst no more wonder, if I deem aright, at thine uprising, than at a river dropping down from a lofty mountain to the base."

Thus both pilgrim and poet continue, even in Paradise, to be on the way, to climb the ladder of light. In a vision in the twenty-first canto, he sees Jacob's ladder, which in Christian speculation was a symbol of the Christian ascension. Everywhere he sees signs of primeval strength and longs for the source itself. He does not reach it until the thirtieth canto.

Ever since the age of nine and the day he first saw Beatrice in the crimson dress, he has seen in her an image of beauty and goodness. He has seen her as a decoy. He has learnt his lesson: after the apple to long for a horse, after the horse a woman, after the woman riches, after the goodness of riches a goodness which endures. Now, in the thirtieth canto, he is parted from her, for he stands before the primeval light that she reflects.

Blake: Dante drinking in the Empyrean from the fount of eternal light. *Paradiso* XXX.

William Blake: The celestial rose, on the petals of which the blessed sit like spectators in an amphitheatre. Angels come down like bees into the flower and rise up again. *Paradiso* XXXI.

Dante sees—as he has often done he borrows the imagery from the Psalms and the book of Revelation here—a river of light flowing between banks "painted with marvellous spring" (*Paradiso,* XXX:63). Out of the river rise sparks of life which sink into the flowers on either side. They are like rubies set in gold. As though intoxicated by the scent that is wafted over the meadows, the sparks leap back into the river, but each time one spark sinks into the water, another issues forth. Dante turns to it like a hungry baby who has overslept and who clutches at its mother's breast for milk. But hardly has his gaze taken in this vision before it changes character, taking the form of a yellow rose which opens its petals under a flood of light. Angels swarm down like bees into the flower and fly up again. On the petals of the rose the blessed sit like the spectators in an amphitheater. The angels have come to visit them. Up to now Dante has not been able to see the blessed, who have been wrapped in light like the silkworm in its silk. Now his eyes are used to the light and he sees their features. It is like being at a masked ball when the moment comes for the guests to take off their masks. In front of Mary, as once on earth, the archangel Gabriel unfolds his wings. Here is Paradise proper, the Empyrean, which is outside time and space and which contains within itself all that has been created. Just as a hill is reflected in the water at its foot as though to revel in its own beauty, Dante now sees a thousand thrones reflected. The rose of Heaven opens its golden heart to the beholder. In the heavenly amphitheater he sees Augustine, whose doctrine of pilgrimship is now triumphantly confirmed. He also sees his beloved, who has resumed her place in the rose which she left for his sake, and he sends her thanks for having led him from thralldom to freedom.

The holy Bernard of Clairvaux, the type of contemplation and "the most intimate fosterling of Our Lady," appears at Dante's side and instructs him concerning the kingdom of love to which he has come, where all chance is abolished, where there is neither sorrow, thirst, nor hunger. Bernard prays to the Virgin Mary that she may grant Dante the joy supreme—to look into the eternal light. Dante gazes upwards. He desires nothing now. His pilgrimage is ended. There is no longer a ladder to climb, there are no footsteps to follow. He says that he cannot remember what he now experienced. It is like waking from a sweet and happy dream and forgetting the details. The feeling of joy is all that is left. He says that he seemed to look into a ray of light, and he was unable to turn his eyes away. Motionless, he gazed into the living light. He saw three circles, of equal size but of different colors, seemingly reflected in each other. They were coincident, yet three. In one of them he glimpsed the likeness of a human face. Just as a mathematician tries to measure a circle but cannot find a solution, the poet tries to find the connection between the circle and the human face. But his wings are not for such a flight. Then his mind is lit by a flash, and he understands. The poem is finished, the words are ended. He has seen the love that moves the sun and the other stars—*l'amor che move il sole e l'altre stelle.*

What, ultimately, *is* Paradise? It is not a place far above the earth, nor is it a reward to souls after death. Paradise is here and now. Man is a piece of coal, but God is fire and heat, writes Angelus Silesius. Those who are not with God are cold, dark, and dead. So Paradise is the moment when the soul's coal burns, and Dante brings that moment to his readers. He builds a Paradise with the aid of the Christian doctrines. He populates it with pious Christians, with angels of varying degree. He shows us the yellow rose, which is an old symbol of contemplation, but which also reminds us of the red rose, the symbol of earthly love that once long ago roused the spirit of life within him. He brings us at last to the three circles, which stand for the triune God, and in one of them we see the face of the Son of Man. It is the mystery of the incarnation, revealed by the light that flashes through his mind.

Dante has constructed for us the mighty rose window of his poem and filled it with figures to the last pane of glass. Now he flings us out towards the source of light. Everything that has been said is merely image and reflection. Everything bears witness to the primordial light and leads us towards it. When Dante, in the last great vision, divines a human face within the circle, we know that it must be there. When man is kindled with love, he is one with the divine light. Paradise is immediate perception. Paradise is a state of love, and those who have attained it know that their banishment is over, that they have come home, that they need no longer move on.

15

THE ANGELS

THE FIRST TIME an angel appears in the Comedy is in the ninth canto of *Inferno*. At the end of the eighth canto the pilgrim and Virgil arrive at the infernal city of Dis, which is surrounded by a high wall. Behind it can be glimpsed towers and glowing mosques. The turbid river of death, the Styx, flows around the city. The two travelers have just been taken across the river by the ferryman Phlegyas and put down before the city gates, which are guarded by fallen angels. When they discover that Dante is still in the flesh, and therefore not their prey, they are incensed (*Inferno,* VIII:84–85): "Who is this man that, never having died, is going through the kingdom of the dead?" Virgil talks to the guards in an effort to make them leave the way free. It is in vain. The devils shout that they will let Virgil in but that, as a penalty for having shown the pilgrim the way, he must stay in their city. Dante, they say, must return alone the "foolish way" (*la folle strada,* line 91) he has come.

At this savage defiance the pilgrim grows more than usually alarmed. He begs Virgil—"O my loved Guide," *O caro duca mio*—not to desert him and is tempted to give up the whole journey through the realms of the dead. Virgil tries to calm him, indicating that someone is coming to rescue them. A moment later the fallen angels withdraw into the city and shut the gates in the travelers' faces.

Dante and Virgil stand in the dark between the wall and the river. Virgil listens, peering out across the black water, but he cannot see far, for the air is thick with fog and vapors (*Inferno,* IX:4–9):

He stopped, attentive, like a man who listens,
For his eye could not take him very far
In that black air and impenetrable fog.
"This is a battle you and I must win,"
He said; "if not . . . someone else has volunteered.
Oh, how time drags till that other comes!"

It is the only time during the journey that Virgil falters, and it terrifies the pilgrim still more; he puts the worst construction on "the broken phrase" (*la parola tronca*). He is by no means reassured when he looks up. Inside the wall glows the top of a high tower, in which three female demons appear; they are girded by green hydras and their tresses are serpents. Virgil utters their names. They are the Furies — Megæra, Alecto, and Tisiphone. They tear their breasts with their talons, smite their faces, and utter fearful shrieks. They call on the Medusa to come and turn the intruder to stone with her ice-eyes so that he can never return to earth. At this point Virgil puts his hands over Dante's eyes to shield him. In depicting this scene, Dante the storyteller has done his utmost to emphasize the resistance that evil mobilizes against those who try to penetrate down into its realm. The road of self-knowledge is a road of horror.

At this moment there is a roar out on the river. "And now there came," Dante tells us, "upon the muddy waves, a crash of fearful sound, at which the shores both trembled; a sound as of a wind, impetuous for the adverse heats, which smites the forest without any stay; shatters off the boughs, beats down, and sweeps away. It rushes along overweeningly in a cloud of dust, making the wild beasts and the shepherds flee. He freed my eyes" (Virgil has been screening them all this time with his hands) "and said: 'Now turn thy nerve of sight [*il nerbo del viso*] across that ancient foam, where the smoke is thickest.' Like frogs darting in all directions through the water before their enemy the serpent until they are squatting on the bottom of the pond, I saw thousands of lost spirits flee before one who crossed the Styx with unwet feet. He waved away the fetid air, often moving his left hand before his face. It seemed to be the only thing that troubled him. I knew that he must be a messenger of heaven and I turned to the master, who made a sign that I should stand still and bow in homage. How full of indignation he seemed! He reached the gate and opened it with a wand, for there was no resistance."

"You contemptible outcasts of heaven!"
He started saying on that fearful threshold.
"Why does this insolence still cling to you?
Why do you stubbornly resist that will
Which can never be divided from its goal
And which has often brought you added pain?
What can you gain from grappling with the Fates?
That Cerberus of yours, if you recall well,
Still bears a skinless chin and throat for trying."
Then he returned along that filthy road,
Said not a word to us, but bore the look
Of one consumed and pressed by other cares
Than those of him who stands in front of him.

(*Inferno,* IX:91-103). This angel is the archangel Michael. The words about Cerberus' neck are an allusion to the story in the *Aeneid* of how Hercules descended into the underworld to liberate Theseus and put a chain about the dog's neck, chafing it raw. The angel who so effortlessly bursts open the ironbound gate in Hell and who reminds Dante of Hercules and of a snake the frogs flee from in panic is part of an Old Testament tradition, as Romano Guardini has shown in his book about the angels in Dante. Angels of this kind appear before the patriarchs. In the book of Samuel an angel like this stretches out his hand to destroy Jerusalem by command of the Lord. Giotto was still painting angels of this mightiness, austerity, and strength, but the race died out during the Renaissance, when the angels declined into the human, decreased in stature, and became mawkish and sugary. It was left to Hölderlin and Rilke to reinstate, if only momentarily, the angels in their former majesty. But those who are interested may read of this in Guardini.

The striking thing about the angel in the ninth canto is his unswerving concentration on his task. He has descended into the underworld in order to help the pilgrim on his way, but he vouchsafes him neither glance nor word. While he is still lashing the demons with his tongue he has begun to plan for his next mission. He is a warrior of God, and no crusader with breastplate and closed vizor on the way to the holy tomb could be more dedicated to God's service.

When the pilgrim arrives in Purgatory he finds on all the terraces angels who are there to help, purify, and enlighten the souls. They no longer look like warriors; they seem more like priests on duty in the great open-air church on the other side of death, Purgatory. But even the angels of Purgatory are exalted and commanding. They are reminiscent of the angels in the New Testament, of Gabriel who said to Mary, "Fear not!" when he appeared to her. One of these angels appears in the second canto of *Purgatorio*. He is standing in the stern of a boat which is bringing blessed souls from the inhabited earth across the ocean to the foot of the Mount of Purgatory. The angel is using his wings as sails. As soon as the boat touches land, the angel makes the sign of the cross over the new arrivals before they hurry ashore and departs as swiftly as he came. He shows the same power of concentration as Michael. A dazzling light shines all about him.

The first eight cantos of *Purgatorio* describe the lower regions of the Mount, which are a kind of forecourt. The pilgrim reaches Purgatorio proper in the ninth canto, and the actual purification begins. As in *Inferno*'s ninth canto, which depicts the entry into the lower infernal city, here too an angel plays an important part. Dante sees a portal in front of him and three steps leading up to it. The first is of white marble, so polished and smooth that in it is his "very image shown." It is a symbol of self-knowledge and repentance. The second step is "of deeper hue than perse" and cracked in its length and breadth. It is confession. The third is as red as blood that spurts from a vein. This is acceptance of atonement. Seated upon the threshold of adamant is a guardian angel with a naked sword in his hand. The pilgrim kneels down at his feet and with the point of his sword the angel inscribes seven "P's" upon Dante's forehead—P for *peccatum,* sin—as a sign that he is not free from any of the seven deadly sins. "Do thou wash these wounds when thou art within" (*Purgatorio,* IX:113–114), the angel says. From under his vesture, the color of "earth which is dug out dry," he takes two keys, one of gold and the other of silver, and with them he unlocks the gate. He says that he has been given the keys by the apostle Peter, who told him to err on the side of leniency when opening it, if only the people fell prostrate at his feet. The pilgrim, with the rush round his brow, already has the necessary humility. The two halves of the heavy portal open with a screech. A half-heard song of praise to God, *Te Deum laudamus,* is the first sound the poet hears; it is like people singing in church—now the words are clear, now they are muffled by the organ's mighty peal.

This scene is an allegory of the Christian's penitence, atonement, and salvation. It is a cathedral we are entering; the cathedral gives a clear picture of the church, just as the angel with the keys represents the priesthood. At the same time the scene has a life of its own, it radiates the indefinable purity that is present throughout Purgatory. The angel has taken one more step towards the human. He is interested in Dante personally and talks to him. But this is not a leading part. In the Comedy all is concentrated on the pilgrim, who is unquestionably the main character. The poem is about his spiritual development and salvation, and neither pilgrim nor poet has time for digressions and arabesques. Just as the archangel Michael, the second he has opened the infernal gate, hastens to his next task, so does the poet Dante. Hardly has a scene been brought to a close before he turns his nerve of sight towards a new one. There is an impatience to move on in the verse itself. Quickly and without a single unnecessary phrase, the storyteller leaves the scenes he has created.

On the various ledges of Purgatory angels appear who wipe out the "P's" on the pilgrim's forehead. But when he reaches Paradise the angels no longer perform individual tasks. Only now do they reveal their inmost nature. The angels we have met in Hell and Purgatory belonged to the

lowest ranks in the angel hierarchy. Comparing them with
the angels in Paradise is like comparing a child's chalk drawings with Rembrandt's paintings.

The pilgrim, with Beatrice at his side, has attained the
ninth celestial sphere, the crystalline heaven (*Paradiso,*
XXVIII:4–9):

> As a man sees in a mirror the torch's
> Flame that is blazing behind him before
> He thinks of it or has it in his sight,
> Then turns round to see that the mirror
> Is telling him the truth, and sees that the two
> Accord the way a note does with its rhythm—

so Dante sees a light reflected in Beatrice's lovely eyes. He
turns round and is aware of a point of such intense radiance
that his eye is dazzled. The point is infinitely small. A star
would seem as big as a moon by comparison. Round the
point whirls a circle of fire so swiftly that not even the inconceivable speed of the crystalline heaven can match it.
Outside this circle spins another, and beyond that another,
and so on—all nine circles (*Paradiso,* XXVIII:16–45):

> A point that gave out such a piercing ray
> That any eye its glare fell on was compelled
> To close from its overpowering brightness.
> That very star, which seems from here the smallest,
> Would seem to be a moon located with it,
> As star with star together are located.
> Perhaps as near as seems the ring encircling
> The luminary that exhibits it,
> When the mist that carries it is densest,
> A ring of fire revolved about the point
> So rapidly, it would have far exceeded
> The motion that circles the cosmos fastest.
> And this was by another circled round;
> That by a third, the third then by a fourth,
> By a fifth the fourth, then by a sixth the fifth.
> Above, a seventh followed, spread out with
> Such vastness that Juno's messenger, even if
> Complete, would be too narrow to contain it.
> And, thus, on to the eighth and ninth, and each

Moved slower according as its distance
From one in number was the greater.
And that circle had the clearest flame
Which was the least distant from that purest spark,
Because, I think, it absorbed more of its truth.
My lady, who saw that I was struggling
With uncertainty, said: "From that point
All Heaven hangs, and all of nature.
Gaze at the circle that is closest to it,
And know that its motion is so rapid
From the fiery love that pierces it."

The quotation is typical of the objectivity so noticeable throughout the Comedy. We almost expect the poet to leave his verse and take to plans and diagrams. It is remarkable that Dante, with his passion for mathematical exactitude, has been wrapped in such clouds of mawkishness and emotionalism. Dante is hard, vigorous, and precise, and ought to discourage sentimentality and "arty" poetics.

The pilgrim, who has studied the nine concentric circles, makes the observation that they operate contrary to the world of sense. God has created the earth in the middle and the heavens around it. The Empyrean, where God dwells, keeps the whole world enclosed, and the ninth heaven, which is the largest and widest, moves with the greatest speed, driven by its longing to unite with God. In the system of circles that Dante now beholds, the center is the pure spark—*la favilla pura.* The circle of fire that is nearest moves the most swiftly, and is equivalent to the crystalline heaven, *Primum Mobile,* which the pilgrim in this *Paradiso* canto has now reached.

Beatrice explains the apparent contradiction. In the world of matter a larger measurement corresponds to a greater power. Therefore, the higher up we come the faster the spheres move and the wider their circumference is. But in the world of spirit—which the pilgrim has now come to—it is just the reverse. Spirit has no extent. It cannot be symbolized better than by means of a point of infinite light.

What Dante has seen is the nine angel hierarchies such

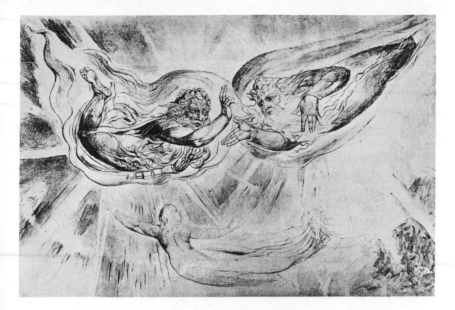

William Blake: The apostles Peter and James greet one another in Paradise. They are clad in mantles of light and resemble heavenly doves.

Sandro Botticelli: Dante and Beatrice in the crystalline heaven. *Paradiso* XXVI.

Gustave Doré is perhaps the Dante illustrator of more recent times who is best known. He illustrated the entire Comedy. Here the host of angels in Paradise.

Although this picture by Gustave Doré is said to be an illustration of the celestial rose such as it is described in *Paradiso* XXXI, it seems more closely allied to the description of the angels' nine hierarchies according to Dionysius, canto XXVIII. See the chapter *The Angels*.

as they are described by the great writer of late antiquity Dionysius the Areopagite, who is mentioned by name in this canto (*Paradiso*, XXVIII: 130). He is a writer who possessed a unique authority during the Middle Ages. Thomas Aquinas and Meister Eckhart quote him with almost the same reverence as they do the Bible. I have studied his angelology chiefly in the works of Hugo Ball and Mazzeo, to which the reader is referred. Dionysius' premise is that the hierarchy is a doctrine of the angels' and the priests' different degrees of light. The angels are purely spiritual powers, intelligences. They represent various stages of spirit on the path between man and God. They have no material form. It is only in our imagination that they take shape. In fact, they cannot be described. They stand for a sacred knowledge and a sacred work. Dionysius' celestial hierarchy can be conceived as a ladder, like the one in Jacob's dream, raised between earth and heaven, an effulgent, living order of rank which at the same time is a picture of God Himself, who manifests Himself in this spiritual and hallowed chain of apparitions.

Dionysius' angels thus have nothing to do with angels like those in Swedenborg. When the Bible talks of angels in the form of celestial bodies or winged beings, when the book of Revelation speaks of angels of wind and fire, when Paul in his letters to the Ephesians and Colossians classifies the angels, it is only because our comprehension is so limited and needs these images. But we must not confuse the images with the purely spiritual powers they symbolize.

We must not, Dionysius says, imagine, as the uneducated masses do, that the celestial spirits have feet and faces, that they are shaped like bulls or lions, that they are equipped with beaks and feathers like the eagle. We must not believe that glowing wheels roll across the sky or that caparisoned steeds and warriors with spears charge across the heavens. When the Revelation speaks of shapeless spirits it makes use of fictions and images so that we mortals may understand.

We must bear the angels' incorporeal nature in mind when we view the various angel apparitions which Dante goes on to describe in the twenty-eighth canto. The angelic

sphere nearest the pure spark is the most holy—seraphim.
The word means "the burning ones." Seraphim are entirely
love. Seraphim, without ever averting their eyes, gaze into
God's light and understand God without the need of any
image of Him. They represent pure perception, a blessed
madness. These angels rush towards God with inconceivable
speed, so that their circle of fire moves more swiftly than
anything else in existence. Beyond seraphim, come cherubim
and beyond cherubim, the thrones. They represent different
degrees of knowledge about the eternal. The next three
angelic circles are the dominions, the virtues, and the powers.
If cherubim and the thrones enjoy God's emanation without
being hampered by the imperfection of the world of
imagination or action and are firmly fixed in the core of their
being, deriving their nourishment direct from eternal beauty,
then the lower grades of angels receive their knowledge
instantly, through contact with the angelic circle lying
within. They represent an indomitable striving to attain the
light. The last three orders of angels are the principalities,
the archangels, and the ordinary angels. Only now do we
come down to a spirituality which can be thought to interest
itself in earthly matters. The principalities give kings advice.
The archangels help nations. The angels intervene in ordinary people's lives.

The whole of the created world through which the pilgrim has journeyed and where he has found a hierarchic
pattern is governed by this host of angels. The crystalline
heaven is ruled by seraphim and the starry heaven by
cherubim. The other seven angel grades correspond to the
seven heavens that follow. Purgatory, equivalent to life on
earth, and Hell, the realm of the damned, are in fact reflections in another life-form of the celestial hierarchy. Below
the ranks of angels comes the ecclesiastical grading with
pope, archbishops, hierarchs, priests, and monks. And in Hell
we find the same military ranking among the fallen angels.
The whole of the medieval conception of the universe has
this passion for order. One of the definitions of God is that

He is order and that evil is disorder, a lack of the harmony that is God's essence.

This hierarchic thinking has one of its roots in the Platonic doctrine of the gradual rising towards the primordial idea, and another in Paul's words about the various grades of angels and about our partial knowledge here on earth compared with the full knowledge which we shall one day attain. In the Comedy, however, it is chiefly Dionysius who lays the hierarchic foundation. In accordance with his teaching the pilgrim is moved from class to class in the big angelic school.

On the inner plane, then, what do the angels represent? Hugo Ball says that the doctrine of the angels is the Christian's doctrine of the superman. The angels are the God-man and his ascent through the spheres. The angels are knowledge of ecstasy which alone can reach the final knowledge of God. The purpose of the angels is the mystery which is available only to feeling. The differences in rank in the angelic world are distinctions of the heart. The angels are a scale of spiritual states, bordering on and overlapping each other.

A basic thought is that the soul, as it rises from a lower to a higher sphere, retains complete awareness of the lower state. Every higher form contains all functions and knowledge from all the lower forms. It is the same thought that Aristotle expressed in his biology—that every form of life includes all the functions of the lower forms plus the function characteristic of itself. The animals have all the functions of plants and in addition consciousness. Man has all the functions of plants and animals and in addition reason. Seraphim thus have all insight and all knowledge possessed by all human and divine hierarchies, and in addition their own capacity of imageless perception. The pilgrim's development takes place in accord with this law. The earlier stages along his life's road are present at every moment. Even in the highest heavens we hear echoes out of Hell, we catch glimpses of the earth and see pictures of Florence in greatness and decline. The ecstasy and the broadening of consciousness that the pilgrim is approaching, do not estrange him from his life

on earth. Everything is present at the same time. The hierarchic thinking has helped Dante to this totality. In this
development he also draws a picture of God Himself, who
contains within Himself all that is created, all the heavens
and the earth with its Hell. God knows all and is present in
all, as well as possessing that which is God alone: absolute
love.

Or let me put it this way: The angels are thus the incarnation of spirit. The light is an image of God and this
light is at the same time love, goodness, and righteousness.
Seraphim represent a love which, having once gazed into the
beloved's eyes, can never turn its eyes away. The angels are
awareness of the human soul's capacity to rise, to win a higher
light, a greater authority, a purer devotion to the only thing
with any meaning. The angels are the power that is moving
towards perfection.

Seraphim's thoughts are not divided. Their perception is
not interrupted, and therefore they have neither memory nor
consciousness. They live bathed in pristine light, which the
pilgrim is making his way towards. In the twenty-ninth canto
Beatrice tells him of this blessed life, thus preparing him for
the last great experience. In the thirtieth canto the vision of
the angels yields. "And as the brightest of the sun's hand-
maidens / Comes ever nearer, so does the sky shut off / Sight
after sight, up to the loveliest" (lines 7–9). The apparition
of the host of angels vanishes before God's pure light, which
Dante has now reached. For one dizzy second he divines seraphim's life, for which no words are adequate. We have passed
the entire scale. It is easier now to understand why Dante
was in constant need of a guide. During the long pilgrimage
he was never alone. First Virgil was at his side, then Beatrice.
In the last cantos he is instructed by Bernard of Clairvaux.
God's being is an everlasting movement up and down, an
effluence of light drawn back to its source. The Christian
has to make his way from stage to stage. It is love's path
which ends in love of God, not because God is good, loving,
and just, not because "every good gift and every perfect gift

. . . cometh down from the Father of lights," but because God is God and worthy of being loved for His own sake.

Do these words concern only the Christian, the man who believes in a personal God? No! The reality that here takes shape can be understood only by those who desist from explaining the divinity and clothing it in images, but who in the Comedy's last cantos recognize a description of the highest spiritual state that we are capable of imagining. Light, love, silence, righteousness—these are merely symbols of the ineffable.

16

THE COMEDY AS A
FREEDOM DRAMA

"TO WORK FROM A MODEL has in all ages and within all branches of art been considered as something very laudable, because it has been beneficial to the end in view, namely, through art to seem like nature. In the literature of today this is not allowed, since there is an imminent risk, especially in small communities: the model will be recognized and the author's characters, which were intended as types, will become persons, who give a new interest, displeasing and by no means deliberate, to his work. . . . The fantasy which one thought to create, that is, make out of nothing, is only the arranging gift which sorts out life's greater or smaller wealth of impressions and experiences and sets them in their place, where with a light in their hands they can show thought its way. . . . The world's greatest writers have been realists. Dante in his famous *Divina Commedia* is something more than a realist, for he does not mask his characters in another guise."

The words are Strindberg's. He jotted them down during the dispute that followed *The New Kingdom,* in which he exposed to ridicule, under a thin disguise, a large number of representatives of official Sweden. Dante, behind whom Strindberg is here taking cover, also had good reason to ponder the displeasing interest that his poem aroused because of the persons named in it. When Dante the pilgrim meets his ancestor Cacciaguida in the crusaders' heaven he asks his advice. Shall I not, he says, get into trouble when I return to earth and reveal in my poem what people I have encountered in somewhat unflattering places? His ancestor exhorts Dante to conceal nothing, explaining that God had a special reason for letting the pilgrim meet only famous people during his journey through the realms of the dead. There is little point in preaching against vice in general terms or pointing out wicked people whom no one knows. Dante's presentation is effective, Cacciaguida says, only when it is illustrated by personal examples known to all.

One result of the pedagogic method expounded by Dante's ancestor is that the Comedy has acquired an upper-class character. On all sides we find nothing but princes, renowned poets, saints, political and religious leaders, knights, founders of orders. A citizen of the twentieth century with its sense of social responsibility may think that the Comedy reflects an unappealing indifference to the fate of nameless folk such as the servants, the common soldiers, the slave workers of Florence's flourishing trade. One would like to have seen not only the noble Piccarda enjoy her reward in Paradise, but also some ill-treated dairymaid or a vagabond frozen to death in a ditch. Dante lives in an aristocratic society, where discrimination of rank is just as strict as in the hierarchies of angels. But Dante's artistic genius and unfailing tact ward off even a latter-day criticism of this kind. Almost as though aware that his poem lacked social balance, he introduces into his detailed similes the everyday affairs of ordinary, anonymous people, who are a welcome contrast to all the high-born princes and their ladies. The peasant stands in the doorway on a day in early spring, looking sorrowfully at the frost glistening in the grass. He thinks that winter has returned and that his animals and himself will be forced to starve. He laments his lot, but consoles himself when the sun comes out and the frost vanishes. Trustingly he turns his beasts out to graze—the shepherd lies down to sleep beside his flock in the mountains—at the great arsenal in Venice the shipyard workers boil sticky pitch in huge cauldrons and caulk the boats drawn up for the winter (*Inferno*, XXI:7 *et seq.*).

Like Strindberg, Dante wants "through art to seem like

nature." When he names persons, he does so in accord with the ethical and esthetical theory he conceived and not from spite or a desire for revenge. Of course personal motives may have played a part; it is likely, for instance, that the repeated abuse of Pope Boniface had its root not only in Dante's conviction that this pope degraded the papal see, but also in the fact that Dante's personal misfortunes were partly due to measures Boniface VIII had taken. But it is certainly true that the lessons Dante wants to bring home to the reader have a stronger impact when each sin and each virtue is associated with a famous person. Here Dante deliberately follows the tradition of the Old Testament prophets, who made no bones about telling mighty lords the truth to their faces.

We therefore have no right to assert that Dante claimed to know the final destination of the people he placed in the realms of the dead. Like Strindberg, he could say that his target was the type and not the person. He branded vice, immorality, dissension in Italy and in the world. The personal examples were the torches he held up to light the way of thought and imagination.

But whether Dante believed he knew what life was like after death for the people in the Comedy or not, there remains a problem of conscience which is not touched on in the conversation between him and Cacciaguida. Strindberg had little difficulty in convincing himself that he was right, and he bore his victims' afflictions with a light heart. True, he did not place them in Hell, but he made sure that they came to a kind of inferno of ignominy, which will endure for as long as his books are read and out of which there is no chance of the captives escaping.

Dante can hardly have believed that those whom he placed in his poem's Hell were also in "reality" tormented in the underworld. But he did know that when he designated people who had been contemporary with him as doomed to the various circles of Hell, this meant distress for relations and friends. And he could not have been insensible to the consequences of his having painted Hell in such hideous colors and thereby adding to the terror in the world—he accepted the thought that justice could be combined with *everlasting* punishment.

As I have emphasized several times, the Comedy is the story of how Dante the pilgrim awakens to an increasingly deep awareness during his journey. In Hell he is often overcome with pity for the sufferers and thereby rebels against God's judgments. But he is not merely a *visitor* to Hell; he is himself a part of this penal institution of suffering. Hell is within him. It thus happens that his thoughts and feelings grow confused, that he is infected with hatred and coarsened. He finds the punishments of some of the sinners justified and behaves cruelly and brutally. The sight of the severest suffering deadens his pity.

In Purgatory this confused state of mind is resolved. A theme hinted at in *Inferno* emerges into the open: Is there a Hell at all? When pilgrim and Virgil arrive at the foot of the Mount of Purgatory Cato comes towards them (*Purgatorio*, I:40–48):

"Who are you who, defying the blind river,
Have escaped from the eternal prison?"
Said he, moving that venerable plumage.
"Who guided you? Who served you as a lamp
When you came out of that profound night which
Keeps the valley of Hell forever black?
Are the laws of the abyss so broken,
Or has there been a change in Heaven's council,
That you who are damned should reach my ledge?"

Cato's words inspire a hope which persists throughout all the *Purgatorio* cantos.

It is true that the design of the poem requires that a hope is kindled at this moment. The pilgrim has risen up from the underworld just as Christ once did. Dante the poet has stressed the parallel by timing the arrival in Purgatory, which represents the new life, for the morning of Easter Day. In the Christian passion drama, the stone is about to be rolled away from the tomb in Jerusalem. The seal of death is broken and the miracle of salvation is a fact. But the reader knows at the same time that only those who believe in Christ and have died reconciled with Him will be saved. Should he perchance have forgotten it, he has been vividly reminded of this basic Christian tenet during the passage through Hell.

In *De Monarchia* Dante had written "that a person who has never heard of Christ, and therefore has no faith, cannot be saved. . . . It makes no difference whether he has practiced all intellectual and moral virtues or not. Human reason cannot unaided understand that this is just. Only with the help of faith can it be understood." But Dante's endeavor—to grapple with this problem without his sense of justice being outraged—is much too great for him to have patience with the argument he develops in *De Monarchia* and which is well-nigh intolerable to any Christian who seeks not only submission to faith, but also righteousness and a clear conscience. He is forced to approve of people being sentenced to punishment when their only crime is that they have never heard of Christ. Moreover, he must approve terms of punishment unacceptable to a normal human sense of justice. He knows that the Christian doctrine of salvation along one road alone leads, when it is taken literally, to hideous consequences. If there is a real Hell and a real Paradise, everything on earth must be subordinate to this idea of salvation. Herein lies the root of the intolerance and the many bloody exterminations of heretics that stain the history of Christianity.

Dante called his poem a Comedy because he had learned from Aristotle that a poetical work which began in woe but had a happy end should be called that. Tragedies, on the other hand, were works which began in happiness and ended in woe. According to this definition, *The Divine Comedy* is aptly named. It is a drama of liberation and its hero, after anguish and purification, attains the highest bliss. But the Comedy is a freedom drama in another way as well: It is a struggle against the belief in the omnipotence of evil, and perhaps a victory.

The pilgrim is already faced with the problem in the

fourth canto of the Comedy; he has just arrived in Hell when he meets the heathens in Limbo. Dante asks Virgil if anyone has ever been saved by his own or by others' merit— *o per suo merto, o per altrui* (*Inferno*, IV:49–50). Virgil, at once grasping the hidden meaning in this question, tells him that Christ after His death descended into the underworld and took with him up to Paradise the great figures of the Old Testament—Adam, Abel, Noah, Moses, David, Abraham, Rachel, and many others. Virgil does not say whether these were saved by their own merits or through grace, and Dante's question thus remains unanswered. It is a consoling thought, however, that *some* were saved even if they did live before Christ. The problem recurs in Purgatory when the pilgrim meets one of those who should have been in Limbo—Cato. Cato asks if the laws of Hell are broken when he sees before him the pagan Virgil and the pilgrim Dante, who is still in the first life. Cato's astonishment seems odd, for he is himself an example of salvation against all Christian rules. To the extent that the Comedy is the recorded minutes of a trial, Cato is a threefold offender. He was a heathen. He was an opponent of Cæsar, who was chosen by God Himself to give the world peace. Furthermore, Cato had committed suicide. Not long before, in the lowest pit of Hell, the pilgrim had seen Brutus and Cassius, who had been traitors to God's instrument, Cæsar. In the suicides' wood Dante had met Emperor Frederick II's noble chancellor, whose only crime was that he had taken his own life.

But Cato, Dante wrote in *Convivio,* lived not for his own sake but for humanity's. He devoted his life to righteousness. He had the moral pivot within himself. He was a man who followed the dictates of his own conscience, even if by doing so he defied the gods. The pilgrim, when he meets Cato, has in fact found the answer to the question he put to Virgil—whether anyone could be saved from Hell by his own merit.

If a man like Cato could be saved, then could not Francesca, Brunetto Latini, and the noble Ghibelline chief, Farinata, also win salvation? Did not they too have nobility of soul? Did not they too act as their consciences told them? Are not all nine circles of Hell at this moment being emptied? Is there a single being left there? For if one man's conscience and one man's reason hold good, all must be acquitted, not only the great personalities, who like Ulysses followed their own star and until the very last evening hours sought "virtue and knowledge," but all the others as well, including the thieves, the hypocrites, the gluttons, the wizards, the violent, and the traitors. If human reason and human justice are allowed their say, there can be no sin which deserves everlasting punishment.

In the heaven of Jupiter are the souls of the just princes, and they appear to the pilgrim in the shape of an eagle. The eagle is a symbol not only of Rome and a righteous govern-ment, but also of the greatest of all rulers, God, whose nature is love as well as justice. In the presence of this im-perial and divine bird, Dante confesses his lifelong doubt. If a man is born on the bank of the Indus and there is none to speak, read, or write of Christ; if this man's deeds are right-eous and good and he is sinless in life and discourse; can he in all fairness be condemned when he dies? (*Paradiso*, XIX: 70–78). In these circumstances, where is his fault if he does not believe? It is the same question that Dante put in *De Monarchia*. The eagle gives him a stern answer. How are human beings, who are but animals of earth with a short vision no longer than a span, to mount the judgment seat? God, the eagle says, is always just and good and everything emanating from Him is right. Dante declares himself as satis-fied with this answer as a fledgling stork which, having been fed, looks up at the mother still hovering over the nest. But oddly enough, the poem goes on as though this answer were not adequate.

The eagle, which stays with Dante and the reader for several cantos, tells in the twentieth canto that its eye is formed by six of the noblest princes the earth has borne: David, Trajan, Hezekiah, Constantine, William the Good, and Ripheus. The presence of Ripheus the Trojan among these *élite* startles Dante with good reason. Ripheus lived long before Christianity. The eagle says of him that in Paradise he has learned that there is much in God's grace which the world cannot grasp. Dante has therefore received an answer to his question, when among the redeemed princes he meets a righteous pagan. But the doubt in his breast still goads him into asking for an explanation. The eagle answers that Ripheus was saved because he set all his love on righteousness, which opened his eyes to salvation. The eagle ends with the words (*Paradiso*, XX:133–138):

"And, you mortal beings, restrain yourselves
From passing judgment, for we who see God
Do not as yet know who all the chosen are.
And such deficiency is sweet to us,
Because our good is bettered in this good,
And whatever God wishes, we wish too."

At moments of excitement Dante uses bird similes. Here, in the kingdom of the righteous rulers, are three pictures all of which express the freedom and the clear conscience that he has at last attained. I mentioned the picture of the baby stork in the nest just now. The second bird simile describes how the falcon, freed from its hood, stretches its neck and opens its wings. The third tells of the lark which suddenly falls silent high in the air, as though rapt with the sweetness of its own song. The eagle has given the pilgrim "a delightful medicine"—*soave medicina*. His shortsightedness has been changed to perception.

It seems therefore as though Dante wanted to tell us that righteousness is a quality which leads to Christ and the triune God even when one has not heard Christianity preached. This is the delightful medicine offered the pilgrim in Paradise. The reader experiences this development as a drama of liberation. But this drama takes form not only inside the fictitious reality, it takes place simultaneously on another and a larger stage. Here too, the movement is towards liberation. Hell is emptied in two ways at the same time. The poem—we must not forget this—is conceived on four parallel planes. Hell's nine circles, the heretics' burning tombs, the

hypocrites' gilded copes of lead, as well as the terraces of
Purgatory and the light-phenomena of Paradise, can be seen
merely as pictures and symbols, as hideous or beautiful
dresses round a purely spiritual truth.

In the fourth canto of *Paradiso* Beatrice told the pilgrim
how the souls showed themselves to him in the various
heavens so that he might understand the nature of their
bliss. She added that the Bible speaks to man in the same
way, "assigning foot and hand to God," though meaning
something else. The church represents Gabriel and Michael
with human traits, although of course this is not literally
correct. In this Beatrice, and through her the pilgrim, are
disciples of Dionysius the Areopagite. It is not only true in
Paradise that what man experiences and imagines there is
merely a series of pictures. Things are signs. Behind every
human being and behind every word is another reality.

As man's thought and feeling rise on the scale of values,
he takes with him knowledge of all the underlying ones.
Therefore even in Paradise both Purgatory and Hell live
within him. But as they gradually become part of a higher
sphere they are transformed, dematerialized. The three mystical planes of meaning are moved into the foreground. Hell
becomes merely an allegory, evil merely a negation, an
absence of light, but even in its deficiency it is organized
in accord with the angel hierarchies. Although God created
the world and the Bible on four planes, His meaning is that
all life shall one day become part of eternity, that the only
plane to possess reality and truth will be that of fulfillment
in Paradise. In the same way, as the Comedy draws to a close
it seems to have annulled itself on the literal plane. In this it
is one stage in a striving within Christianity during these
centuries to free itself from the metaphorical, to dematerial-
ize doctrine, to fight against the many brutal and supersti-
tious tendencies.

The Gothic cathedral stands as a visible monument to
this striving. The stone flings itself aloft, vanishing in tracery,
spires, and pinnacles. The windows with their tall pointed
arches eat up the walls and gather in all the light of Heaven.

The entire nave is filled with reflections and intersecting sunbeams. The church is built for the sake of light—in fact the Gothic cathedral is chiseled light, and that which is not light is unreal. The church is on the way towards resolving itself and becoming nothing but light. The monsters pressed down under the pillars, the fabulous winged beasts sitting crouched on the parapets, the whirls of color in the rose windows—all help to create an impression of imminent transformation. *The Divine Comedy* is a link in the same endeavor. One plane of meaning bursts its cocoon and unfolds its wings on a higher plane.

The words "Middle Ages" have an unpleasant ring and in many people's minds are connected with superstition, bigotry, and fanaticism. But during these centuries Christianity shows a striving for liberation. In Dante's time there was still freedom of creation within Christianity. The doctrine was not dead, it was not a casket with precious stones formed for all time. The teaching was growing, breaking old bounds, seeking liberation from the images that wanted to materialize themselves round it and enslave it. The people who were active in this creative process were not slaves of their religion but masters of it.

There is no doubt that Dante, if asked, would have declared that revelation took precedence over reason. But at the same time he conceived that reason would one day wholly understand and accept the truths of faith. Virgil in Limbo is quite aware that Christianity represents a higher truth just as Newton in the Limbo of modern mathematics would realize that Einstein had come farther than he had. In this respect Dante's idea of the universe was optimistic; it saw no gap between faith and reason. Faith was, so to say, reason on a higher level.

But Dante is also a person for whom righteousness plays a predominant part. He finds it hard to allow what his own reason cannot accept. We see this in the Comedy, which is filled with an explosive force which acts from within. We are used to seeing the Renaissance as an awakening. A period of fantastic expansion begins. A civilization is built up which today seems ready to lay other planets than our own under its rule. But at the same time as the bright new light was being directed towards outer reality and all power was given to Ulysses, who together with Columbus, Copernicus, Galileo, Newton, and Einstein, penetrates undismayed into worlds once closed, the light is put out on the stage where the drama of man's soul was enacted. The thirteenth century sees man as the center of the universe. Round him arch the ten heavens which at last exist only in his own mind. Nature and history are creations of a God who holds everything together with the mighty power of His love, and the conceptions of this God, such as He appears in time and space, are at last merely projections of man's own thoughts and feelings. The great explorations go down into man's soul. Dante's journey through the three realms of the dead is one of them. The knowledge he acquires of man's potential for good and evil and of a religion which is not a museum piece or a Sunday school lesson, but a development, is such that Dante still seems to belong to a vanguard. I should be happy indeed, if one day I were to catch up with it.

Bibliography

Bibliographical Notes on Dante and
His Comedy

A personal choice of books available in English.

Erich Auerbach. *Mimesis.* trans. Willard R. Trask. Double-
day, Anchor paperback edition, 1957.

This collection of essays contains a detailed, very well-
informed, and helpful analysis of the Farinata episode—the
tenth canto of *Inferno.*

————. Dante, *Poet of the Secular World.* trans. Ralph
Manheim. University of Chicago Press, 1960.

Michael Barbi. *Life of Dante.* trans. and ed. Paul G. Ruggiers.
University of California Press paperback edition, 1954.

This work offers an admirably concentrated—132 pages—
summary of Dante's life. In addition it presents Dante's
works. The last chapter is called "The Reputation and Study
of Dante" and is an excellent starting-point for the beginner,
who is given good advice as to where to look for information
about Dante and his time. The book, in a paperback edition,
costs only $1.25.

Thomas G. Bergin. *Dante.* Houghton Mifflin paperback edition, 1965.

A useful book for beginners which was published after I had
completed my work.

William Blake. *Illustrations to the Divine Comedy of Dante.*
1922.

In 1824, at the age of sixty-seven, Blake began work on these
illustrations, which in my view are superior to all other attempts to express Dante's vision in picture form. It is the

fierceness, the enlargements, the awfulness of the monsters, the excess of suffering, the violence of movement which are so Dantean. Nearly every picture pierces to the marrow. We feel that the pilgrim really is in danger, that both literally and morally he is fighting for his life.

Johan Chydenius. *The Typological Problem in Dante, a Study in the History of Medieval Ideas.* Helsinki, 1958.

One of the few important works about Dante to be published in the North. Chydenius defines typology as ". . . the understanding of past events as types foretokening other, future events." The book is amusing and is brimming with ideas. It follows several big "types" in the Bible and in the Comedy, among them Jerusalem, Paradise, and the bride. What Chydenius says about the influence of the crusades on the fourfold interpretation of the Bible is particularly noteworthy.

Concordance.

There are several Dante concordances which facilitate study. The one I have used is Edward Allen Fay. *Concordance of the Divina Commedia.* The Dante Society. Cambridge, Massachusetts, 1888. This work includes all words—the Italian ones, of course—in the Comedy except the more common pronouns, prepositions, adverbs, and conjunctions and the commonest forms of the verbs *avere* and *essere*. Since I published my book, a splendid volume has appeared —*A Concordance to the Divine Comedy of Dante Alighieri.* Edited by Ernest Hatch Wilkins and Thomas Goddard Bergin. The Belknap Press of Harvard University Press.

Umberto Cosmo. *A Handbook to Dante Studies.* trans. David Moore. Oxford: Basil Blackwell, 1950.

This work is the best help one could wish for in finding one's way about the Dante literature. Umberto Cosmo was one of the leading modern Dante scholars. He has divided his work up into a section which gives general aids, bibliographies, and historical sources. Another section comprises the literature about Dante's life. Then, in chapters in which he also discusses the worth and credibility of various writings, he gives a detailed description of the literature that deals with Dante's various works. The emphasis is of course on the Comedy.

Benedetto Croce. *The Poetry of Dante.* trans. Douglas Ainslie. Holt, 1922.

Croce's Italian original was published in 1920. Mazzeo says, with some justification, that Croce sees the Comedy as a series of lyrical *bravura* numbers interspersed with indifferent lectures on philosophy and theology. To this, however, should be added the fact that the great passages on which Croce concentrates are interpreted with a genius which excuses his indifference to the Comedy as a whole and its beauty.

Ernst Robert Curtius. *European Literature and the Latin Middle Ages.* trans. Willard R. Trask. Harper, Torchbook paperback edition, 1953.

This mighty pioneer work is of vital importance to the understanding not only of medieval culture, but of our own. One of the principal ideas is that Europe as a concept should be seen as the combination of the ancient Mediterranean culture and the modern Western culture. It is provincial to think that modern Europe began about 1500. Curtius pays special attention to the Latin literature of the Middle Ages. He shows how antiquity lives on here. Dante, who occupies a central place in Curtius' book, has one of his roots in this Latin Middle Age, which is a direct continuation of the ancient culture. It may be practical to speak of renaissances, but actually the ancient cultural substance was never lost. The Comedy is a vast academy in which all the great figures of western culture appear. It forms an essential part of mankind's road, the same road we are traveling today. I warmly recommend Curtius' book to all who like a bold approach, a wide horizon, a feeling that the seeming past is part of the present.

Charles Till Davis. *Dante and the Idea of Rome.* Oxford, 1957.

This work discusses in detail the influence of Augustine, Orosius, Brunetto Latini, and Virgil on Dante's political thinking.

T. S. Eliot. *Dante.* London, 1929.

Earlier in my book I have several times gratefully referred to and quoted from Eliot's *Dante* book. I urge all those interested in Dante to read it. Eliot says that we grow out of the greater part of all poems just as we grow out of the greater part of the human passions. "Dante is one of those whom I hope to grow up towards at the end of my life." I wish the same.

————. *On Poetry and Poets.* Farrar, Straus, 1957.

The essay "What Is a Classic?" found in this collection discusses Virgil regarded as a classical writer before all others and his importance to Dante.

A. P. d'Entrèves. *Dante as a Political Thinker.* London, 1952.

The author devotes himself almost exclusively to discussing Dante's political views, taking as his starting-point *De Monarchia, Convivio,* and the letters. He considers the Comedy's allegorical and symbolic language as far too ambiguous. One of d'Entrèves' principal ideas is that Dante radically changed his views between *De Monarchia* and the Comedy. In the former work Dante, he thinks, saw a final goal for mankind in the world empire. In the latter, he saw earthly happiness and earthly peace merely as a station on the way towards heavenly bliss.

Francis Fergusson. *Dante's Drama of the Mind. A Modern Reading of the Purgatorio.* Princeton University Press, 1953.

As the title suggests, this American Dante scholar concentrates his attention on *Purgatorio,* which he regards as the center of the poem. Fergusson takes great pains to show how Dante the pilgrim's journey through the realms of the dead always takes place on two planes simultaneously. Each step the pilgrim advances corresponds to a step towards greater understanding. Fergusson also lays great stress on the difference between Dante the pilgrim and Dante the storyteller. He writes:

> Dante writes the poem as the record of a journey which he once took and now remembers. He writes in the first person; and yet the distinction between Dante speaking

as the author, and Dante the Pilgrim, is fundamental
to the whole structure. The author, when he reminds us
of his existence, is outside the fictive world of the
poem; the Pilgrim is the protagonist of the drama, the
center of each scene. The author knows the whole story
in advance, the Pilgrim meets everything freshly, for the
first time. The two perspectives together produce a sort
of stereoptical effect, that of an objective and partially
mysterious reality. The shifting tensions between the
two make the complex movement of the poem, and
sustain its suspense. The Pilgrim is very much like one
of Henry James's central intelligences, visible himself
as a particular individual, yet revealing to the reader
both the story and its meaning as he learns it. The
Pilgrim's awareness is always moving toward the
author's, but when they coincide, in the very strange and
wonderful close of the *Paradiso Terrestre,* all narrative
movement, and all growth of understanding, cease.
While the poem unfolds, the Pilgrim's awareness is the
moving center of the composition.

Fergusson discusses in detail the difference between
Dante's view of poetry in *Convivio* and in the Comedy:

When Dante wrote the *Convivio* he was trying to think
of poetry in terms of his 'allegory of poets'; when he
wrote the *Commedia* he conceived his poem-making in
terms of the 'allegory of theologians,' as he explains to
Can Grande. He was no longer trying to make his
style obedient to reason only; he had a still more ambitious purpose and criterion: to make it obedient to
God as revealed in Christianity. He wanted to make a
poem which would be true as he believed Scripture was
true. He wanted it to reflect the drama of man's life
in the real world, in actual history, and in hidden but
perpetual relation to God, as the Christian faith sees that
drama. Thus in the *Commedia* a cosmic and historic
drama replaces the abstract truths of reason as the
ultimate meaning of the poem, and a dramatic conception of form replaces rationality as the basis of its style,
or art.

In the last chapter of his book Fergusson gives a piece of
advice to Dante interpreters which I think it is wise to bear

in mind. When the experts disagree as to the meaning of a Dante figure, it is usually safest to assume that they are all right up to a point. For Dante creates his work with the aid of concrete and multi-dimensional elements which, just like living human beings, may have many different kinds of intentions and meanings.

Etienne Gilson. *Dante and Philosophy.* Harper, Torchbook pocketbook edition, 1963.

The Swedish reader notes with envy that this special work has appeared in an English translation in a cheap edition. Gilson is a Frenchman and one of the world's foremost specialists in medieval philosophy and theology—Thomas Aquinas in particular. In this work he studies the philosophical ideas in all Dante's works. He is a witty and very entertaining writer.

C. H. Grandgent. *Dante.* London, 1920.

A work which concentrates on putting Dante and the Comedy in the medieval frame.

C. G. Hardie. *Dante's Comedy as Self-Analysis on Integration.* London, 1959.

This work consists of only twenty-four pages but contains many amusing and bold—too bold, perhaps—opinions. Hardie is convinced that the three prophecies in the Comedy —the greyhound, the figure 515, and the man at the court of Verona—are connected and that they should be regarded as fulfilled in that the Comedy has come into being. In other words, it is the Comedy which is the liberator who puts the she-wolf to flight and kills her. All the more important persons in *Inferno* and *Purgatorio* reflect different aspects of Dante, and Dante himself was aware of this. In *Paradiso* the pilgrim realizes that he has seen himself in the others. In *Inferno,* Dante the poet lets Dante the pilgrim treat Filippo Argenti harshly. The storyteller has not yet allowed it to dawn on the pilgrim that it is himself he sees in the shades he meets. Only when he enters the Earthly Paradise does he discover that everything was a dramatization of himself—the vision in the Earthly Paradise when Beatrice stands on the chariot, when the chariot is destroyed by the eagle, the fox, and the dragon, this too is an image of Dante's own soul and by no means, as most scholars contend, an allegory of the Church and its relationship to the pope-emperor. Dante intentionally hints at such an interpretation, but this is not the purpose when Beatrice's apparition is before him. The procession comes alive for us when we understand that in it Beatrice holds up a glass to Dante to show him that everything he accused others of in the outer world was present within himself.

The three beasts in the first canto of the Comedy—the leopard, the lion, and the she-wolf—are not symbols of the vices outlined in Hell. The beasts, just like Virgil, try to persuade Dante to descend into Hell. The beasts should be conceived as a single one, a dream beast, a symbol of Dante's poetic instinct. The beasts are transformed into Virgil, who speaks of the greyhound, the poet to be, who is represented by the shade of Virgil. Hardie is not sure, however, that Dante was quite clear as to the meaning of the three beasts in Hell.

Nancy Lenkeith. *Dante and the Legend of Rome*. London, 1952.

A leading thought in this work, of help to the Dante reader, is that the Italians during the Middle Ages regarded themselves as Romans. The popes regarded themselves as carrying on Roman culture, the Church became Roman, and in imagination the apostles merge with the senate.

Joseph Antony Mazzeo. *Medieval Cultural Tradition in Dante's Comedy*. Cornell University Press, 1960.

This work is also of great value. It deals chiefly with the metaphysics of light, with hierarchic thought, and with the analogous form of presentation in the Comedy.

———. *Structure and Thought in the Paradiso*. Cornell University Press, 1958.

I owe a particular debt of gratitude to this excellent book. It was the book which made me familiar with the methods and results of modern Dante research. As the title says, Mazzeo concentrates on the *Paradiso* cantos, but the structural principles he lays down apply to the whole work.

Edward Moore. *Studies in Dante*. First Series. Oxford, 1896.

The subject of this work is Dante's references to the Bible and the classical authors and at the end there is an index which shows where the quotations occur in Dante. The writers—apart from the Vulgate—included here are: Aristotle, Plato, Homer, Virgil, Horace, Ovid, Lucanus, Statius, Juvenal, Cicero, Livy, Orosius, Boëthius, Seneca, Augustine, and some minor authors.

Leonardo Olschki. *The Myth of Felt*. University of California Press, 1949.

In the first canto of *Inferno,* Dante's meeting with Virgil is described. Dante has been driven from the right path by a savage she-wolf. Virgil tells him that he must take another way, for the wolf will let no one past. Virgil prophesies that one day she will be killed by the greyhound (*il veltro*). This animal, said to subsist on wisdom, love, and virtue and to have its origin between *feltro* and *feltro* (*tra feltro e feltro*) will save unhappy Italy and drive the she-wolf out of every city and finally back to Hell. Virgil's prophecy is one of the big stumbling blocks of Dante research. Who is the greyhound? A contemporary politician? Dante's friend Can Grande della Scala, perhaps, for "Can" means dog? Christ who is to redeem the world? And what is the significance of the twice-repeated word *feltro?* Earlier Dante scholars have generally looked for a solution on an exterior, geographical-historical plane. During our century the autobiographical element in the Comedy has been stressed more and more. The Comedy has been seen as a self-realization, as a journey not so much in the realms of the dead as in Dante's own being. It is natural that the greyhound problem has also been discussed from this new viewpoint. Leonardo Olschki gives a remarkable contribution in his book *The Myth of Felt*. *Feltro* means "felt" and felt had a symbolic meaning for many of the eastern races. The Mongols lifted up their ruler on a felt rug as a sign that they acknowledged him. Felt had once been the shepherds' protection against the cold, and the nomadic tribes retained it as a symbol. A Mongolian emperor could therefore be said to rule from felt to felt. We know that Genghis Khan was placed on a felt rug when he was proclaimed emperor, as were Chinese rulers. But the earliest commentators—including both Dante's son Pietro and Benvenuto—thought that *feltro* in the Comedy had something to do with Heaven. Castor and Pollux, the famous heavenly twins, wear felt caps as a sign of a pastoral origin. Dante was born in 1265 under the zodiac sign of Gemini. He too was born between felt and felt. Often, for example on ancient coins, the twins were denoted merely by two felt caps crowned by two stars. When Virgil now says that the hound that is to drive out the she-wolf has its origin between felt and felt, he wants in this way to indicate, according to Olschki, that the liberator will be influenced by the virtues that the twins, the Dioscuri, symbolized. The twins were a popular symbol of liberty. They also symbolized the triumph of wisdom, virtue, and love that Virgil spoke of. Who, then, is the liberator? He must be a man in the spirit of the Dioscuri. He should therefore be born between their stars. He should have come under the same sign as Dante himself. During the Middle Ages the twins were thought to have an effect on the wisdom that is given through poetry and science. In the inseparable heavenly brothers was seen a symbol of brotherly love. In his prophecy Dante was not thinking of any particular man but of a human being with the twins' virtues. The greyhound becomes an allegorical counterpart to the she-wolf. The hunting scene in the first canto takes on a moral significance and acquires universal proportions. It is freedom and fellowship which the greyhound represents, and he chases the she-wolf, which is avarice and selfish ambition, down into the abyss. It can be added that even three hundred years before Christ the felt cap of Castor and Pollux became a symbol of liberty. When a slave was freed he wore a felt cap. Dante's work is about freedom. His journey is from slavery to freedom and, as we have seen, it takes place on many planes simultaneously.

Giovanni Papini. *Dante Vivo.* trans. Eleanor Hammond Broadus and Anna Benedetti. London, 1934.

Papini asserts that one must be an artist, a Roman Catholic, and a Florentine in order to understand Dante, and he leaves us in no doubt that he himself fulfills these conditions. He abuses many of his predecessors, especially Carlyle, in an amusing way. He stresses that in Dante one should see not only an Italian but also a Hebrew prophet, an Etruscan priest, and a Roman imperialist. The Etruscans were obsessed by the thought of life after death. In their religion the demons are more numerous than in the Hellenic and Roman religions. In this the Etruscans influenced Dante, Papini contends.

Papini disputes with those who in Dante see a fossil from the dead Middle Ages, who regard Dante's work as a monument from a city in ruins which is worthy of interest only on account of the beauty of certain pillars, bas-reliefs, and arches. The reverse is true, Papini says—Dante is entirely living and contemporary. He shares Dante's view that the church should not have political power. The church is responsible only for the salvation of the soul. I don't know whether this declaration of Papini's had anything to do with his being awarded a Mussolini prize in 1933.

Papini's book is high-flown, lively, sometimes superficial. All too often Dante appears to take on Papini's own features. But the book affords witty reading.

Ezra Pound. *The Spirit of Romance.* New Directions, 1958.

This book first appeared in 1910. It contains much that helps us to understand Dante. One essay is devoted entirely to Dante and is full of perceptive, self-willed, and pioneering viewpoints. Pound is convinced that Dante conceived of Hell, Purgatory, and Paradise as states and not as places. Pound considers the last six cantos of *Purgatorio* as one of the pinnacles of the poem. He has been followed by Eliot in this evaluation. Pound amuses himself by comparing Dante with Milton, and when he has finished there is not much left of the latter. Dante's God is high divinity, while Milton's God is a meddlesome old man with a hobby. Dante is a metaphysician, while Milton is a sectarian.

Dorothy Sayers. *Introductory Papers on Dante.* Harpers, 1954.

Witty essays by the famous writer of detective stories who translated the Comedy.

Charles S. Singleton. *Dante Studies I. Commedia Elements of Structure.* Harvard University Press paperback edition, 1954.

Singleton is one of the pioneers in interpreting the Comedy in the light of the medieval view of the Bible. In this he has greatly helped our understanding of the poem's basic structure. The allegorical element is put aside and the analogous aspect appears instead.

—————. *An Essay on the Vita Nuova.* Harvard University Press, 1949.

Dante's youthful work, all too often sentimentalized, is here subjected to a penetrating analysis in the spirit of the new criticism. Singleton emphasizes that the story moves forward on two planes of time, that the meaning leaps like a spark between the two temporal poles. Singleton sees the miraculous in Beatrice and her connection with the Holy Trinity and with Jesus. In this she differs very much from the women whose praises were sung by the troubadours. Singleton's view is that even in *Vita Nuova* Dante, as a poet, wants to resemble God. Amor, the god of love who appears in *Vita Nuova,* disappears and is succeeded by the God of Christianity, who is love. The troubadours saw a goal in their beloved. Beatrice, on the other hand, is a way to God, part of the tradition in which the greatest names are Augustine and Bernard of Clairvaux.

Bernard Stambler. *Dante's Other World.* New York University Press, 1957.

This excellent work has the subtitle, "The *Purgatorio* as Guide to the Divine Comedy." It contains a discussion on the principles of criminal law on which the "punishments" and purgings in Purgatory are based. The reader will find a very clear presentation of the Comedy's fourfold meaning on p. 54 *et seq.*

W. B. Stanford. *The Ulysses Theme. A Study in the Adaptability of a Traditional Hero.* 2nd ed. Oxford: Basil Blackwell, 1963.

This work, by an ingenious Irish scholar, follows the development of the Ulysses figure in myth and poetry from pre-Homer days via Virgil, Ovid, and Seneca to our time. Among the modern writers whose Ulysses figures are analyzed are Joyce, Kazantzakis, and Eyvind Johnson.

Paget Toynbee. *Dante Alighieri, His Life and Works.* Macmillan, 1910.

Ezra Pound states in his Dante essay that this work of Toynbee's gives all the commentary that the reader of the Comedy needs, and all the elementary facts which enable him to find his way.

————. *A Dictionary of Proper Names and Notable Matters in the Works of Dante.* Oxford: The Clarendon Press, 1898.

This book contains information about all the persons and important events in Dante's works. It is generally considered very reliable. Toynbee is a man who has done great service to Dante research. His dictionary also includes pedigrees of all the princely families named in the Comedy. In one table the reader can see which princes were Dante's contemporaries.

Karl Vossler. *Medieval Culture, An Introduction to Dante and His Times,* 2 vols. trans. William Cranston Lawton. Ungar, 1958.

I read this voluminous work—over 800 pages—in an English translation. It is extremely varied, for Vossler deals with every imaginable writer and every conceivable influence on Dante and his work.

Philip H. Wicksteed. *Early Lives of Dante and of his Poetical Correspondence with Giovanni del Virgilio.* 1898.

The most important part of this book is the three early biographies of Dante, reprinted in their entirety in an English translation. Some of the statements in these biographies are fantastic. Boccaccio, for instance, tells that Dante's mother during her pregnancy dreamt of a laurel tree in a green meadow beside a clear spring. Under the tree she was delivered of a son, who subsisted on the berries of the tree and water from the spring, grew up into a shepherd and strove to reach the leaves of the tree under which he was born. As she watched him he fell, and when he picked himself up he was changed into a peacock. Villani, the famous chronicler, tells that at the time of Dante's conception a huge comet appeared in the sky. On the whole, however, it can be said that the information in these oldest biographies and that given by the early commentators has emerged more and more from its former disrepute, and that modern research has shown that statements in the earlier biographies nearly always deserve to be investigated seriously. Lionardo Bruni Aretino's biography is the least important, but contains the interesting statement that Dante fought valiantly at the battle of Campaldino. Villani has critical words for Dante's arrogance and scornful manner, but treats him with great respect. He asserts that Dante studied not only at Bologna but also in Paris. Boccaccio's biography is the most valuable. It is he who has given us the information we have about Beatrice.

Charles Williams. *The Figure of Beatrice.* London, 1943.

Despite the title, this is a work which deals with Dante's whole life and all his works. Williams sees Beatrice chiefly as a way to the eternal light. Williams is pious—over-pious in fact—but he writes with devotion. Those who are interested in Wordsworth will find particular profit in this book, for Williams is fond of drawing a parallel between Wordsworth and Dante.

W. B. Yeats. *Ideas of Good and Evil.* London, 1903.

There is an interesting essay in this collection which is called "William Blake and his Illustrations to the Divine Comedy." Yeats rightly values Blake's illustrations very highly and criticizes those who hold that Doré is the foremost Dante illustrator. There are those who say that some illustrators give us the real Dante while others offer us only their own fantasies.

About the Author

Olof Lagercrantz is in many ways himself a Renaissance man. A well-known Swedish writer, he has published a novel, four volumes of verse, three biographies, two volumes of literary essays, and A DIARY that have enjoyed great success in his own country. He holds a doctorate in the History of Literature from the University of Stockholm, and is currently a chief editor of Stockholm's leading daily newspaper, *Dagens Nyheter*. He recently received the Nordic Literary Prize, often called the "Nordic Nobel Prize," for FROM HELL TO PARADISE.

About the Translator

Alan Blair has earned a wide reputation for his numerous translations from Finnish and Swedish. His works include PEOPLE IN THE SUMMER NIGHT by F. E. Sillanpää, MEN FROM THE SEA by K. M. Wallenius, THE TONGUE OF FIRE by Mika Waltari, RALLI by Eeva Joenpelto, BARABBAS by Pär Lagerkvist, and A BURNT CHILD by Stig Dagerman. He currently resides in Sweden.